SIXTH EDITION
ACCOUNTING 1

STUDENT WORKBOOK

GEORGE SYME, B. Com., C.A.

TIM IRELAND, B.P.E.

Harraj Sandhu

Mr. Scorcia – Grade 11

Prentice
Hall

Toronto

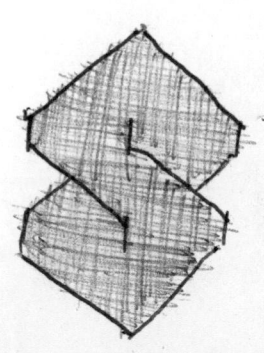

ISBN: 0-13-092333-8

Publisher: Reid McAlpine

Editor: Marg Bukta

Production Coordinator: Denise Wake

Cover Design: Alex Li

Interior Design & Page Layout: Artplus Limited

Printed and bound in Canada

13 WEB 11

Disclaimer

An honest attempt has been made to secure permission for and acknowledge contributions of all material used. If there are errors or omissions, these are wholly unintentional and the publisher will be grateful to learn of them.

Contents

Note:

The following pages are *not* in the Student Workbook:

Chapter 7	pages 133–136 and 139–142
Chapter 9	pages 263–268
Chapter 10	pages 312–313
Chapter 11	pages 380–381
Chapter 12	pages 444–445
Chapter 14	pages 537–538
Summary Exercises	pages 554–559 and 583–596

The missing pages relate to the Computer Exercises in the Student Textbook, where all work is done on a computer and does not require Workbook pages.

These pages *are* included in the Teacher's Key with answers to the Computer Exercises.

Name _____ Date _____

ANSWERS TO CHAPTER 1 REVIEW QUESTIONS (text p. 10)

1. _____
   _____
   _____
   _____
   _____

2. _____

3. _____
4. _____
5. _____
   _____
   _____

6. _____
7. _____
   _____

8. _____
9. _____
10. _____
    _____

11. _____
12. _____
    _____

13. _____
14. _____
15. _____
16. _____
17. _____
18. _____
19. _____
    _____

20. _____
    _____

ANSWERS TO CHAPTER I REVIEW EXERCISES (text p. 11)

Exercise 1, p. 11   **Using Your Knowledge**

a. _____   g. _____

b. _____   h. _____

c. _____   i. _____

   _____   j. _____

d. _____   k. _____

e. _____   l. _____

f. _____   m. _____

Exercise 2, p. 12

Complete each sentence using either **accountant**, **accounting**, or **accounting clerk**.

a. The work of an _____ is clerical in nature.

b. The work of an _____ is concerned with routine matters.

c. An _____ ensures that the supporting documents are present and correct for every transaction.

d. An _____ ensures that generally accepted accounting principles are followed.

e. An _____ records the accounting entries in the books of account.

f. An _____ makes the payroll calculations.

g. An _____ prepares reports based on the data produced by the accounting system.

h. An _____ carries out all the necessary banking transactions.

i. An _____ participates in management meetings.

j. A professional _____ has a high-level position.

k. For centuries, all _____ was handwritten.

l. Many small businesses still do their _____ by hand.

Exercise 3, p. 12

Underline the correct answer.

1. Which of the following statements does not fit the job title?
   a. An accounting clerk verifies source documents.
   b. An accounting clerk ensures that the ledger balances.
   c. An accounting clerk works neatly to guard against errors.
   d. An accounting clerk studies tax bulletins to keep up to date.

2. Which of the following statements does not fit the job title?
   a. An accounting clerk works out accounting entries.
   b. An accounting clerk, together with the owner, compares this year's and last year's income statements.
   c. An accounting clerk records accounting entries in the books.
   d. An accounting clerk inquires about a suspected error made by the bank.

ANSWERS TO SECTION 2.1 EXERCISES (cont.)

Exercise 5, p. 17

Assets

Liabilities

Equity

_____

Exercise 6, p. 18

Assets

Liabilities

Equity

_____

ANSWERS TO SECTION 2.2 REVIEW QUESTIONS (text p. 24)

The Balance Sheet

1. _____
_____

2. _____

3. _____
_____

4. _____
_____

5. _____

6. _____

7. _____

8. _____
_____

9. _____

10. _____

11. _____

12. _____

13. _____

14. _____

15. _____

16. _____

17. _____

ANSWERS TO SECTION 2.2 EXERCISES (text p. 24)

Exercise 1, p. 24

A. _____
_____
_____

Name _____ Date _____

Exercise 1 (cont.)

B. _____
_____
_____
_____

Exercise 2, p. 25

_____
_____
_____

Exercise 3, p. 25

_____
_____

ANSWERS TO SECTION 2.3 REVIEW QUESTIONS (text p. 27)

Claims against the Assets

1. _____
   _____
   _____

2. _____

3. _____

4. _____

5. _____

ANSWERS TO SECTION 2.3 EXERCISES (text p. 27)

Exercise 1, p. 27

A. _____
   _____
   _____
   _____
   _____
   _____
   _____
   _____
   _____
   _____
   _____
   _____
   _____
   _____
   _____
   _____
   _____
   _____
   _____

B. _____
   _____
   _____
   _____
   _____
   _____
   _____
   _____

ANSWERS TO SECTION 2.3 EXERCISES (cont.)

Exercise 2, p. 28

A. _____

_____

_____

B. _____

_____

_____

ANSWERS TO SECTION 2.4 REVIEW QUESTIONS (text p. 30)

Generally Accepted Accounting Principles

1. _____

_____

_____

2. _____

3. _____

4. _____

_____

5. _____

_____

6. _____

_____

_____

Name _____ Date _____

ANSWERS TO SECTION 2.4 EXERCISES (text p. 30)

Exercise 1, p. 30

ASSETS	AMOUNT	BUSINESS	PERSONAL
Accounts Receivable	$ 27 460		
Boat and Motor	16 520		
Business Bank Balance	1 852		
Business Automobiles	48 054		
Furniture and Appliances	6 528		
Government Bonds of Owner	20 000		
House and Lot	99 600		
Office Furniture and Equipment	18 324		
Office Supplies	3 545		
Owner's Automobiles	18 657		
Paving Materials	55 326		
Personal Bank Balance	1 258		
Plant Property and Buildings	125 358		
Summer Cottage	65 874		
Trucks and Equipment	285 657		
Total Assets			

LIABILITIES			
Accounts Payable	3 500		
Business Bank Loan	56 000		
Mortgage on Plant Property	75 000		
Mortgage on House and Lot	60 000		
Mortgage on Summer Cottage	22 300		
Owed to Finance Co.—Business Equipment	136 522		
Total Liabilities			

OWNER'S EQUITY/PERSONAL NET WORTH

Cases for Further Thought, p. 31

1. a. _____

   b. _____

   _____

2. a. _____

   b. _____

   _____

   _____

   _____

ANSWERS TO SECTION 2.4 EXERCISES (cont.)

Cases for Further Thought (cont.)

3. a. _____

    b. _____

    _____

    _____

    _____

4. a. _____

    b. _____

    _____

    _____

5. a. _____

    b. _____

    _____

    _____

6. a. _____

    b. _____

    _____

    _____

ANSWERS TO SECTION 2.5 COMPUTER REVIEW QUESTIONS (text p. 35)

A Spreadsheet for Personal Balance Sheets

1. _____

2. _____

3. _____

4. _____

    _____

5. _____

    _____

6. _____

    _____

7. _____

    _____

    _____

    _____

8. _____

9. _____

10. _____

    _____

ANSWERS TO SECTION 2.5 COMPUTER EXERCISES (text p. 35)

Exercise 1, p. 35

You will create a new spreadsheet file in this exercise. Instructions begin on page 32 in the text.

A. to D.

E. _____

_____

_____

_____

_____

_____

_____

_____

Extending Your Computer Skills (text p. 37)

  1.

Communicate it (text p. 37)

ANSWERS TO CHAPTER 2 REVIEW EXERCISES (text p. 38)

Exercise 1, p. 38   **Using Your Knowledge**

For each of the following questions, write the letter that represents the best possible answer.

A.   The financial position of a business is: _____
    a. the difference between total assets and total liabilities.
    b. represented by the assets, the liabilities, and the capital.
    c. the same as the net worth of the business.

ANSWERS TO CHAPTER 2 REVIEW EXERCISES (cont.)

Exercise 1 (cont.)

B. If the total assets increase by $10 000 and the total liabilities decrease by $10 000, the capital will: _____
   a. increase by $20 000.
   b. be unchanged.
   c. decrease by $20 000.

C. Which one of the following is not true? _____
   a. A − E = L
   b. A − L = E
   c. A + L = E
   d. A = L + E

D. A balance sheet shows: _____
   a. all of the owner's assets and liabilities.
   b. a financial picture of the business on a certain date.
   c. the progress of the business over a period of time.

E. Which one of the following is not true? _____
   a. The heading of a balance sheet shows the date as of which it was prepared.
   b. Assets are listed in the order of their liquidity.
   c. Accounts receivable are considered to be a liquid asset.
   d. Personal assets have no place on the business balance sheet.
   e. A truck that cost $10 000 and for which $6 000 is owed is listed on the balance sheet at $4 000.

F. Abbreviations may be used on financial statements: _____
   a. when it is necessary to crowd things to conserve space.
   b. to save time in preparing the statements.
   c. in a company name if the abbreviation is a formal part of the name.

G. Which one of the following is least true? _____
   Columnar paper helps the accountant to:
   a. add columns more accurately.
   b. make records easier to read.
   c. make the records more appealing.
   d. make recordkeeping go more quickly.

H. Which one of the following is not true? _____
   Ruled lines are:
   a. used to underline headings.
   b. used to indicate that columns of numbers are to be totalled.
   c. necessary to separate sections of the balance sheet.
   d. doubled to indicate a final total.

I. Before a business is closed down, the equation for it is:
   Assets ($125 000) = Liabilities ($37 000) + Equity ($88 000)
   If assets of $70 000 are sold for $20 000, assets of $50 000 are sold for $90 000,
   and the remaining assets stay the same the equation will become: _____
   a. $ 55 000 = $37 000 + $18 000
   b. $ 115 000 = $37 000 + $78 000
   c. $ 75 000 = $37 000 + $38 000
   d. $ 135 000 = $47 000 + $88 000
   e. $ 115 000 = $27 000 + $88 000

ANSWERS TO CHAPTER 2 REVIEW EXERCISES (cont.)

Exercise 1 (cont.)

J. Which of the following is not true? _____
- **a.** In the liability section on a balance sheet, accounts payable may be listed first.
- **b.** On a balance sheet there are three main totals.
- **c.** On a balance sheet the owner's name appears only in the heading.
- **d.** On a balance sheet the final totals are always on the same line.

Exercise 2, p. 39

_____

Exercise 3, p. 39

_____

Exercise 4, p. 39

_____

Exercise 5, p. 40

A.
- "Assets" should be the subtitle in the place of "Accounts Receivable"
- Underline under "Owner's Equity"
- Line for sum should be right above "Total Assets"
- There shouldn't be a double underline beneath "Total Liabilities"
- "Cash" should be above "Accounts Receivable"
- There shouldn't be decimals in the Assets column before the cents
- There shouldn't be decimals in the Liabilities column before the cents
- "Nina's Creations" should be above "Tse Networks"
- "Total Assets" should be a line down
- "Balance Sheet" should be above the date
- Under "Owner's Equity" it should be the owner's name, not the Company's
- Under "Owners Equity" it should say capital
- above all the creditors, it should have a sub-subtitle that should say Accounts Payable

Name *Harraj Sandhu*   Date *Fri. Sept. 15/2011*

ANSWERS TO CHAPTER 2 REVIEW EXERCISES (cont.)

Exercise 5 (cont.)

B.

Carmen's Web Creations
Balance Sheet
September 30, 20 —

Assets						Liabilities				
Cash	3	6	5	2	80					
Accounts Receivable										
Nina's Creations		4	6	0	50					
Tse Networks	1	7	8	0	—					
Equipment	6	5	0	0	30					
Supplies		9	0	0	25					
Total Assets	13	2	9	3	85					

Exercise 6, p. 40

_____
_____
_____
_____
_____

Exercise 7, p. 41

A. _____
_____
_____

B. _____
_____

Questions for Further Thought, p. 41

1. _____
_____

2. _____
_____

3. _____
_____
_____

ANSWERS TO CHAPTER 2 REVIEW EXERCISES (cont.)

Questions for Further Thought (cont.)

4. _____
_____

5. _____

6. _____
_____
_____
_____

7. _____
_____

8. _____
_____

9. _____

CASE STUDIES (text p. 42)

Case 1 *Is Money Better?*, p. 42

_____
_____
_____
_____
_____
_____
_____
_____
_____
_____

Case 2 *Can you Spend the Equity?*, p. 43

_____
_____
_____
_____
_____

CASE STUDIES (cont.)

Challenge Case 3 *Are the Assets Always Worth What the Balance Sheet Says?*, p. 43

1. _____
   _____
   _____

2. _____
   _____
   _____
   _____

3. _____
   _____
   _____

4. _____
   _____
   _____

5. _____
   _____
   _____

6. _____
   _____

Co-operative Learning Case 4 *Should Your Friends Purchase This Business?*, p. 44

Here are some good questions to ask:

1. What condition is the equipment in and is it really worth $67 000? _____
2. _____

CASE STUDIES (cont.)

Co-operative Learning Case 4 (cont.)

3. _____
4. _____
5. _____
6. _____
7. _____
8. _____
9. _____
10. _____
11. _____

Career **JULIA STAVREFF, CA/FOUNDER OF ACCOUNTING FIRM GORY & STAVREFF CHARTERED ACCOUNTANTS**

ANSWERS TO DISCUSSION QUESTIONS (text p. 47)

1. _____
_____

2. _____
_____
_____
_____
_____
_____
_____
_____
_____
_____
_____

3. _____
_____
_____

4. _____
_____
_____
_____
_____

Chapter 3   Analyzing Changes in Financial Position

ANSWERS TO SECTION 3.1 REVIEW QUESTIONS (text p. 50)

Business Transactions

1. _____
2. _____
   _____
3. _____
   _____
4. _____
   _____
   _____
5. _____
   _____
6. _____
7. _____
   _____
   _____
   _____
   _____

ANSWERS TO SECTION 3.1 EXERCISES (text p. 50)

Exercise 1, p. 50

A. Yes

B. Yes

C. No

D. Yes

E. Yes

F. Yes

G. Yes

H. No

Exercise 2, p. 51

A. Yes

B. No

C. No

D. Yes

E. No

F. Yes

G. Yes

H. No

Exercise 3, p. 51

A. CAMPBELL & ASSOCIATES

B. Smokey Valley Ski Club

C. July 22, 20—

D. Auditing the records of the club for the year ended April 15, 20—
   Preparing therefrom financial statements as at that date, and reporting thereon

E. Yes, because it shows the price

Name *Harraj Sandhu*   Date *Mon. Sept. 19/2011*

ANSWERS TO SECTION 3.1 EXERCISES (cont.)

Exercise 4, p. 52

A. THE DAVEY COMPANY

B. Smokey Valley Ski Club

C. Dec. 5, 20 —

D. 12/5, CPX

E. 30 Days

F. Name Tags

G.

H. It includes everything

Exercise 5, p. 53

A.

B.

ANSWERS TO SECTION 3.2 REVIEW QUESTIONS (text p. 59)

Equation Analysis Sheet

1.

2.

3.

4.

5.

ANSWERS TO SECTION 3.2 EXERCISES (text p. 59)

Exercise 1, p. 59   Transaction

	Assets					Liabilities		Owner's Equity
	Cash	Accounts Receivable	Supplies	Office Furniture	Truck	Accounts Payable		S. Kostiuk, Capital
		D. Murray				Ace Supply	Pine Motors	
Opening balances	1 000	50						1 050
Trans 1			75			75		
New Balance	1000	50	75			75		1050
Trans 2	−450			450				
N.B.	550	50	75	450		75		1050
Trans 3	50	−50						
N.B.	600		75	450		75		1050
Trans. 4	100							100
N.B.	700		75	450		75		1150
Trans 5	−500				6500		6000	
N.B.	200		75	450	6500	75	6000	1150
Trans 6	−75					−75		
N.B.	125		75	450	6500		6000	1150
Trans 7.	−100							
N.B.	25		75	450	6500		6000	1150

Name _Harraj Sandhu_   Date _____

ANSWERS TO SECTION 3.2 EXERCISES (cont.)

Exercise 2, p. 60

A., B.

	Assets					Liability	Owner's Equity

C. _____

_____

_____

Name _Harraj Sandhu_   Date _____

ANSWERS TO SECTION 3.2 EXERCISES (cont.)

Exercise 3, p. 61

A., B.

	Assets						Liabilities		Owner's Equity

C. _____

_____

_____

ANSWERS TO SECTION 3.3. REVIEW QUESTIONS (text p. 62)

Summary of Steps in Analyzing a Transaction

1. _____

_____

_____

Name _____ Date _____

ANSWERS TO SECTION 3.3. REVIEW QUESTIONS (con't.)

_____

_____

_____

2. _____

_____

3. _____

_____

4. _____

_____

5. _____

ANSWERS TO SECTION 3.3. EXERCISES (text p. 62)

Exercise 1, p. 62

	STEP ONE				STEP TWO			
	ASSETS		LIABILITIES		EQUITY			
					Increase	*Decrease*	*No Change*	
	Item	$ Change	Item	$ Change				$Change
1. Bought $350 of supplies with cash.	Supplies	+350						
	Cash	−350					✓	
2. Paid telephone bill, $45 cash.	Cash	−45				✓		−45
3. Paid $500 to reduce the bank loan.	Cash	−500						
			Bank Loan	−500			✓	
4. Sold services for $1000 cash.								
5. An accounts receivable customer pays us $600.								
6. Paid wages, $800.								
7. Sold services for $2000 on credit.								
8. Paid an accounts payable vendor $750.								
9. Bought $4500 of equipment on credit.								
10. Furniture valued at $400 was destroyed.								
		A =	L		+		OE	

ANSWERS TO SECTION 3.3 EXERCISES (cont.)

Exercise 2, p. 63

A. _____

B. _____

C. _____

_____

D. _____

E. _____

F. _____

_____

Exercise 3, p. 64

A. _____

B. _____

C. _____

_____

D. _____

E. _____

F. _____

_____

ANSWERS TO SECTION 3.4 REVIEW QUESTIONS (text p. 67)

Using a Computer: A Spreadsheet for Transaction Analysis

1. _____

2. _____

3. _____

4. _____

_____

_____

5. _____

_____

_____

_____

6. _____

_____

7. _____

_____

8. _____

ANSWERS TO SECTION 3.4 EXERCISES (text p. 68)

Exercise 1, p. 68

Continue working with the ANNA spreadsheet model that you started on page 64.

Extending Your Computer Skills (text p. 72)

Exercise 1, p. 68

Cell Display Continue working with the ANNA file you completed in exercise 1 above.

ANSWERS TO SECTION 3.4 EXERCISES (cont.)

Exercise 1 (cont.)

Balance Sheet

Exercise 2, p. 69

Communicate It (text p. 69)

_____
_____
_____
_____
_____
_____
_____
_____
_____
_____
_____

ANSWERS TO CHAPTER 3 REVIEW EXERCISES (text p. 70)

Exercise 1, p. 70   **Using Your Knowledge**

1. _____
2. _____
3. _____
4. _____
5. _____

Name _____ Date _____

ANSWERS TO CHAPTER 3 REVIEW EXERCISES (cont.)

Exercise 2, p. 71

1. _____
   _____

2. _____
   _____
   _____

3. _____
4. _____
5. _____

Exercise 3, p. 71

Year	Assets	Liabilities		Equity
20-0	$ 85 000	Step 1		$60 000
20-1	$115 000	Step 2	Step 3	

Make the calculations in the order shown: Step 1, Step 2, then Step 3.

Exercise 4, p. 71

_____
_____
_____
_____
_____

Exercise 5, p. 71

_____
_____
_____

Exercise 6, p. 71

A. _____
B. _____
C. _____
D. _____

E. _____
   _____
   _____
   _____

CASE STUDIES (cont.)

Case 1 (cont.)

4. _____

_____

Case 2   *Checking Out a New Customer*, p. 74

1. _____
2. _____

_____

_____

_____

_____

_____

_____

_____

3. _____

_____

Challenge Case 3   *The Balance Sheet Shuffle*, p. 75

1. The revised amounts are: Total Assets _____

Total Liabilities _____

_____

_____

_____

_____

_____

_____

2. _____
3. _____

_____

_____

4. _____

_____

_____

_____

Career   **LARRY LANCEFIELD, CA, IFA, CFE/FORENSIC ACCOUNTANT**

ANSWERS TO DISCUSSION QUESTIONS (text p. 76)

1. _____
   _____

2. _____
   _____
   _____

3. _____
   _____

4. _____
   _____
   _____
   _____
   _____
   _____
   _____
   _____

5. _____
   _____

Chapter 4   The Simple Ledger

ANSWERS TO SECTION 4.1 REVIEW QUESTIONS (text p. 82)

Ledger Accounts

1. _____
   _____

2. _____

3. _____
   _____
   _____
   _____
   _____

4. _____
   _____

5. _____
   _____

6. _____

7. _____
   _____

ANSWERS TO SECTION 4.1 EXERCISES (text p. 82)

Exercise 1, p. 82

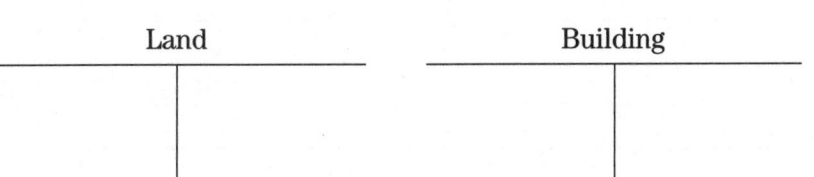
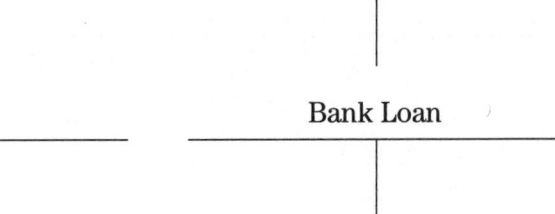
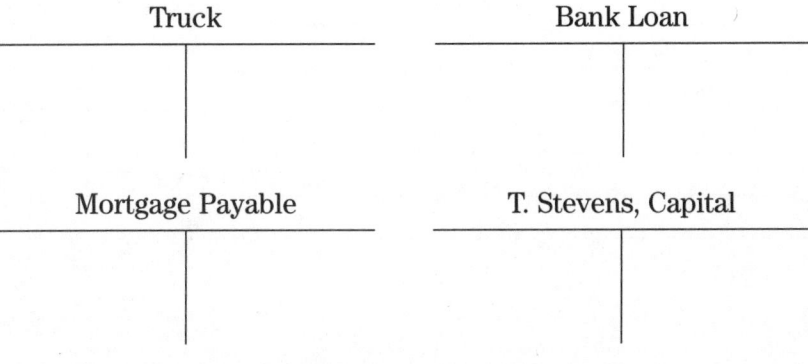

Cash	A/R — A. Marks	A/R — C. Prentice
Land	Building	Equipment
Truck	Bank Loan	A/P — Gem Lumber
Mortgage Payable	T. Stevens, Capital	

ANSWERS TO SECTION 4.1 EXERCISES (cont.)

Exercise 2, p. 83

Cash	A/R — P. Auul	A/R — S. Wouke

Supplies	Furniture and Equipment	Automobile

A/P — A.B. Associates	A/P — Medico Supply	Pauline Inaba, Capital

Exercise 3, p. 83

Assets: _____

Liabilities: _____

Equity: _____

ANSWERS TO SECTION 4.2 REVIEW QUESTIONS (text p. 90)

Debit and Credit Theory

1. _____
2. _____
   _____
3. _____
4. _____
5. _____
6. _____
7. _____
   _____
8. _____
   _____
9. _____
10. _____
11. _____
12. _____
   _____
   _____
   _____

ANSWERS TO SECTION 4.2 EXERCISES (text p. 91)

Exercise 1, p. 91

Assets		=	Liabilities		+	Owner's Equity	
Debit	Credit		Debit	Credit		Debit	Credit

Exercise 2, p. 91

A/R — K. Mak

1000	
Increases	Decreases

Exercise 3, p. 91

Transaction No.	Account Names	Account Classification: Asset, Liability, or Owner's Equity	Increase (+) or Decrease (−)	Debit or Credit	Amount	
1	Cash	Asset	+	DR	300	−
	A/R — J. Parker	Asset	−	CR	300	−

ANSWERS TO SECTION 4.2 EXERCISES (cont.)

Exercise 4, p. 92

Transaction No.	Account Names	Account Classification: Asset, Liability, or Owner's Equity	Increase (+) or Decrease (−)	Debit or Credit	Amount	

ANSWERS TO SECTION 4.3 REVIEW QUESTIONS (text p. 96)

Account Balances and Terminology

1. _____
   _____
   _____
   _____

2. The two steps are:
   _____
   _____
   _____

ANSWERS TO SECTION 4.3 REVIEW QUESTIONS (cont.)

3. _____
   _____
   _____
   _____
   _____

4. _____

5. _____
   _____

6. _____

7. Two examples of situations that result in an exceptional balance are:

   1. _____
   2. _____

8. _____
   _____

9. _____
   _____
   _____
   _____
   _____

ANSWERS TO SECTION 4.3 EXERCISES (text p. 96)

Exercise 1, p. 96

Bank		A/R — H. Devrie		A/P — P. Helka		R. Smart, Capital	
250	190	25	175	30	75	150	3 140
1 210	48	150		45	40		
360	512	70			175		
29		35		*75*	*290*		*(2 990)*
1 849	*750*	*280*	*175*		*(215)*		
(1099)		*(105)*					

A. *Owes $105 / Debit side means Assets*

B. *Credit side means the right side*

Exercise 2, p. 97

A. _____
   _____
   _____
   _____
   _____
   _____

ANSWERS TO SECTION 4.3 EXERCISES (cont.)

Exercise 2 (cont.)

B. Possible causes for exceptional balances:

_____

_____

_____

_____

Exercise 3, p. 97

	Debit	Credit

a. The left side of an account.

b. The balance of an account receivable.

c. The balance of a supplier's account.

d. A decrease in a liability.

e. An exceptional balance in the Bank account.

f. The balance in the Equipment account.

g. The right side of an account.

h. The balance in the Bank Loan account.

i. An exceptional balance in an account payable.

j. The larger side of a liability account.

k. A creditor's account.

l. A customer's account.

m. An increase in an asset.

n. A debtor's account.

o. The effect on accounts receivable when we sell on account.

p. The effect on accounts payable when we pay on account.

q. The effect on accounts receivable when we have a receipt on account.

r. The effect on accounts payable when we purchase on account.

ANSWERS TO SECTION 4.4 REVIEW QUESTIONS (text p. 101)

Trial Balance

1. _____

_____

_____

_____

_____

ANSWERS TO SECTION 4.4 REVIEW QUESTIONS (cont.)

2. To balance a ledger:
   1. _____
   2. _____
   3. _____

3. _____
   _____
   _____

4. _____
   _____
   _____
   _____
   _____

5. _____
6. _____
7. a. _____
   b. _____
   c. _____
   d. _____

ANSWERS TO SECTION 4.4 EXERCISES (text p. 101)

Exercise 1, p. 101

_____
_____
_____

ACCOUNTS	DEBIT	CREDIT

ANSWERS TO SECTION 4.4 EXERCISES (cont.)

Exercise 2, p. 102

_____

_____

_____

ACCOUNTS	DEBIT	CREDIT

Exercise 3, p. 103

_____

_____

ACCOUNTS	DEBIT	CREDIT

ANSWERS TO SECTION 4.5 REVIEW QUESTIONS (text p. 106)

Accounting Software: Ledger Accounts and the Trial Balance

1. _____
_____
_____

2. _____
_____
_____

3. _____
_____
_____

4. _____
_____
_____

5. _____
_____
_____

ANSWERS TO SECTION 4.5 EXERCISES (text p. 107)

Exercise 1, p. 107

A.

Bank	A/R — Infield Flyers	A/R — Remdal Red Sox

Supplies	Equipment	Bank Loan

A/P — Cannon Sports	A/P — Ewert Equipment	A/P — Sandhu Sporting Goods

S. Lucas, Capital

ANSWERS TO SECTION 4.5 EXERCISES (cont.)

Exercise 1 (cont.)

B. _____

_____

_____

ACCOUNTS	DEBIT	CREDIT

C. a. _____

_____

_____

_____

_____

_____

b. _____

c. _____

_____

d. _____

_____

Extending Your Computer Skills (text p. 108)

_____

_____

_____

_____

_____

_____

ANSWERS TO SECTION 4.5 EXERCISES (cont.)

Communicate It (text p. 108)

Write down the main points of your letter, then use a word-processing program to compose it.

_____

_____

_____

_____

_____

_____

_____

_____

_____

_____

_____

_____

ANSWERS TO CHAPTER 4 REVIEW EXERCISES (text p. 109)

Using Your Knowledge

Exercise 1, p. 109

Indicate whether each of the following statements is true or false by entering a "T" or an "F" in the box indicated. Explain the reason for each "F" response in the space provided.

A. A number of individual balance sheet items may appear on one account page, as long as they are shown separately.

B. Many accountants use the equation analysis sheet instead of the ledger.

C. There is a page in the ledger for the total assets figure.

D. T-accounts are ideal for small businesses.

E. The first dollar amount recorded in an account is placed on the same side as it appears on a simple balance sheet.

F. There is no account for capital because it can always be found by subtracting the total assets from the total liabilities.

G. A transaction analysis sheet is a permanent accounting record.

H. For every transaction, there is always one debit amount and one credit amount, which are equal.

I. A balanced accounting entry is a correct accounting entry.

J. The balance of an account that is not zero must be either a debit or a credit.

K. The J.R. Dahl account in the ledger of C. Jacob is either an account payable or an account receivable.

L. Eric Lai's account has a credit balance. This means that he purchased our services on credit.

ANSWERS TO CHAPTER 4 REVIEW EXERCISES (cont.)

Exercise 1 (cont.)

M. An exceptional balance is opposite to what would be normal. ☐

N. A customer is given a refund because of unsatisfactory service. The account of this customer will now have an exceptional balance. ☐

O. A ledger contains an exceptional balance. A trial balance cannot be taken until the exceptional item is transferred to another part of the ledger. ☐

P. A trial balance that is in balance proves that there are no errors in the accounts. ☐

Q. A trial balance is taken using a printing calculator. When the "total" key is pressed, the figure 89.00 comes up. This is the amount of the error. ☐

R. The business buys supplies and pays cash. The accounting entry made in the accounts is Dr Bank and Cr Supplies. This causes the ledger to be out of balance. ☐

Explanations for "F" Responses

_____

_____

_____

_____

_____

_____

_____

_____

_____

_____

_____

_____

_____

_____

_____

Exercise 2, p. 110

A. _____

_____

_____

_____

B. _____

_____

C. _____

ANSWERS TO CHAPTER 4 REVIEW EXERCISES (cont.)

Exercise 6 (cont.)

Office Supplies	Furniture and Equipment	Properties Owned	Automobile
1 115	11 916	18 042	27 965

Bank Loan	A/P — Pioneer Furniture	A/P — Tuck Corporation	Cathy Geraci, Capital
19 000		1 520	*

* Calculate opening capital

ACCOUNTS	DEBIT	CREDIT

This page is left blank intentionally.

Name _____ Date _____

ANSWERS TO CHAPTER 4 REVIEW EXERCISES (cont.)

Challenge Exercise, p. 112

1. Name of Business: _____

2. Transactions:

1. _____
   _____

2. _____
   _____

3. _____
   _____

4. _____
   _____

5. _____
   _____

6. _____
   _____

ANSWERS TO CHAPTER 4 REVIEW EXERCISES (cont.)

Challenge Exercise (cont.)

7. _____

_____

8. _____

_____

9. _____

_____

10. _____

_____

11. _____

_____

12. _____

_____

_____

_____

_____

ACCOUNTS	DEBIT	CREDIT

ANSWERS TO CHAPTER 4 REVIEW EXERCISES (cont.)

Challenge Exercise (cont.)

3. Your Answer Key to Your Computer Exercise

ACCOUNTS		DEBIT	CREDIT

ANSWERS TO CHAPTER 4 REVIEW EXERCISES (cont.)

Questions for Further Thought, p. 112

1. _____
   _____
   _____
   _____

2. _____
   _____

3. _____
4. _____
   _____
   _____
   _____

5. _____
   _____
   _____

6. _____
   _____

7. _____
8. _____
9. _____
   _____
   _____

10. _____
    _____

CASE STUDIES (text p. 113)

Case 1   *Are Debits and Credits Confusing?*, p. 113

1. _____
   _____
   _____

2. _____
3. _____
   _____
   _____

CASE STUDIES (con't.)

Case 2 *Property Value: A Matter of Opinion?*, p. 113

1. _____

_____

_____

_____

_____

_____

_____

_____

_____

2. _____

_____

_____

_____

3. _____

_____

_____

_____

Challenge Case 3 *Choosing between Two Companies*, p. 114

1. _____

2. _____

_____

_____

_____

3. _____

_____

_____

_____

_____

_____

_____

_____

Name _____ Date _____

Career   **MELANIE APPLEYARD/CO-OPERATIVE EDUCATION STUDENT**

ANSWERS TO DISCUSSION QUESTIONS (text p. 115)

1. _____
   _____
   _____
   _____
   _____
   _____
   _____

2. _____
   _____
   _____

3. a. _____
      _____
      _____

   b. _____
      _____
      _____
      _____

   c. _____
      _____
      _____
      _____

4. _____
   _____
   _____

5. _____
   _____

Name _____ Date _____

Chapter 5 The Expanded Ledger

ANSWERS TO SECTION 5.1 REVIEW QUESTIONS (text p. 131)

Expanding the Ledger

1. _____

2. _____
   _____
   _____

3. _____
   _____

4. _____
   _____

5. _____
   _____

6. _____
   _____
   _____
   _____

7. _____

8. _____
   _____
   _____
   _____
   _____

9. _____
   _____
   _____
   _____
   _____
   _____
   _____
   _____

ANSWERS TO SECTION 5.1 EXERCISES (text p. 124)

Exercise 1, p. 124

A.

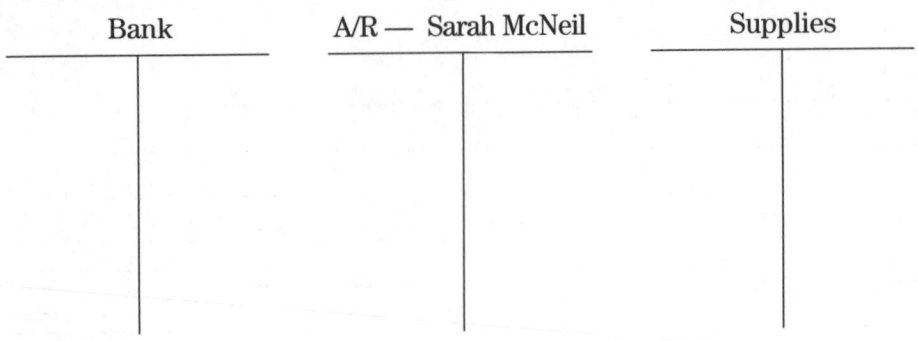

Bank	A/R — Sarah McNeil	Supplies

Bank Loan	A/P — Percy's Office Outfitters	A/P — Northern Utilities	A. Dodds, Capital

B. Total debits: _____   Total credits: _____

C. Expanded Ledger

A. Dodds, Capital	A. Dodds, Drawings	Fees Earned	Rent Expense

Telephone Expense	Wages Expense	Utilities Expense

ANSWERS TO SECTION 5.1 EXERCISES (cont.)

Exercise 1 (cont.)

D. Sum of credit balances: $ _____

Sum of debit balances: _____

Difference $ _____

The total of $2 440 matches the balance in A. Dodds, Capital in Part 1 above.

E. _____

_____

_____

_____

Exercise 2, p. 125

A business has the beginning financial position recorded in the schedule below. Ten simple transactions are listed in the left-hand column. **Work out the revised totals for assets, liabilities, and owner's equity after each transaction. Enter these totals below. Complete the last two columns of the chart by recording: a) the amount of change in equity (if any), and b) whether the change in equity represents revenue, expense, or drawings.**

Transactions	Total Assets	Total Liabilities	Owner's Equity	Change in Equity	Revenue? Expense? Drawings?
Beginning financial position	10 000	6 000	4 000	–	–
1. Purchased $400 of supplies for future use and paid cash.					
2. Reduced bank loan by $1 000.					
3. Received $800 cash from a debtor.					
4. Sold services for $900 cash.					
5. Sold services on credit, $1 500.					
6. Paid hydro for month just ended, $125.					
7. Owner withdrew $750 cash for personal use.					
8. Paid employee's wages, $600.					
9. Purchased truck on credit, $20 000.					
10. Owner took supplies for personal use, $250					

ANSWERS TO SECTION 5.1 EXERCISES (cont.)

Exercise 3, p. 126

| Date | Debits | | Credits | |
	Account(s)	Amount	Account(s)	Amount

Exercise 4, p. 127

a. The Bank account normally has a _____ balance.

b. A revenue account normally has a _____ balance.

c. An expense account normally has a _____ balance.

d. Paying a creditor involves a _____ entry to the creditor's account.

e. The Drawings account receives a _____ entry when the owner withdraws money for personal use.

f. A lawyer gives a cash refund to a customer. The Bank account will receive a _____ entry and the Revenue account will receive a _____ entry.

g. Supplies are bought on credit. The Supplies account will receive a _____ entry and the supplier's account payable will receive a _____ entry.

h. The Drawings account will not normally receive _____ entries.

i. An increase in equity can be thought of as a _____ to the Capital account.

j. Net income can be thought of as a _____ to the Capital account.

k. Net loss can be thought of as a _____ to the Capital account.

l. The owner takes a computer from the business for his personal (permanent) use. The Drawings account will receive a _____ entry.

ANSWERS TO SECTION 5.1 EXERCISES (cont.)

Exercise 5, p. 127

No.	Asset		Liability		Revenue (Equity) (Increase)	Expense (Equity) (Decrease)	Drawings (Equity) (Decrease)
	Increase	Decrease	Decrease	Increase			
1.	✓				✓		
2.							
3.							
4.							
5.							
6.							
7.							
8.							
9.							
10.							

ANSWERS TO SECTION 5.2 REVIEW QUESTIONS (text p. 133)

The Income Statement

1. _____

2. _____

3. _____

4. _____

5. _____

6. _____

7. _____

8. _____

9. _____

ANSWERS TO SECTION 5.2 REVIEW QUESTIONS (cont.)

10. _____

_____

11. _____

_____

12. _____

_____

_____

13. _____

_____

_____

ANSWERS TO SECTION 5.2 EXERCISES (text p. 134)

Exercise 1, p. 134

1. _____

_____

_____

_____

_____

_____

2. _____

_____

_____

ANSWERS TO SECTION 5.2 EXERCISES (cont.)

Exercise 2, p. 134

A. _____

_____

_____

ANSWERS TO SECTION 5.2 EXERCISES (cont.)

Exercise 2 (cont.)

B.

E. Stokaluk Chart of Accounts

Assets	No.	Equity	No.
_____	___	_____	___
_____	___	_____	___
_____	___		
_____	___	_____	___
_____	___	_____	___
_____	___		
_____		_____	___

Liabilities	No.		
_____	___	_____	___
_____	___	_____	___
_____	___	_____	___
		_____	___
		_____	___
		_____	___

Name _____ Date _____

ANSWERS TO SECTION 5.2 EXERCISES (cont.)

Exercise 2 (cont.)

C. _____

_____

_____

Name Harraj _____   Date _____

ANSWERS TO SECTION 5.2 EXERCISES (cont.)

Exercise 3, p. 135

1.

Express Air Service Chart of Accounts

Assets	No.	Equity	No.
Airplanes	105	Karen Kay	300
Automobiles	110	Karen Kay	305
Bank	115		
Building	120	Revenue - Freight	400
Accounts Receivable	100	Revenue - Passengers	405
Equipment	125		
Land	130	Advertising Expense	500
Supplies	135	Bank Charges Expense	505
		Building Repairs Expense	510
		General Expense	515
Liabilities	**No.**	Insurance Expense	520
Accounts Payable	200	Legal Expense	525
Mortgage Payable	250	Salaries Expense	530
		Supplies Expense	535
		Telephone Expense	540
		Wages Expense	545

Exercise 4, p. 135

Assets = Liabilities + Owner's Equity

Assets		Liabilities		Capital		Revenue	
Debit	Credit	Debit	Credit	Debit	Credit	Debit	Credit
increase	decrease	decrease	increase	decrease	increase	decrease	increase

Drawings		Expense	
Debit	Credit	Debit	Credit
increase	decrease	increase	decrease

ANSWERS TO SECTION 5.2 EXERCISES (cont.)

Exercise 5, p. 135

A.

Atlas Associates
Income Statement
Month Ended November 30, 20-

Revenue								
Fees Earned						31	700	—
Expenses								
Advertising Expense			600	—				
Car Expense	3	760	—					
General Expense	1	200	—					
Rent Expense	6	000	—					
Salaries Expense	13	400	—					
Utilities Expense	3	500	—					

B. _____

_____

_____

C. _____

_____

D. _____

_____

ANSWERS TO SECTION 5.3 REVIEW QUESTIONS (text p. 139)

Equity Relationships and the Balance Sheet

1. _____
2. _____
3. _____
4. _____
5. _____
6. _____
7. _____

Name _Harraj Sandhu_   Date _Wed Sept. 8 20m_

ANSWERS TO SECTION 5.3 EXERCISES (text p. 140)

Exercise 1, p. 140

Complete the schedule below by filling in the blanks.

Items	Opening Capital	Net Income or Net Loss (−)	Drawings	Ending Capital
a.	$30 000	$15 000	$10 000	$ 35,000
b.	50 000	−2 000	7 000	41000
c.	70 000	32 000	26,500	75 500
d.	36,700	16 000	19 500	33 200
e.	56 000	14,000	30 000	40 000
f.	45 000	39,955	25 000	15 000
g.	22 000	16,000	10 000	28 000
h.	35,000	25 000	18 000	42 000
i.	120 000	42 000	50,000	112 000

Exercise 2, p. 140

Complete the following schedule by filling in the blanks for each of the five separate equity section relationships.

Financial Information	Company 1	Company 2	Company 3	Company 4	Company 5
Beginning capital	$ 6 000	$ 6 000	$15 000	$ 5000	$62 000
Total revenues	10 000	25000	29 000	50,000	80000
Total expenses	8 000	11 000	18,000	30 000	35 000
Net income or loss (−)	2000	14 000	11 000	20 000	−5 000
Drawings	3 000	12 000	17,000	15 000	−5000
Increase or decrease (−) in equity	1000	2000	−6 000	5000	−10 000
Ending capital	5000	9000	9,000	10 000	52,000

Exercise 3, p. 140

G. Benvie, Capital														
Balance Jan. 1, 20−					27	0	4	2	62					
Net Income		39	1	7	1	04								
Drawings		35	0	0	0	−								
Increase in Capital							4	1	7	04				
Balance Dec 31, 20−											31	2	1	3 66

ANSWERS TO SECTION 5.3 EXERCISES (cont.)

Exercise 3 (cont.)

S. Robb, Capital																		
Balance Jan. 1, 20-									19	6	4	1	25					
Net Loss	22	4	6	2	67													
Drawings	25	5	7	5	-													
Decrease in Capital									3	1	1	2	39					
Balance March 31, 20-														16	5	2	8	92

J. Bedford, Capital																		
Balance May 1, 20-	0	-							20	1	9	6	74					
Net Loss	3	7	5	0	20													
Drawings	10	0	4	7	17													
Decrease in Capital									13	7	9	7	37					
Balance May 31, 20-														6	3	9	9	37

ANSWERS TO SECTION 5.4 REVIEW QUESTIONS (text p. 144)

Simply Accounting, Spreadsheets, and the Expanded Ledger

1. _____

   _____

2. _____

   _____

3. _____

4. _____

   _____

   _____

5. _____

   _____

   _____

6. _____

   _____

ANSWERS TO SECTION 5.4 EXERCISES (text p. 144)

Challenge Exercises 1 and 2, p. 144 and 145

Use spreadsheet software and the files named BoaIncome.xls and BoaBal.xls to complete these exercises. **Note:** If you are using the first printing of the text, the instructions for exercise 1 direct you to Figure 5.2 on page 119. The correct illustration to examine is Figure 5.3 on page 120.

ANSWERS TO SECTION 5.4 EXERCISES (cont.)

Challenge Exercises 1 and 2 (cont.)

ANSWERS TO CHAPTER 5 REVIEW EXERCISES (text p. 146)

Exercise 1, p. 146

A. _____

_____

_____

_____

_____

_____

B. _____

_____

Name _____   Date _____

Exercise 2, p. 147

Using the table below on the left, complete the exercise to its right. **Show the effect of the accounting entry for each transaction**. The first transaction is done for you.

1. Asset debit	**a.** Purchase a new car on account.		
2. Asset credit	**b.** Receive payment on account from a customer.		
3. Liability debit	**c.** Owner withdraws cash for personal use.		
4. Liability credit	**d.** Owner starts a new business by investing cash.		
5. Capital debit	**e.** The car is repaired and paid for in cash immediately.		
6. Capital credit	**f.** Perform a service for a customer for cash.		
7. Drawings debit	**g.** Perform a service for a customer on account.		
8. Drawings credit	**h.** Purchase supplies for cash.		
9. Revenue debit	**i.** Receive a bill for gas and oil for the car.		
10. Revenue credit	**j.** Pay a creditor on account.		
11. Expense debit	**k.** Throw out some ruined supplies.		
12. Expense credit			

	DR	CR
a.	1	4
b.		
c.		
d.		
e.		
f.		
g.		
h.		
i.		
j.		
k.		

Exercise 3, p. 147

_____

_____

_____

Exercise 4, p. 148

1.

Bank	A/R — P. Alder	A/R — A. Jackson	Supplies
1745	50	70	610

ANSWERS TO CHAPTER 5 REVIEW EXERCISES (cont.)

Exercise 4 (cont.)

Equipment	Automobiles	A/P — B & B Stone	A/P — Century Finance
5 000	7 900	110	5 500

P. Garside, Capital	P. Garside, Drawings	Revenue	Car Expense
5 625	200	11 920	500

Utilities Expense	Rent Expense	Wages Expense	
280	300	6 500	

	Debits		Credits	
	Account(s)	**Amount**	**Account(s)**	**Amount**

2. The corrected net income will be _____ .

Exercise 5, p. 148

End of	Assets	=	Liabilities	+	Beginning Capital	+	Revenue	−	Expenses	−	Drawings
Year 1	100	=	20	+	70	+	60	−	45	−	5
Year 2	120	=	30	+	80	+	90	−	60	−	20
Year 3	130	=	35	+	90	+	105	−	80	−	20
Year 4	130	=	30	+	95	+	110	−	95	−	10

ANSWERS TO CHAPTER 5 REVIEW EXERCISES (cont.)

Exercise 6 (cont.)

	Assets	Liabilities	Equity
End of 20-1		$27 400	
End of 20-2			$19 300

Exercise 7, p. 149   **Comprehensive Exercise**

A.

Date	Debits		Credits	
	Account(s)	Amount	Account(s)	Amount
1.				
2.				
3.				
4.				
5.				
6.				
7.				
8.				
9.				
10.				
11.				
12.				
13.				
14.				
15.				
16.				

Name _Hanaj Sandhu_   Date _____

ANSWERS TO CHAPTER 5 REVIEW EXERCISES (cont.)

Exercise 7 (cont.)

A., B.

Bank	
5000	① 300
⑤ 175	② 50
⑦ 300	⑥ 100
~~175~~	⑧ 1,100
	⑨ 120
	⑪ 750
	⑫ 120
	⑬ 50
	⑭ 600
	⑮ 70
	⑯ 500

A/R — Jenkins and Co.	
④ 900	⑦ 300
	⑭ 600

Office Supplies	
① 300	
③ 1,100	
⑫ 120	

Office Equipment

Automobile	
18,000	

A/P — Office Supply Company	
③ 1,100	③ 1,100

N.A. James, Capital

N.A. James, Drawings	
⑩ 200	

Fees Earned	
⑦ 300	④ 900
⑩ 200	⑤ 175

Advertising Expense	
② 50	
⑬ 50	

Car Expense	
⑨ 120	

Donations Expense	
⑥ 100	

Miscellaneous Expense	
⑮ 70	

Rent Expense	
⑪ 750	

Name _____ Date _____

ANSWERS TO CHAPTER 5 REVIEW EXERCISES (cont.)

Exercise 7 (cont.)

C. _____

_____

_____

ACCOUNTS	DEBIT	CREDIT

Name _____ Date _____

ANSWERS TO CHAPTER 5 REVIEW EXERCISES (cont.)

Exercise 7 (cont.)

D. _____

_____

_____

E. _____

_____

_____

Name _____   Date _____

ANSWERS TO CHAPTER 5 REVIEW EXERCISES (cont.)

Questions for Further Thought, p. 151

1. _____
   _____

2. _____
   _____

3. _____
   _____

4. _____
   _____
   _____

5. _____

6. _____
   _____

7. _____
   a. _____
   b. a doctor: _____
   c. a loan company: _____
   d. a photographer: _____
   e. a real estate company: _____
   f. a hair dresser: _____
      a dry cleaning company: _____

8. _____
   _____
   _____
   _____
   _____
   _____
   _____
   _____
   _____
   _____

9. _____
   _____

10. _____
    _____

11. _____
    _____

ANSWERS TO CHAPTER 5 REVIEW EXERCISES (cont.)

Questions for Further Thought (cont.)

12. _____
13. _____
14. _____
    _____

CASE STUDIES (text p. 152)

Case 1 *"Timing Is Everything,"* p. 152

1. _____
   _____
   _____
   _____

2. _____
   _____
   _____

3. _____
   _____

4. _____
   _____
   _____
   _____

Case 2 *Pumping Profits,* p. 152

1. _____
   _____
   _____
   _____

2. _____
   _____
   _____
   _____

3. _____
   _____

CASE STUDIES (cont.)

Challenge Case 3 *Revenue Roulette*, p. 153

1. _____
   _____
   _____

2. _____
   a. _____
   b. _____
   _____

3. _____
   _____
   _____
   _____

Group Discussion Case 4 *Perspective on Financial Statements*, p. 154

1. _____
   _____
   _____

2. _____

3. _____
   _____

4. _____
   _____

5. _____
   _____

6. _____
   _____

7. _____
   _____

8. _____
   _____
   _____
   _____
   _____

Career **NICHOLAS SCHMIDT/SOLE PROPRIETOR**

ANSWERS TO DISCUSSION QUESTIONS (text p. 155)

1. _____
   _____
   _____
   _____

2. _____

3. _____

4. _____
   _____
   _____
   _____

5. _____

6. _____

7. _____
   _____
   _____

8. _____
   _____
   _____
   _____
   _____
   _____
   _____
   _____

Chapter 6 The Journal and Source Documents

ANSWERS TO SECTION 6.1 REVIEW QUESTIONS (text p. 161)

The Journal

1. _____
_____
_____
_____
_____

2. _____
_____

3. _____
_____

4. _____
_____

5. _____

6. _____
_____

7. _____
_____
_____
_____

8. _____

9. a. _____
   b. _____
   c. _____
   d. _____
   e. _____

10. _____

11. _____

12. _____
_____
_____

13. _____

14. _____
_____

Name Harraj Sandhu   Date _____

ANSWERS TO SECTION 6.1 EXERCISES (text p. 161)

Exercise 1, p. 161

GENERAL JOURNAL   PAGE

DATE		PARTICULARS	P.R.	DEBIT	CREDIT
Feb.	3	Rent Expense			

ANSWERS TO SECTION 6.1 EXERCISES (cont.)

Exercise 1 (cont.)

GENERAL JOURNAL

PAGE

DATE		PARTICULARS	P.R.	DEBIT	CREDIT

Exercise 2, p. 162

A. _____

_____

_____

Name _Harraj Sandhu_   Date _____

Exercise 2 (cont.)

B. and C.

GENERAL JOURNAL   PAGE

DATE	PARTICULARS	P.R.	DEBIT	CREDIT
20xx June 1	← Bank		2 500 —	
	← Law Library		3 500 —	
	← Office Equipment		8 250 —	
	← Automobile		16 500 —	
	→ A/P-Acme Finance Company			8 750 —
	→ A/P-The Stationary Store			3 250 —
	→ P. Perma, Capital			18 750 —
	→ Opening financial position of P. Perma			
1	Rent Expense		500 —	
	Bank			500 —
	Paid the rent			
2	Office Supplies		375 —	
	A/P - The Stationary Store			375 —
	Purchased typing and stationary supplies on account			
3	Bank		200 —	
	Fees Earned			200 —
	Performed a legal service			
5	A/R-R. Spooner		350 —	
	Bank			350 —
	Performed a legal service on account			
8	A/P- The Stationary Store		1 000 —	
	Bank			1 000 —
	Paid cash on account			
10	A/R -T. & R. Builders			
	Bank			

Name _____ Date _____

ANSWERS TO SECTION 6.1 EXERCISES (cont.)

Exercise 2 (cont.)

C.

GENERAL JOURNAL   PAGE

DATE		PARTICULARS	P.R.	DEBIT	CREDIT

Name _Karaj Sandhu_   Date _____

ANSWERS TO SECTION 6.2 REVIEW QUESTIONS (text p. 173)

Source Documents

1. _____
   _____
   _____
   _____

2. _____
   _____

3. _____
4. _____
5. _____
   _____

6. _____
   _____

7. _____
8. _____
   _____

9. _____
10. _____
11. _____
    _____

12. _____
    _____

13. _____
    _____
    _____

14. _____
    _____

15. _____
    _____

16. _____
17. _____
    _____

18. _____
    _____

19. _____

ANSWERS TO SECTION 6.2 REVIEW QUESTIONS (cont.)

20. _____

21. _____

22. _____

23. _____

24. _____
25. _____

ANSWERS TO SECTION 6.2 EXERCISES (text p. 174)

Exercise 1, p. 174

a. Cash Reciepts Daily Summary

b. To list the money coming in from customers, the cash reciepts are listed

c. _____

d. _____

e. _____

ANSWERS TO SECTION 6.2 EXERCISES (cont.)

Exercise 1 (cont.)

f.

DATE		PARTICULARS	DEBIT	CREDIT

g. _____

Exercise 2, p. 175

a. _____

b. _____

_____

c. _____

d. _____

_____

e.

DATE		PARTICULARS	DEBIT	CREDIT

Exercise 3, p. 176

a. _____

b. _____

c. _____

d.

DATE		PARTICULARS	DEBIT	CREDIT

ANSWERS TO SECTION 6.2 EXERCISES (cont.)

Exercise 3 (cont.)

e.

DATE		PARTICULARS	DEBIT	CREDIT

Exercise 4, p. 176

a. _____

b. _____

c. _____

d. _____

e. _____
_____

f.

DATE		PARTICULARS	DEBIT	CREDIT

g. _____

Exercise 5, p. 177

a. _____

b. _____

c.

DATE		PARTICULARS	DEBIT	CREDIT

ANSWERS TO SECTION 6.3 REVIEW QUESTIONS (text p. 181)

Provincial Sales Tax

1. _____

2. _____
_____

ANSWERS TO SECTION 6.3 REVIEW QUESTIONS (text p. 181)

3. _____
   _____

4. _____

    1. _____

    2. _____

    3. _____

    4. _____

5. _____

6. _____

7. _____

8. _____
   _____
   _____
   _____
   _____

ANSWERS TO SECTION 6.3 EXERCISES (text p. 181)

Exercise 1, p. 181

A.

	Amount before PST	PST at 8 per cent	Total Amount
1.	$ 75.00		
2.	$120.00		
3.	$ 58.60		
4.	$ 98.00		
5.	$130.75		

ANSWERS TO SECTION 6.3 EXERCISES (cont.)

Exercise 1 (cont.)

B.

GENERAL JOURNAL   PAGE ____

DATE		PARTICULARS	P.R.	DEBIT	CREDIT

ANSWERS TO SECTION 6.3 EXERCISES (cont.)

Exercise 2, p. 182

A.

GENERAL JOURNAL

PAGE

DATE		PARTICULARS	P.R.	DEBIT	CREDIT

B.

GENERAL JOURNAL

PAGE

DATE		PARTICULARS	P.R.	DEBIT	CREDIT

Exercise 3, p. 182

A. _____
_____
_____
_____
_____
_____
_____

B. _____

Exercise 4, p. 182

A. _____
B. _____
C. _____
D. _____
E. _____
F.

DATE		PARTICULARS	DEBIT	CREDIT

ANSWERS TO SECTION 6.3 EXERCISES (cont.)

Exercise 5, p. 183

A.

MOORE'S MARINA			**16 HARBOURFRONT RD.** **VANCOUVER, B.C.** **V7C 8T8** **Phone: 888-6666** **Fax: 888-6645**

Date: *Feb. 28, 20–*

Name: *Valerie Miniaci*

Address: *Bear Island, Alberta*

Qty	Description	Price	Amount
RECEIVED ABOVE IN GOOD ORDER		PST	
		Total	
	SALES SLIP		9124

B.   Journal entry:

GENERAL JOURNAL   PAGE

DATE	PARTICULARS	P.R.	DEBIT	CREDIT

ANSWERS TO SECTION 6.4 REVIEW QUESTIONS (text p. 190)

The Goods and Services Tax

1. _____

2. _____
   _____

3. _____
   _____

4. _____

5. _____
   _____

6. _____

7. _____
   _____

8. _____

9. _____

10. _____

11. _____

12. _____

13. _____

14. _____

15. _____

16. _____

17. _____

18. _____

19. _____

ANSWERS TO SECTION 6.4 EXERCISES (text p. 190)

Exercise 1, p. 190   Complete the following schedule.

End of period	GST Recoverable	GST Payable	Amount of remittance	Refund claim	Due date
Mar. 31	$ 904.72	$1 507.20			
Sep. 30	$1 565.20	$2 074.21			
Dec. 31	$ 700.40	$ 608.32			
Aug. 31	$2 764.35	$1 964.32			
Jan. 31	$3 750.00	$4 209.64			

ANSWERS TO SECTION 6.4 EXERCISES (cont.)

Exercise 2, p. 191

GENERAL JOURNAL   PAGE ____

DATE		PARTICULARS	P.R.	DEBIT	CREDIT

ANSWERS TO SECTION 6.4 EXERCISES (cont.)

Exercise 3, p. 192

A.

CUSTODIAL SERVICES	INVOICE NUMBER
	953

900 LANSDOWNE AVENUE
TORONTO, ON
M6K 2V7
Phone: 416-767-8569 Fax: 416-767-8533

GST No. 102620110	Terms Net 30	Date *April 26, 20—*	
To:	*Oakridge Ski Club*		
	Box 500		
	Medonte, Ontario		
	L4M 4Y8		
For:	*2 #152 Floor Mops @ $12*		*$24.00*
	6 gals. Floor Cleaner @ $15		*$90.00*
		GST 7%	
		PST 8%	
		TOTAL	

B.

GENERAL JOURNAL   PAGE

DATE		PARTICULARS	P.R.	DEBIT	CREDIT

C.

GENERAL JOURNAL   PAGE

DATE		PARTICULARS	P.R.	DEBIT	CREDIT

ANSWERS TO SECTION 6.4 EXERCISES (cont.)

Exercise 4, p. 192

| | GENERAL JOURNAL | | | PAGE 6 |

DATE		PARTICULARS	P.R.	DEBIT	CREDIT

ANSWERS TO SECTION 6.5 REVIEW QUESTIONS (text p. 197)

Building Spreadsheet Models

1. _____
   _____

2. _____
   _____

3. _____

4. _____

5. _____
   _____

6. _____

7. _____

Computer Exercise

ANSWERS TO CHAPTER 6 REVIEW EXERCISES (text p. 199)

Using Your Knowledge

Exercise 1, p. 199

Complete the following summary.

Nature of Transaction	Source Document(s)	Required Journal Entry	
		Accounts Debited	Accounts Credited
Payment on account			
Sale on account			
Bank service charge			
Cash payment of phone bill			
Cash received on account			
Purchase of equipment on account			
Cash sale			

ANSWERS TO CHAPTER 6 REVIEW EXERCISES (cont.)

Exercise 2, p. 199

Source Document	Document Number	Transactions	Document Number
Bank credit memo	1	1. Owner withdraws money.	
Bank debit memo	2	2. Purchase of equipment on account.	
Cheque copy	3	3. Payment on account.	
Cash sales slip	4	4. Cash sale.	
Sales invoice	5	5. Sale on account.	
Purchase invoice	6	6. Cheques received from customers on account.	
Cash receipts list	7	7. Increase bank loan.	
Owner's written memo.	8	8. Owner invests additional money in the business.	
Bank statement	9	9. Bank service charge.	

Exercise 3, p. 200

Indicate whether each of the following statements is true or false by placing a "T" or an "F" in the box provided. Explain the reason for each "F" response in the space provided.

A. Anyone in the business can initiate a business transaction.

B. Every journal entry is based on a source document.

C. The only purpose of source documents is to provide the basis for a journal entry.

D. A business that sells to its customers on a cash basis does not normally use a sales invoice.

E. Journal entries for all cash sales slips are essentially the same.

F. Sales invoices are used by businesses that make most of their sales on account.

G. For every sales invoice, there is a debit to an account receivable.

H. The transaction log that is produced by a POS terminal is used by an accounting clerk to record a debit to Bank and a credit to Sales.

I. Every sales invoice is also a purchase invoice.

J. The debit entry for every purchase invoice is always the same.

K. The supporting document for a payment on account is the tear-off portion of a cheque.

L. The credit entry for every cheque copy payment is always the same.

M. Cheques received are considered to be cash received.

N. The bank has no right to make deductions from the accounts of its customers.

O. We debit Bank when we receive a bank debit memo.

P. The cost principle states that every asset acquired is to be recorded at its cost price.

ANSWERS TO CHAPTER 6 REVIEW EXERCISES (cont.)

Exercise 3 (cont.)

Q. The best objective evidence of a purchase is a purchase invoice received from an independent supplier. ☐

R. Only provincial governments are allowed to levy retail sales taxes. ☐

S. The purchaser of goods or services is required to make accounting entries for provincial sales tax. ☐

T. The PST account is an expense account. ☐

Explanations for "F" Responses:

_____

_____

_____

_____

_____

_____

_____

_____

_____

_____

_____

_____

Exercise 4, p. 200   **Comprehensive Exercise**

$600 Purchase				
	PST	**GST**	**HST**	**Total Price**
Alberta				
Manitoba				
Newfoundland and Labrador				
Ontario				
Quebec				
Saskatchewan				

Name _____ Date _____

Sales — selling on account
Invoice

Exercise 5, p. 201   Comprehensive Exercise

GENERAL JOURNAL   PAGE 7

DATE		PARTICULARS	P.R.	DEBIT	CREDIT
20— Nov.	4	A/R — R. Chevrier		3 1 0 75	
		Fees Earned			2 75
		HST Payable			3 5 75
		Sales Invoice No. 571			
	6	Photo Supplies		2 65 —	
		HST Recoverable		3 4 45	
		A/P — Black's Photo			2 9 9 45
		Purchase Invoice for photo supplies			
	9	Automobile Expense		1 65 —	
		HST Recoverable		2 1 45	
		A/P — Petro Canada			1 8 6 45
		Purchase Invoice for fuel			
	10	Wayne Siebert, Drawings		3 25 —	
		Bank			3 25 —
		Cheque Copy No. 652			
	12	Bank		1 63 85	
		Fees Earned			1 45
		HST Payable			1 8 85
		Cash Sales Slip No. 214			
	15	Bank Charges Expense		3 5 50	
		Bank			3 5 50
		Bank Debit Memo			
	20	Photo Supplies		75 —	
		HST Recoverable		9 10	
		Bank			8 4 10

ANSWERS TO CHAPTER 6 REVIEW EXERCISES (cont.)

Exercise 5 (cont.)

GENERAL JOURNAL   PAGE 8

DATE		PARTICULARS	P.R.	DEBIT	CREDIT
20- Nov.	22	Bank		4 1 2 —	
		A/R-H.Walker			4 1 2 —
		Cash Reciept			
	25	W. Siebert, Drawings		8 4 10	
		Photo Supplies			7 5 —
		HST Recoverable			9 10

ANSWERS TO CHAPTER 6 REVIEW EXERCISES (cont.)

Exercise 6, p. 202   **Comprehensive Exercise**

GENERAL JOURNAL   PAGE ⑫

DATE	PARTICULARS	P.R.	DEBIT	CREDIT

ANSWERS TO CHAPTER 6 REVIEW EXERCISES (cont.)

Exercise 6 (cont.)

GENERAL JOURNAL   PAGE

DATE		PARTICULARS	P.R.	DEBIT	CREDIT

ANSWERS TO CHAPTER 6 REVIEW EXERCISES (cont.)

Exercise 7, p. 203   **Comprehensive Exercise**

A.

GENERAL JOURNAL   PAGE *36*

DATE		PARTICULARS	P.R.	DEBIT	CREDIT

Name _____ Date _____

ANSWERS TO CHAPTER 6 REVIEW EXERCISES (cont.)

Exercise 7 (cont.)

GENERAL JOURNAL

PAGE _____

DATE	PARTICULARS	P.R.	DEBIT	CREDIT

ANSWERS TO CHAPTER 6 REVIEW EXERCISES (cont.)

Exercise 7 (cont.)

GENERAL JOURNAL   PAGE

DATE		PARTICULARS	P.R.	DEBIT	CREDIT

B.

Canada Customs and Revenue Agency	Agence des douanes et du revenu du Canada	GST/HST RETURN (NON-PERSONALIZED)			001800		Part 2

Reporting period   GST62-5 E

YOU MUST COMPLETE THIS AREA.

Business Number

		Year	Month	Day		Year	Month	Day
From:					To:			

Sales and other revenue	**101**	0 0	Total GST/HST and adjustments for period	**105**	
Instalments and net tax already remitted	**110**		Total ITCs and adjustments	**108**	
Rebates	**111**		Net tax	**109**	
GST/HST due on acquisition of taxable real property	**205**		Refund claimed	**114**	
Other GST/HST to be self-assessed	**405**		Payment enclosed	**115**	

I certify that the information given in this return and in any attached documents is, to the best of my knowledge, true, correct and complete in every respect, and that I am the person required to file this return, or that I am authorized to sign on behalf of the person. **It is a serious offence to make a false return.**

_____   _____/_____/_____
Authorized Signature   Date

⑆1220⑈117⑈   96

Questions for Further Thought, p. 204

1. _____
_____

ANSWERS TO CHAPTER 6 REVIEW EXERCISES (cont.)

Questions for Further Thought (cont.)

2. _____
_____
_____
_____

3. _____
_____

4. _____
_____
_____
_____
_____
_____
_____
_____
_____

5. _____
_____
_____

6. _____

7. _____

8. _____
_____
_____
_____

9. _____
_____
_____

10. _____
_____
_____
_____

11. _____
_____
_____
_____

12. _____
_____

ANSWERS TO CHAPTER 6 REVIEW EXERCISES (cont.)

Cases for Further Thought, p. 204

1. _____
   _____
   _____

2. _____
   _____

3. _____
   _____
   _____

4. _____
   _____
   _____

5. _____
   _____
   _____

6. _____
   _____
   _____

CASE STUDIES (text p. 205)

Challenge Case 1   *Accounting for a Package Deal*, p. 205

1. _____
   _____
   _____
   _____
   _____
   _____
   _____

2. _____
   _____

3. _____

4. _____

Name _____ Date _____

CASE STUDIES (cont.)

Challenge Case 1 (cont.)

Item	Appraised Values in Dollars per Item	Appraised Values in Fractions of Total	Times	Total Cost Price	Cost Price per Item
_____	_____	_____	×	_____	_____
_____	_____	_____	×	_____	_____
_____	_____	_____	×	_____	_____
_____	_____	_____	×	_____	_____
_____	_____	_____	×	_____	_____
_____	_____	_____	×	_____	_____
_____	_____	_____	×	_____	_____
_____	_____	_____	×	_____	_____

5.

DATE	PARTICULARS	DEBIT	CREDIT

6. _____

_____

_____

_____

_____

_____

_____

_____

_____

_____

_____

Group Discussion Case 2 *Is a Profit Always a Profit?*, p. 206

1. _____

2. _____

_____

_____

CASE STUDIES (cont.)

Group Discussion Case 2 (cont.)

3. _____

4. _____

_____

_____

_____

_____

_____

5. _____

_____

_____

6. _____

7. _____

_____

_____

_____

_____

_____

Career   **PHIL QUACKENBUSH/PRESIDENT, Q.W. PAGE ASSOCIATES**

ANSWERS TO DISCUSSION QUESTIONS (text p. 207)

1. _____

_____

_____

_____

2. _____

_____

_____

_____

_____

_____

3. _____

_____

_____

4. _____

_____

Chapter 7 | Posting

ANSWERS TO SECTION 7.1 REVIEW QUESTIONS (text p. 219)

Posting

1. _____
2. _____
3. _____
4. _____
5. _____

_____
_____
_____

6. _____
7. _____
8. _____
    1. _____
    2. _____
    3. _____
    4. _____
    5. _____
9. _____
10. _____

_____
11. _____
    1. _____
    2. _____
    3. _____
12. _____
13. _____

_____
14. _____
15. _____

_____
16. _____
    1. _____
    2. _____
    3. _____
    4. _____

ANSWERS TO SECTION 7.1 EXERCISES (text p. 219)

Exercise 1, p. 219

A. Asset

Debit		Credit		DR/CR	Balance Amount	
1 000	00				1	000 —
250	00				1	250 —
310	00			DR	1	560 —
		1 250	00	DR		310
200	00			DR		510
350	00			DR		860
		860	00	DR		0
850	00			DR		850
		1 000	00	CR		150
1 500	00			DR		1350
200	00			DR		1550

B. Liability

Debit		Credit		DR/CR	Balance Amount	
		3 500	00			
		1 600	00			
3 500	00					
1 000	00					
		2 000	00			
600	00					
2 000	00					
		450	00			
500	00					
		50	00			
		375	00			

ANSWERS TO SECTION 7.1 EXERCISES (cont.)

Exercise 2, p. 219   (Workbook Exercise)

The journal and ledger of C. Fries appear below and on the following pages. **Post the journal entries to the ledger accounts**. When this is completed, **take off a trial balance to ensure your work is accurate**.

GENERAL JOURNAL   PAGE 40

DATE		PARTICULARS	P.R.	DEBIT	CREDIT
20-2 Jan.	4	Bank		8 0 5 —	
		Revenue			7 0 0 —
		GST Payable			4 9 —
		PST Payable			5 6 —
		Cash sale			
	7	Wages Expense		1 5 0 0 —	
		Bank			1 5 0 0 —
		Wages for week			
	10	Bank		3 7 0 —	
		A/R — P. Berry			3 7 0 —
		Received on account			
	15	Supplies		1 1 0 0 —	
		GST Recoverable		7 7 —	
		A/P — General Supply Co.			1 1 7 7 —
		Paper products			
	21	A/R — P. Berry		5 7 5 —	
		Revenue			5 0 0 —
		GST Payable			3 5 —
		PST Payable			4 0 —
		Sale on account			
	25	C. Fries, Drawings		8 0 0 —	
		Bank			8 0 0 —
		For personal use			
	30	General Expense		2 4 0 —	
		GST Recoverable		1 6 80	
		Bank			2 5 6 80
		Materials used			

ANSWERS TO SECTION 7.1 EXERCISES (cont.)

Exercise 2 (cont.)

GENERAL LEDGER

ACCOUNT *Bank*   No. *105*

DATE		PARTICULARS	P.R.	DEBIT	CREDIT	DR/CR	BALANCE
20-1 Dec.	31	Forwarded	–			DR	1 9 0 0 –

ACCOUNT *A/R — P. Berry*   No. *110*

DATE		PARTICULARS	P.R.	DEBIT	CREDIT	DR/CR	BALANCE
20-1 Dec.	31	Forwarded	–			DR	3 7 0 –

ACCOUNT *Supplies*   No. *115*

DATE		PARTICULARS	P.R.	DEBIT	CREDIT	DR/CR	BALANCE
20-1 Dec.	31	Forwarded	–			DR	1 4 2 0 –

ACCOUNT *Equipment*   No. *120*

DATE		PARTICULARS	P.R.	DEBIT	CREDIT	DR/CR	BALANCE
20-1 Dec.	31	Forwarded	–			DR	9 0 7 5 –

ACCOUNT *A/P — General Supply Company*   No. *205*

DATE		PARTICULARS	P.R.	DEBIT	CREDIT	DR/CR	BALANCE
20-1 Dec.	31	Forwarded	–			CR	2 0 3 0 –

ANSWERS TO SECTION 7.1 EXERCISES (cont.)

Exercise 2 (cont.)

ACCOUNT *GST Payable*   No. *210*

DATE		PARTICULARS	P.R.	DEBIT	CREDIT	DR/CR	BALANCE
20-1 Dec.	31	Forwarded	–			CR	1 0 5 –

ACCOUNT *GST Recoverable*   No. *215*

DATE		PARTICULARS	P.R.	DEBIT	CREDIT	DR/CR	BALANCE
20-1 Dec.	31	Forwarded	–			DR	7 5 –

ACCOUNT *PST Payable*   No. *220*

DATE		PARTICULARS	P.R.	DEBIT	CREDIT	DR/CR	BALANCE
20-1 Dec.	31	Forwarded	–			CR	1 2 0 –

ACCOUNT *C. Fries, Capital*   No. *305*

DATE		PARTICULARS	P.R.	DEBIT	CREDIT	DR/CR	BALANCE
20-1 Dec.	31	Forwarded	–			CR	10 5 8 5 –

ACCOUNT *C. Fries, Drawings*   No. *310*

DATE		PARTICULARS	P.R.	DEBIT	CREDIT	DR/CR	BALANCE

ANSWERS TO SECTION 7.1 EXERCISES (cont.)

Exercise 2 (cont.)

ACCOUNT *Revenue*   No. *400*

DATE	PARTICULARS	P.R.	DEBIT	CREDIT	DR/CR	BALANCE

ACCOUNT *General Expense*   No. *500*

DATE	PARTICULARS	P.R.	DEBIT	CREDIT	DR/CR	BALANCE

ACCOUNT *Wages Expense*   No. *505*

DATE	PARTICULARS	P.R.	DEBIT	CREDIT	DR/CR	BALANCE

_____

_____

_____

ACCOUNTS	DEBIT	CREDIT

ANSWERS TO SECTION 7.1 EXERCISES (cont.)

Exercise 3, p. 219 (Workbook Exercise)

The Bank account page shown below is filled. **Forward the balance to a new account page.**

ACCOUNT *Bank*   No. *101*

DATE		PARTICULARS	P.R.	DEBIT	CREDIT	DR/CR	BALANCE
20— Jul.	1		J1	1 9 0 0 —		DR	1 9 0 0 —
	7		J1	1 9 0 0 —		DR	3 8 0 0 —
	13		J1		5 0 0 —	DR	3 3 0 0 —
	19		J2		2 7 5 —	DR	3 0 2 5 —
	21		J2		5 0 —	DR	2 9 7 5 —
	25		J2		7 5 —	DR	2 9 0 0 —
	27		J3	1 0 0 0 —		DR	3 9 0 0 —
	29		J3		1 0 0 —	DR	3 8 0 0 —

ACCOUNT   No.

DATE		PARTICULARS	P.R.	DEBIT	CREDIT	DR/CR	BALANCE

ANSWERS TO SECTION 7.2 REVIEW QUESTIONS (text p. 222)

Trial Balance Out of Balance

1. _____

_____

2. _____

   1. _____

_____

   2. _____

_____

   3. _____

_____

   4. _____

_____

3. _____

4. _____

ANSWERS TO SECTION 7.2 REVIEW QUESTIONS (cont.)

5. _____
_____
_____

6. _____
_____
_____

7. _____
_____
_____

8. _____
_____

9. _____

10. _____

11. _____

    1. _____
    2. _____
    3. _____
    4. _____
    5. _____

12. _____

ANSWERS TO SECTION 7.2 EXERCISES (text p. 223)

Exercise 1, p. 223   (Workbook Exercise)

The exercise below, involving a journal, ledger, and trial balance, has errors in it. **Locate and correct the errors and balance the trial balance.**

GENERAL JOURNAL

PAGE *12*

DATE		PARTICULARS	P.R.	DEBIT	CREDIT
20— Nov.	4	Automobile	125	13 5 0 0 —	
		GST Recoverable	215	1 0 1 5 —	
		Bank	105		4 0 0 0 —
		A/P — Ace Finance	205		11 5 1 5 —
		Purchase of new car for $15 515 incl. tax			
	6	Furniture	120	9 0 0 —	
		GST Recoverable	215	3 6 —	
		Bank	105		9 3 6 —
		Purchase of new desk for $936 incl. tax			
	7	A/R — A. Boyd	110	4 6 0 —	
		Revenue	400		4 0 0 —
		GST Payable	210		2 8 —
		PST Payable	220		3 2 —
		Sale on account			
	10	Bank	105	3 4 5 —	
		Revenue	400		3 0 0 —
		GST Payable	210		2 1 —
		PST Payable	220		2 4 —
		Cash sale			
	12	Rent Expense	510	7 0 0 —	
		GST Recoverable	215	4 9 —	
		Bank	105		7 4 9 —
		Rent for the month			
	15	Car Expense	505	2 0 0 —	
		GST Recoverable	215	1 4 —	
		Bank	105		2 1 4 —
		Car repairs paid by cash			

Assume that $36 is correct GST

ANSWERS TO SECTION 7.2 EXERCISES (cont.)

Exercise 1 (cont.)

GENERAL LEDGER

ACCOUNT *Bank*   No. 105

DATE		PARTICULARS	P.R.	DEBIT				CREDIT				DR/CR	BALANCE					
20— Oct.	31	Forwarded	–									DR	12	0	4	8	88	
Nov.	4		J12					4	0	0	0	–	DR	8	0	4	8	88
	6		J12						9	3	6	–	DR	7	1	1	2	88
	10		J12		2	4	5	–					DR	7	3	5	7	88
	12		J12						7	4	9	–	DR	6	6	0	8	88
	15		J12						2	1	4	–	DR	6	3	9	4	88

ACCOUNT *A/R — A. Boyd*   No. 110

DATE		PARTICULARS	P.R.	DEBIT				CREDIT				DR/CR	BALANCE			
20— Nov.	7		J12		4	6	0	–					DR		4	6	0	–

ACCOUNT *Supplies*   No. 115

DATE		PARTICULARS	P.R.	DEBIT				CREDIT				DR/CR	BALANCE			
20— Oct.	31	Forwarded	–									DR		5	7	0	–

ACCOUNT *Furniture*   No. 120

DATE		PARTICULARS	P.R.	DEBIT				CREDIT				DR/CR	BALANCE			
20— Oct.	31	Forwarded	–									DR	1	9	7	1	50
Nov.	6		J12		9	0	0	–					DR	2	8	7	1	50

ACCOUNT *Automobile*   No. 125

DATE		PARTICULARS	P.R.	DEBIT				CREDIT				DR/CR	BALANCE			
20— Nov.	4		J12	13	5	0	0	–					DR	13	5	0	0	–

ANSWERS TO SECTION 7.2 EXERCISES (cont.)

Exercise 1 (cont.)

ACCOUNT *A/P — Ace Finance*   No. 205

DATE		PARTICULARS	P.R.	DEBIT	CREDIT	DR/CR	BALANCE
20— Nov.	4		J12		11 5 1 5 –	CR	11 5 1 5 –

ACCOUNT *GST Payable*   No. 210

DATE		PARTICULARS	P.R.	DEBIT	CREDIT	DR/CR	BALANCE
20— Oct.	31	Forwarded	–			CR	2 5 1 90
Nov.	7		J12		2 8 –	CR	2 7 9 90

ACCOUNT *GST Recoverable*   No. 215

DATE		PARTICULARS	P.R.	DEBIT	CREDIT	DR/CR	BALANCE
20— Oct.	31	Forwarded	–			DR	1 9 3 50
Nov.	4		J12	1 0 1 5 –		DR	1 2 0 8 50
	6		J12	3 6 –		DR	1 2 4 4 50
	10		J12	2 1 –		DR	1 2 6 5 50
	12		J12	4 9 –		DR	1 3 1 4 50
	15		J12	1 4 –		DR	1 3 2 8 50

ACCOUNT *PST Payable*   No. 220

DATE		PARTICULARS	P.R.	DEBIT	CREDIT	DR/CR	BALANCE
20— Oct.	31	Forwarded	–			CR	3 6 5 –
Nov.	7		J12		2 3 –	CR	3 8 8 –

ACCOUNT *A. Holmes, Capital*   No. 305

DATE		PARTICULARS	P.R.	DEBIT	CREDIT	DR/CR	BALANCE
20— Oct.	31	Forwarded	–			CR	9 0 2 4 44

ANSWERS TO SECTION 7.2 EXERCISES (cont.)

Exercise 1 (cont.)

ACCOUNT *Revenue*   No. *400*

DATE		PARTICULARS	P.R.	DEBIT	CREDIT	DR/CR	BALANCE
20— Oct.	31	Forwarded	–			CR	19 4 0 9 –
Nov.	7		J12		4 0 0 –	CR	19 7 0 9 –
	10		J12		3 0 0 –	CR	20 0 0 9 –

ACCOUNT *Car Expense*   No. *505*

DATE		PARTICULARS	P.R.	DEBIT	CREDIT	DR/CR	BALANCE
20— Oct.	31	Forwarded	–			DR	2 9 6 4 30
Nov.	15		J12		2 0 0 –	DR	3 1 6 4 30

ACCOUNT *Rent Expense*   No. *510*

DATE		PARTICULARS	P.R.	DEBIT	CREDIT	DR/CR	BALANCE
20— Oct.	31	Forwarded	–			DR	7 0 0 0 –
Nov.	12		J12	7 0 0 –		DR	7 7 0 0 –

ACCOUNT *Wages Expense*   No. *515*

DATE		PARTICULARS	P.R.	DEBIT	CREDIT	DR/CR	BALANCE
20— Oct.	31	Forwarded	–			DR	4 3 0 2 16

ANSWERS TO SECTION 7.2 EXERCISES (cont.)

Exercise 1 (cont.)

A. Holmes

Trial Balance

November 15, 20—

ACCOUNTS	DEBIT	CREDIT
Bank	6 3 9 4 88	
A/R — A. Boyd	4 6 0 —	
Supplies	5 7 0 —	
Furniture	2 8 7 1 50	
Automobile	13 5 0 0 —	
A/P — Ace Finance		11 5 1 5 —
GST Payable		2 7 9 90
GST Recoverable		1 3 2 8 50
PST Payable		3 8 8 —
A. Holmes, Capital		9 0 2 4 44
Revenue		20 0 0 9 —
Car Expense	3 1 6 4 30	
Rent Expense	7 7 0 0 —	
Wages Expense	4 3 0 2 16	
	38 9 6 2 84	42 5 4 4 84

ANSWERS TO SECTION 7.2 EXERCISES (cont.)

Exercise 2, p. 223

1. Why does it not balance?

Journal

DATE		PARTICULARS	DEBIT	CREDIT
20— Jan.	1	Bank	4 500 —	
		Equipment	3 600 —	
		Capital		8 100 —
	3	Supplies	73 —	
		Accounts Payable		73 —
	6	Expense	47 —	
		Bank		47 —
	10	Bank	195 —	
		Revenue		195 —
	15	Drawings	100 —	
		Bank		100 —
	19	Accounts Receivable	63 —	
		Revenue		63 —
	24	Supplies	38 —	
		Bank		38 —

Ledger

Bank

4 500	47
195	100
	38
4 695	185
(4 510)	

Accounts Receivable

63	

Supplies

73	
38	
(111)	

Equipment

3 600	

Accounts Payable

	73

Capital

	8 100

Drawings

100	

Revenue

	159
	63
	(222)

Expense

47	

Trial Balance

DR	CR
4 510	73
63	8 100
111	222
3 600	
100	
47	
8 431	8 395

Description of the error and how you found it:

_____

_____

_____

_____

_____

_____

_____

_____

_____

ANSWERS TO SECTION 7.2 EXERCISES (cont.)

Exercise 2 (cont.)

2. Why does it not balance?

Journal

DATE		PARTICULARS	DEBIT	CREDIT
20— Feb.	3	Bank	3 000 –	
		Equipment	2 000 –	
		Capital		5 000 –
	5	Supplies	490 –	
		Bank		490 –
	9	Accounts Receivable	155 –	
		Revenue		155 –
	15	Expense	56 –	
		Bank		56 –
	25	Expense	72 –	
		Accounts Payable		72 –
	28	Bank	312 –	
		Revenue		312 –
	29	Drawings	97 –	
		Bank		97 –

Ledger

Bank

3 000	490
312	56
	97
3 312	643
(2 669)	

Accounts Receivable

155	

Supplies

490	

Equipment

2 000	

Accounts Payable

	72

Capital

	5 000

Drawings

97	

Revenue

	155
	312
	(467)

Expense

56	

Trial Balance

DR	CR
2 669	72
155	5 000
490	467
2 000	
97	
56	
5 467	5 539

Description of the error and how you found it:

_____

_____

_____

_____

_____

_____

_____

_____

ANSWERS TO SECTION 7.2 EXERCISES (cont.)

Exercise 2 (cont.)

3. Why does it not balance?

Journal

DATE		PARTICULARS	DEBIT	CREDIT
20—				
Apr.	3	Bank	2 5 0 0 —	
		Equipment	7 0 0 0 —	
		Capital		9 5 0 0 —
	4	Accounts Receivable	3 7 1 —	
		Revenue		3 7 1 —
	8	Bank	2 6 9 —	
		Revenue		2 6 9 —
	10	Supplies	5 3 —	
		Accounts Payable		5 3 —
	11	Drawings	1 2 7 —	
		Bank		1 2 7 —
	13	Expense	8 6 —	
		Bank		8 6 —
	17	Expense	4 9 —	
		Accounts Payable		4 9 —

Ledger

Bank

2 500	127
269	86
2 769	213
(2 556)	

Accounts Receivable

371	

Supplies

53	

Equipment

7 000	

Accounts Payable

	53
	49
	(102)

Capital

	9 500

Drawings

127	

Revenue

	371
	269
	(540)

Expense

86	
49	
(135)	

Trial Balance

DR	CR
2 556	102
371	9 500
53	540
7 000	
127	
135	
10 242	10 142

Description of the error and how you found it:

_____

_____

_____

_____

_____

_____

_____

_____

_____

ANSWERS TO SECTION 7.2 EXERCISES (cont.)

Exercise 2 (cont.)

4. Why does it not balance?

Journal

DATE		PARTICULARS	DEBIT	CREDIT
20—Jul.	4	Bank	4000 –	
		Equipment	3000 –	
		Capital		7000 –
	5	Supplies	216 –	
		Accounts Payable		216 –
	10	Accounts Receivable	321 –	
		Revenue		321 –
	15	Expense	73 –	
		Bank		73 –
	20	Expense	34 –	
		Accounts Payable		34 –
	25	Drawings	41 –	
		Bank		41 –
	30	Bank	150 –	
		Accounts Receivable		150 –

Ledger

Bank	
4 000	73
150	41
4 150	114
(4 036)	

Accounts Receivable	
321	150
(171)	

Supplies	
216	

Equipment	
3 000	

Accounts Payable	
	216
	34
	(250)

Capital	
	7 000

Drawings	
41	

Revenue	
	321

Expense	
73	
34	
(107)	

Trial Balance

DR	CR
4 036	250
171	7 000
216	41
3 000	321
107	
7 530	7 612

Description of the error and how you found it:

_____

_____

_____

_____

_____

_____

_____

_____

ANSWERS TO SECTION 7.3 COMPUTER REVIEW QUESTIONS (text p. 237)

Comparing Accounting Software Programs to Manual Accounting

1. _____

2. _____

3. _____
   _____

4. _____
   _____
   _____
   _____
   _____

5. _____
   _____
   _____

ANSWERS TO SECTION 7.3 COMPUTER EXERCISES (text p. 237)

Using Simply Accounting to complete the activity in Section 7.3 (Sam's Softball City)

ANSWERS TO SECTION 7.3 COMPUTER EXERCISES (cont.)

This page is left blank intentionally.

Note: page 137 follows next.

ANSWERS TO SECTION 7.3 COMPUTER EXERCISES (cont.)

Exercise 1, p 237   **Kalley's Database Developments**

Business Background

Shaun Kalley is an entrepreneur whose current enterprise grew out of his knowledge of computers and his concern for the environment. Shaun is aware of the enormous volume of paper used by business and government organizations, at considerable expense. He also knows that paper documents can be converted to electronic documents.

Shaun did some initial research and found that organizations were receptive to his ideas. First, he will scan paper documents. Then, he will use software to convert the scanned images to text that a computer can recognize. Finally, he will develop electronic databases from the text. His customers will save paper and space, and they will take advantage of the efficient search engine features of electronic databases.

Required

1. Load the Simply Accounting files named **kalley.sdb**. Display the trial balance on your monitor. You will discover that accounts and opening balances have been entered for you.

2. Use Simply Accounting to enter the transactions for the first month of this business (May 2002). Before starting, you may find it helpful to change the Session Date to the end of the month— May 31, 2002. Take care to record the proper date for each transaction.

May

1 *Memorandum*

Shaun Kalley, the owner, invested an additional $4 000 of his personal funds into the business.

1 *Cheque Copy*

No. 001 to Myrtle Holdings Ltd. for rent, $1 900.00 plus GST of $133.00, total $2 033.00.

1 *Purchase Invoice*

No. 8932 from Automated Office Supplies on 30-day terms. Supplies purchased amounted to $513.64 plus GST of $35.95, total $549.59.

1 *Cheque Copy*

No. 002 to RISC Computers Ltd. for a flat-bed scanner, $2 456.90 plus GST of $171.98, total $2 628.88.

1 *Purchase Invoice*

No. 221A from Virtual Computers for a computer and laser printer, net 30 days, $9 045.67 plus GST of $633.20, total $9 678.87.

3 *Sales Invoice*

No. S001. Sold services to Ontario's Office of the Registrar General. (Started scanning and converting birth registrations to electronic form.) Amount of the sale was $20 000.00 plus GST of $1 400.00, total $21 400.00. A down payment of $5 000.00 was received.

(**Note:** You are to record all of the $20 000.00 as revenue, even though Kalley's Database Developments did not complete all of the services on May 3. The senior accountant, paying close attention to generally accepted accounting principles, will adjust your entry at a later time. In Chapter 9, you will cover GAAPs in more detail and learn to make similar adjustments.)

ANSWERS TO SECTION 7.3 COMPUTER EXERCISES (cont.)

Exercise 1 (cont.)

3   *Cheque Copy*

No. 003 to Fast Touch Software Ltd. for a variety of computer programs. The cost was $2 352.04 plus GST of $164.64, for a total of $2 516.68. (**Note:** Canada Customs and Revenue Agency allows 100 per cent of a software purchase to be immediately claimed as an expense.)

9   *Purchase Invoice*

No. 9041 from Automated Office Supplies for a fax machine and filing cabinets, $1 987.32 plus GST of $139.11, total $2 126.43.

14   *Memorandum*

From the owner regarding a used filing cabinet sold at a loss. It had been included in the Equipment account at a value of $250.00. It was sold for $150.00 (ignore GST).

17   *Cheque Copy*

No. 004 to the owner for personal use, total $900.00.

23   *Remittance Advice*

No. R001, from the Government of Ontario in partial payment of its account, total $10 000.00.

23   *Sales Invoice*

No. S002. Sold services to Utility Gas Co. (converting policy and procedure manuals to electronic form). Amount of sale was $5 000.00 plus GST of $350.00, total $5 350.00; terms are net 30 days.

23   *Purchase Invoice*

No. 5435 from Mackie's Garage regarding gasoline and oil used in the company car, $87.00 plus GST of $6.09, total $93.09.

24   *Memorandum*

From the owner, advising that he instructed the bank to reduce the bank loan by $2 500.00.

31   *Cheque Copies*

No. 005 to Automated Office Supplies for $549.59 in payment of Invoice 8932.
No. 006 to Virtual Computers for $9 678.87 in full payment of account.
No. 007 to AGB Telephone Company for monthly charges, $36.45 plus GST of $2.55, total $39.00.

31   *Bank Debit Memos*

For monthly service charges ($16.98) and interest on the demand loan ($81.25), total $98.23.

31   *Cheque Copies*

No. 008 for $42 worth of postage stamps plus GST of $2.94, total $44.94.
No. 009 for the personal use of the owner in the amount of $600.00.
No. 010 to Leanne Tan (an employee) for wages of $2 100.00.

3. Print the journal entries, the trial balance, the income statement for May, and the balance sheet.

Note: page 143 follows next.

ANSWERS TO SECTION 7.3 COMPUTER EXERCISES (cont.)

This page is left blank intentionally.

ANSWERS TO SECTION 7.3 COMPUTER EXERCISES (cont.)

Exercise 1 (cont.)

Communicate It (text p. 237)

Write down the main points of your letter before you prepare it with a word-processing program.

_____

_____

_____

_____

_____

_____

_____

_____

_____

ANSWERS TO CHAPTER 7 REVIEW EXERCISES (text p. 238)

Exercise 1, p. 238   Using Your Knowledge

Indicate whether each of the following statements is true or false by placing a "T" or an "F" in the space indicated. Explain the reason for each "F" response in the space provided.

A. The chief advantage of the balance-column account is that there is room for the account balance. ☐

B. Both sides of an account page (front and back) are used for the same item (for example, Bank). ☐

C. Entering the journal page number in the account is the sixth step in the posting process. ☐

D. The step described in question c above is performed in the journal. ☐

E. The process of setting up an account is known as "forwarding." ☐

F. The fourth step in the accounting cycle, as we know it, is the taking off of a trial balance. ☐

G. It is not possible for the ledger to be out of balance and also to be correct. ☐

H. If the trial balance difference is an even amount, the error could not be a transposition error. ☐

I. If the trial balance difference is zero, the ledger is correct. ☐

J. Posting a debit item incorrectly as a credit produces a trial balance credit total that is smaller than the debit total by twice the amount of the error. ☐

K. Very rarely does a transaction affect only one account. ☐

L. Ledger accounts are arranged alphabetically to make them easier to find. ☐

M. The presence of the account number in the journal indicates that the posting of an item has been completed. ☐

ANSWERS TO CHAPTER 7 REVIEW EXERCISES (cont.)

Exercise 1 (cont.)

Explanations for "F" Responses:

_____

_____

_____

_____

_____

_____

_____

_____

_____

_____

_____

_____

_____

_____

_____

_____

_____

_____

_____

_____

_____

_____

_____

_____

_____

_____

_____

_____

_____

_____

_____

_____

ANSWERS TO CHAPTER 7 REVIEW EXERCISES (cont.)

Exercise 2, p. 239

Error situations	Trial Balance will not balance		Trial Balance will balance but will not be correct
	Debits greater than credits by ($$)	Credits greater than debits by ($$)	
a. An entire journal entry is posted as $400 instead of $100.			
b. A debit of $200 is posted twice.			
c. A debit of $150 is posted as a credit.			
d. The Bank account is over-added by $80.			
e. The Drawings account balance of $5 500 is missed when preparing the trial balance.			
f. The Revenue account balance of $72 000 is listed on the trial balance as a debit.			
g. An entire general journal entry for $325 is not posted.			
h. An entire general journal entry for $50 is posted in reverse.			
i. A $40 debit is not posted.			
j. A $500 credit is posted as $50.			
k. A debit of $60 to Bank was posted to a customer's account instead of to Bank.			
l. A $40 debit is posted as $400.			

Exercise 3, p. 240

_____

_____

_____

_____

_____

_____

_____

ANSWERS TO CHAPTER 7 REVIEW EXERCISES (cont.)

Exercise 4, p. 240

_____

_____

_____

_____

_____

_____

_____

_____

_____

_____

_____

Exercise 5, p. 240

_____

_____

_____

_____

_____

_____

_____

Exercise 6, p. 240

_____

_____

_____

_____

_____

_____

_____

_____

_____

ANSWERS TO CHAPTER 7 REVIEW EXERCISES (cont.)

Exercise 7, p. 240   Comprehensive Exercise

A., B.

Buy - Recoverable
Sell - Payable

GENERAL JOURNAL   PAGE 1

DATE		PARTICULARS	P.R.	DEBIT	CREDIT
20- August	31	Bank	101	2 0 0 0 —	
		Supplies	120	1 4 5 0 —	
		Equipment	125	14 7 3 8 —	
		Automobiles	130	28 9 5 7 —	
		Bank Loan	201		20 0 0 0 —
		P. Schelling, Capital	300		27 1 3 9 —
Sep.	1	Rent Expense	520	9 0 0 —	
		GST Recoverable	225	6 3 —	
		Bank	101		9 6 3 —
		Cheque Copy for Rent			
	3	Supplies	120	2 3 5 —	
		GST Recoverable	225	1 6 45	
		A/P-Home Hardware	213		2 5 1 45
		Purchase Invoice from Home Hardware			
	5	A/R-W.J. Thomson	117	4 0 2 5 —	
		GST Payable	220		2 4 5 —
		PST Payable	230		2 8 0 —
		Service Revenue	401		3 5 0 0 —
		Sales Invoice to W.J. Thomson			
	5	A/R-L-Pero	111	2 3 0 0 —	
		GST Payable	220		1 4 0 —
		PST Payable	230		1 6 0 —
		Service Revenue	401		2 0 0 0 —
		Sales Invoice to L. Pero			

ANSWERS TO CHAPTER 7 REVIEW EXERCISES (cont.)

Exercise 7 (cont.)

GENERAL JOURNAL

PAGE 2

DATE		PARTICULARS	P.R.	DEBIT	CREDIT
20– Sep.	9	Bank			

ANSWERS TO CHAPTER 7 REVIEW EXERCISES (cont.)

Exercise 7 (cont.)

GENERAL JOURNAL   PAGE 3

DATE		PARTICULARS	P.R.	DEBIT	CREDIT

Name _____ Date _____

ANSWERS TO CHAPTER 7 REVIEW EXERCISES (cont.)

Exercise 7 (cont.)

GENERAL JOURNAL   PAGE 4

DATE	PARTICULARS	P.R.	DEBIT	CREDIT

ANSWERS TO CHAPTER 7 REVIEW EXERCISES (cont.)

Exercise 7 (cont.)

GENERAL LEDGER

ACCOUNT *Bank*   No. *101*

DATE		PARTICULARS	P.R.	DEBIT	CREDIT	DR/CR	BALANCE
20— August	31	Opening Entry	J1	2000 —		DR	2000 —
Sep	1		J1		963 —	DR	1037 —

ACCOUNT *A/R — L. Pero*   No. *111*

DATE		PARTICULARS	P.R.	DEBIT	CREDIT	DR/CR	BALANCE
20— Sep.	5		J1	2300 —		DR	2300 —

ACCOUNT *A/R — K. Puna*   No. *113*

DATE		PARTICULARS	P.R.	DEBIT	CREDIT	DR/CR	BALANCE

ANSWERS TO CHAPTER 7 REVIEW EXERCISES (cont.)

Exercise 7 (cont.)

ACCOUNT *A/R — Spectrum Co.*   No. *115*

DATE	PARTICULARS	P.R.	DEBIT	CREDIT	DR/CR	BALANCE

ACCOUNT *A/R — W. J. Thomson*   No. *117*

DATE	PARTICULARS	P.R.	DEBIT	CREDIT	DR/CR	BALANCE
20— Sep. 5		J1	4 025 —		DR	4 025 —

ACCOUNT *Supplies*   No. *120*

DATE	PARTICULARS	P.R.	DEBIT	CREDIT	DR/CR	BALANCE
20— Aug. 31	Opening Entry	J1	1 450 —		DR	1 450 —
Sep 1		J1	235 —		DR	1 685 —

ACCOUNT *Equipment*   No. *125*

DATE	PARTICULARS	P.R.	DEBIT	CREDIT	DR/CR	BALANCE
20— Aug. 31	Opening Entry	J1	14 732 —		DR	14 732 —

ACCOUNT *Automobiles*   No. *130*

DATE	PARTICULARS	P.R.	DEBIT	CREDIT	DR/CR	BALANCE
	Opening Entry		28 957 —		DR	28 957 —

ANSWERS TO CHAPTER 7 REVIEW EXERCISES (cont.)

Exercise 7 (cont.)

ACCOUNT *Bank Loan*   No. *201*

DATE		PARTICULARS	P.R.	DEBIT	CREDIT	DR/CR	BALANCE
20—Aug	31	Opening Entry	J1		20 000 —	CR	20 000 —

ACCOUNT *A/P — Imperial Garage*   No. *211*

DATE	PARTICULARS	P.R.	DEBIT	CREDIT	DR/CR	BALANCE

ACCOUNT *A/P — Home Hardware*   No. *213*

DATE		PARTICULARS	P.R.	DEBIT	CREDIT	DR/CR	BALANCE
20—Sep	1		J1		25 1 45	CR	25 1 45

ACCOUNT *GST Payable*   No. *220*

DATE		PARTICULARS	P.R.	DEBIT	CREDIT	DR/CR	BALANCE
20—Sep.	5		J1		2 45 —	CR	2 45 —
	5		J1		1 40 —	CR	3 8 5 —

ANSWERS TO CHAPTER 7 REVIEW EXERCISES (cont.)

Exercise 7 (cont.)

ACCOUNT *GST Recoverable*   No. 225

DATE		PARTICULARS	P.R.	DEBIT	CREDIT	DR/CR	BALANCE
20– Sep.	1		J1	63 —		DR	63 —
	1		J1	16 45		DR	79 45

ACCOUNT *PST Payable*   No. 230

DATE		PARTICULARS	P.R.	DEBIT	CREDIT	DR/CR	BALANCE
20– Sep	5		J1		280 —	CR	280 —
	5		J1		160 —	CR	440 —

ACCOUNT *Pat Schelling, Capital*   No. 301

DATE		PARTICULARS	P.R.	DEBIT	CREDIT	DR/CR	BALANCE
20– Aug	31	Opening Entry	J1		27 139 —	CR	27 139 —

ACCOUNT *Pat Schelling, Drawings*   No. 302

DATE	PARTICULARS	P.R.	DEBIT	CREDIT	DR/CR	BALANCE

ANSWERS TO CHAPTER 7 REVIEW EXERCISES (cont.)

Exercise 7 (cont.)

ACCOUNT *Service Revenue* No. *401*

DATE	PARTICULARS	P.R.	DEBIT	CREDIT	DR/CR	BALANCE
20-Sep. 5		J1		3 500 —	CR	8 500 —
5		J1		2 000 —	CR	5 500 —

ACCOUNT *Automobile Expense* No. *505*

DATE	PARTICULARS	P.R.	DEBIT	CREDIT	DR/CR	BALANCE

ACCOUNT *Bank Charges Expense* No. *510*

DATE	PARTICULARS	P.R.	DEBIT	CREDIT	DR/CR	BALANCE

ACCOUNT *General Expense* No. *515*

DATE	PARTICULARS	P.R.	DEBIT	CREDIT	DR/CR	BALANCE

ACCOUNT *Rent Expense* No. *520*

DATE	PARTICULARS	P.R.	DEBIT	CREDIT	DR/CR	BALANCE
20-Sep. 1		J1	900 —		DR	900 —

ANSWERS TO CHAPTER 7 REVIEW EXERCISES (cont.)

Exercise 7 (cont.)

ACCOUNT *Telephone Expense*   No. *525*

DATE		PARTICULARS	P.R.	DEBIT	CREDIT	DR/CR	BALANCE

ACCOUNT *Wages Expense*   No. *530*

DATE		PARTICULARS	P.R.	DEBIT	CREDIT	DR/CR	BALANCE

ACCOUNT *Loss on Sale of Equipment*   No. *535*

DATE		PARTICULARS	P.R.	DEBIT	CREDIT	DR/CR	BALANCE

ANSWERS TO CHAPTER 7 REVIEW EXERCISES (cont.)

Exercise 7 (cont.)

C. _____

_____

_____

ACCOUNTS	DEBIT	CREDIT

ANSWERS TO CHAPTER 7 REVIEW EXERCISES (cont.)

Exercise 7 (cont.)

D. _____

_____

_____

Name _____ Date _____

ANSWERS TO CHAPTER 7 REVIEW EXERCISES (cont.)

Exercise 7 (cont.)

E. _____
_____
_____

ANSWERS TO CHAPTER 7 REVIEW EXERCISES (cont.)

Exercise 8, p. 243

A.

GENERAL JOURNAL
PAGE 28

DATE		PARTICULARS	P.R.	DEBIT	CREDIT

ANSWERS TO CHAPTER 7 REVIEW EXERCISES (cont.)

Exercise 8 (cont.)

GENERAL JOURNAL

PAGE _____

DATE	PARTICULARS	P.R.	DEBIT	CREDIT

ANSWERS TO CHAPTER 7 REVIEW EXERCISES (cont.)

Exercise 8 (cont.)

GENERAL JOURNAL

PAGE

DATE	PARTICULARS	P.R.	DEBIT	CREDIT

ANSWERS TO CHAPTER 7 REVIEW EXERCISES (cont.)

Exercise 8 (cont.)

GENERAL JOURNAL

PAGE _____

DATE		PARTICULARS	P.R.	DEBIT	CREDIT

ANSWERS TO CHAPTER 7 REVIEW EXERCISES (cont.)

Exercise 8 (cont.)

GENERAL LEDGER

ACCOUNT *Bank*   No. *100*

DATE		PARTICULARS	P.R.	DEBIT	CREDIT	DR/CR	BALANCE
20— Sep.	30	Forwarded	–			DR	3 7 5 0 20

ACCOUNT *Supplies — Golf Course*   No. *105*

DATE		PARTICULARS	P.R.	DEBIT	CREDIT	DR/CR	BALANCE
20— Sep.	30	Forwarded	–			DR	10 2 3 6 –

ANSWERS TO CHAPTER 7 REVIEW EXERCISES (cont.)

Exercise 8 (cont.)

ACCOUNT *Supplies — Office*   No. *110*

DATE		PARTICULARS	P.R.	DEBIT	CREDIT	DR/CR	BALANCE
20— Sep.	30	Forwarded	—			DR	3 2 6 5 25

ACCOUNT *Property*   No. *115*

DATE		PARTICULARS	P.R.	DEBIT	CREDIT	DR/CR	BALANCE
20— Sep.	30	Forwarded	—			DR	95 0 0 0 —

ACCOUNT *Buildings*   No. *120*

DATE		PARTICULARS	P.R.	DEBIT	CREDIT	DR/CR	BALANCE
20— Sep.	30	Forwarded	—			DR	85 3 6 0 —

ACCOUNT *Automotive Equipment*   No. *125*

DATE		PARTICULARS	P.R.	DEBIT	CREDIT	DR/CR	BALANCE
20— Sep.	30	Forwarded	—			DR	40 9 5 6 —

ACCOUNT *Maintenance Equipment*   No. *130*

DATE		PARTICULARS	P.R.	DEBIT	CREDIT	DR/CR	BALANCE
20— Sep.	30	Forwarded	—			DR	22 6 5 0 60

ACCOUNT *Bank Loan*   No. *201*

DATE		PARTICULARS	P.R.	DEBIT	CREDIT	DR/CR	BALANCE
20— Sep.	30	Forwarded	—			CR	120 0 0 0 —

ANSWERS TO CHAPTER 7 REVIEW EXERCISES (cont.)

Exercise 8 (cont.)

ACCOUNT *A/P — Blair's Automotive*   No. 205

DATE		PARTICULARS	P.R.	DEBIT	CREDIT	DR/CR	BALANCE

ACCOUNT *A/P — Main Supply*   No. 210

DATE		PARTICULARS	P.R.	DEBIT	CREDIT	DR/CR	BALANCE
20— Sep.	30	Forwarded	—			CR	1 8 9 0 65

ACCOUNT *A/P — Pro Equipment*   No. 215

DATE		PARTICULARS	P.R.	DEBIT	CREDIT	DR/CR	BALANCE
20— Sep.	30	Forwarded	—			CR	3 5 8 2 10

ACCOUNT *GST Payable*   No. 220

DATE		PARTICULARS	P.R.	DEBIT	CREDIT	DR/CR	BALANCE
20— Sep.	30	Forwarded	—			CR	7 1 0 —

ANSWERS TO CHAPTER 7 REVIEW EXERCISES (cont.)

Exercise 8 (cont.)

ACCOUNT *GST Recoverable*   No. *225*

DATE		PARTICULARS	P.R.	DEBIT	CREDIT	DR/CR	BALANCE
20— Sep.	30	Forwarded	–			DR	1 8 5 –

ACCOUNT *PST Payable*   No. *230*

DATE		PARTICULARS	P.R.	DEBIT	CREDIT	DR/CR	BALANCE
20— Sep.	30	Forwarded	–			CR	2 5 0 50

ACCOUNT *Mortgage Payable*   No. *240*

DATE		PARTICULARS	P.R.	DEBIT	CREDIT	DR/CR	BALANCE
20— Sep.	30	Forwarded	–			CR	100 0 0 0 –

Name _____   Date _____

Exercise 8 (cont.)

ACCOUNT *Shirley Ng-A-Kien, Capital*   No. 301

DATE		PARTICULARS	P.R.	DEBIT	CREDIT	DR/CR	BALANCE
20— Sep.	30	Forwarded	—			CR	37 0 2 7 46

ACCOUNT *Shirley Ng-A-Kien, Drawings*   No. 305

DATE		PARTICULARS	P.R.	DEBIT	CREDIT	DR/CR	BALANCE
20— Sep.	30	Forwarded	—			DR	18 0 0 0 —

ACCOUNT *Revenue — Golf*   No. 401

DATE		PARTICULARS	P.R.	DEBIT	CREDIT	DR/CR	BALANCE
20— Sep.	30	Forwarded	—			CR	52 6 5 5 —

ACCOUNT *Revenue — Food*   No. 405

DATE		PARTICULARS	P.R.	DEBIT	CREDIT	DR/CR	BALANCE
20— Sep.	30	Forwarded	—			CR	9 2 5 0 50

ACCOUNT *Automotive Expense*   No. 500

DATE		PARTICULARS	P.R.	DEBIT	CREDIT	DR/CR	BALANCE
20— Sep.	30	Forwarded	—			DR	5 9 6 3 01

ANSWERS TO CHAPTER 7 REVIEW EXERCISES (cont.)

Exercise 8 (cont.)

ACCOUNT *Bank Charges Expense*   No. *505*

DATE		PARTICULARS	P.R.	DEBIT	CREDIT	DR/CR	BALANCE
20— Sep.	30	Forwarded	–			DR	6 8 4 2 25

ACCOUNT *Utilities Expense*   No. *510*

DATE		PARTICULARS	P.R.	DEBIT	CREDIT	DR/CR	BALANCE
20— Sep.	30	Forwarded	–			DR	2 8 5 0 45

ACCOUNT *Maintenance Expense*   No. *515*

DATE		PARTICULARS	P.R.	DEBIT	CREDIT	DR/CR	BALANCE
20— Sep.	30	Forwarded	–			DR	7 2 3 0 85

ACCOUNT *Miscellaneous Expense*   No. *520*

DATE		PARTICULARS	P.R.	DEBIT	CREDIT	DR/CR	BALANCE
20— Sep.	30	Forwarded	–			DR	1 5 2 5 75

ACCOUNT *Mortgage Interest Expense*   No. *525*

DATE		PARTICULARS	P.R.	DEBIT	CREDIT	DR/CR	BALANCE
20— Sep.	30	Forwarded	–			DR	4 5 0 0 –

ANSWERS TO CHAPTER 7 REVIEW EXERCISES (cont.)

Exercise 8 (cont.)

ACCOUNT *Telephone Expense*   No. *530*

DATE		PARTICULARS	P.R.	DEBIT	CREDIT	DR/CR	BALANCE
20— Sep.	30	Forwarded	–			DR	6 8 5 55

ACCOUNT *Wages Expense*   No. *535*

DATE		PARTICULARS	P.R.	DEBIT	CREDIT	DR/CR	BALANCE
20— Sep.	30	Forwarded	–			DR	16 3 6 5 30

Name —————————————————— Date ——————————————————

ANSWERS TO CHAPTER 7 REVIEW EXERCISES (cont.)

Exercise 8 (cont.)

B. ——————————————————————————
——————————————————————————
——————————————————————————

ACCOUNTS	DEBIT	CREDIT

ANSWERS TO CHAPTER 7 REVIEW EXERCISES (cont.)

Exercise 8 (cont.)

C. _____

_____

_____

ANSWERS TO CHAPTER 7 REVIEW EXERCISES (cont.)

Exercise 8 (cont.)

D. ———————————————————————————

ANSWERS TO CHAPTER 7 REVIEW EXERCISES (cont.)

Questions for Further Thought, p. 245

1. _____

2. _____

3. _____

4. _____

5. _____

6. _____

7. _____

ANSWERS TO CHAPTER 7 REVIEW EXERCISES (cont.)

Questions for Further Thought (cont.)

8. _____
_____
_____
_____

9. _____
_____
_____
_____

CASE STUDIES (text p. 258)

Case 1 *A Stitch in Time...*, p. 246

1. _____
_____
_____
_____
_____

2. _____
_____
_____
_____
_____
_____
_____

Case 2 *Does the Order of Accounts Matter?* p. 246

1. _____
_____
_____
_____

CASE STUDIES (cont.)

Case 2 (cont.)

2. _____

_____

_____

ACCOUNTS	DEBIT	CREDIT

Challenge Case 3   *Frustration for the Auditor*, p. 247

1.

GENERAL JOURNAL   PAGE

DATE	PARTICULARS	P.R.	DEBIT	CREDIT

CASE STUDIES (cont.)

Challenge Case 3 (cont.)

1. (cont.)

GENERAL JOURNAL   PAGE

DATE		PARTICULARS	P.R.	DEBIT	CREDIT

CASE STUDIES (cont.)

Challenge Case 3 (cont.)

2. _____

_____

_____

_____

_____

_____

_____

_____

_____

_____

_____

_____

Group Discussion Case 4   *To Fire or Not To Fire?*, p. 248

1. _____

_____

_____

_____

_____

2. _____

3. _____

_____

4. _____

_____

5. _____

_____

_____

_____

_____

_____

6. _____

_____

_____

Career   **FRED BRANCH, HEAD OF INFORMATION SYSTEMS, GLOBE, GLOBAL ENTERPRISE EXCELLENCE, NESTLÉ SA**

ANSWERS TO DISCUSSION QUESTIONS (text p. 250)

1. _____
   _____
   _____

2. _____

3. _____
   _____
   _____
   _____
   _____
   _____
   _____
   _____
   _____
   _____

4. _____

Chapter 8   The Work Sheet and Financial Statements

ANSWERS TO SECTION 8.1 REVIEW QUESTIONS (text p. 260)

The Six-Column Work Sheet

1. _____
   _____
2. _____
3. _____
   _____
4. _____
5. _____
   _____
   _____
6. _____
7. _____
8. _____
9. _____
   _____
   _____
10. _____
11. _____
12. _____
   _____
   _____
   _____
   _____
13. _____
   _____
   _____
14. _____
15. _____
   _____
16. 1. _____
    2. _____
    3. _____
    4. _____
    5. _____
    6. _____

Name _____ Date _____

ANSWERS TO SECTION 8.1 EXERCISES (text p. 260)

Exercise 1, p. 260

Indicate to which column in the work sheet each account should be extended by placing a check mark in the appropriate column.

Account	Income Statement Debit	Income Statement Credit	Balance Sheet Debit	Balance Sheet Credit
Accounts Payable				
Miscellaneous Expense				
Revenue				
Advertising Expense				
Wages Expense				
Mortgage Payable				
Utilities Expense				
Equipment				
G. Rojek, Capital				
Delivery Expense				
GST Recoverable				
Bank Loan				
Accounts Receivable				
Automobile				
Bank				
G. Rojek, Drawings				
Sales				
Bank Charges Expense				
Rent Expense				
Supplies				
Trucks				
GST Payable				

ANSWERS TO SECTION 8.1 EXERCISES (cont.)

Exercise 2, p. 261

WORK SHEET

Month Ended April 30, 20—

N. Foreman and Company

ACCOUNTS	TRIAL BALANCE DEBIT	TRIAL BALANCE CREDIT	INCOME STATEMENT DEBIT	INCOME STATEMENT CREDIT	BALANCE SHEET DEBIT	BALANCE SHEET CREDIT
Bank	7 5 0 20					
Accounts Receivable	15 3 7 5 10					
Supplies	1 2 5 0 —					
Equipment	18 5 0 0 —					
Automobiles	29 3 0 0 88					
Bank Loan		30 0 0 0 —				
Accounts Payable		5 3 3 1 —				
GST Payable		1 0 6 17				
GST Recoverable	7 4 12					
PST Payable		1 2 1 33				
N. Foreman, Capital		24 7 7 2 50				
N. Foreman, Drawings	3 0 0 0 —					
Fees Revenue		18 2 0 0 —				
Bank Charges	2 5 0 —					
Car Expense	1 7 5 0 —					
Miscellaneous Expense	5 1 2 20					
Light and Heat Expense	7 4 6 —					
Rent Expense	1 1 0 0 —					
Telephone Expense	2 7 6 50					
Wages Expense	5 6 4 6 —					
	78 5 3 1 —	78 5 3 1 —				

ANSWERS TO SECTION 8.1 EXERCISES (cont.)

Exercise 3, p. 261

WORK SHEET

Collision Bodywork and Repairs

Year Ended December 31, 20—

ACCOUNTS	TRIAL BALANCE		INCOME STATEMENT		BALANCE SHEET	
	DEBIT	CREDIT	DEBIT	CREDIT	DEBIT	CREDIT

Name _____   Date _____

ANSWERS TO SECTION 8.1 EXERCISES (cont.)

Exercise 4, p. 262

A.

The Arthur Company

WORK SHEET

Month Ended October 31, 20—

ACCOUNTS	TRIAL BALANCE DEBIT	TRIAL BALANCE CREDIT	INCOME STATEMENT DEBIT	INCOME STATEMENT CREDIT	BALANCE SHEET DEBIT	BALANCE SHEET CREDIT
Bank	1722 16				1722 16	
A/R — H.Chan	116 -				116 -	
A/R — M.Watson	72 -				72 -	
A/R — J.Young	323 -				323 -	
Supplies	1255 -				1255 -	
Office Equipment	5863 -				5863 -	
Automobiles	13200 -				13200 -	
A/P — City Hydro		116 42				116 42
A/P — O.K. Supply		421 72				421 72
A/P — Slick Oil Co.		331 19				331 19
Bank Loan		10000 -				10000 -
P. Arthur, Capital		10504 82				10504 82
P. Arthur, Drawings	1000 -				1000 -	
Consulting Fees		4903 17		4903 17		
Advertising Expense	465 12		465 12			
Automobile Expense	270 -		270 -			
Bank Charges Expense	56 40		56 40			
Miscellaneous Expense	113 74		113 74			
Rent Expense	400 -		400 -			
Salaries Expense	1280 -		1280 -			
Telephone Expense	25 60		25 60			
Utilities Expense	115 30		115 30			
	26277 32	26277 32	2726 16	4903 17	23551 16	21374 15
Net Income			2177 01			2177 01
			4903 17	4903 17	23551 16	23551 16

ANSWERS TO SECTION 8.1 EXERCISES (cont.)

Exercise 4 (cont.)

B. Accounts Receivable Control   _____

Accounts Payable Control   _____

ANSWERS TO SECTION 8.2 REVIEW QUESTIONS (text p. 266)

How Accountants Use Income Statements

1. _____
   _____

2. _____
   _____
   _____

3. _____

4. _____
   _____
   _____
   _____

5. _____
   _____

ANSWERS TO SECTION 8.2 EXERCISES (text p. 266)

Exercise 1, p. 266

A., B.

Professional Engineering and Consulting
Income Statement
Years Ended June 30, 20-2 and 20-1

Revenues	20-2	20-1	Increase or Decrease (−)	% Change
Consulting	$ 62 250	$ 60 402	_____	____
Construction	202 365	290 201	_____	____
Designing	35 250	36 603	_____	____
Total Revenue	$299 865	$387 206	_____	____
Operating Expenses				
Advertising Expense	$ 3 520	$ 3 400	_____	____
Automobiles Expense	25 025	16 350	_____	____
Bank Charges Expense	15 850	11 200	_____	____
Building Expense	4 200	3 700	_____	____
Equipment Maintenance Expense	1 525	1 750	_____	____
Insurance Expense	5 014	3 000	_____	____
Light, Heat, and Water Expense	3 124	3 107	_____	____
Miscellaneous Expense	312	250	_____	____
Property Taxes Expense	1 215	950	_____	____
Telephone Expense	1 507	904	_____	____
Wages Expense	102 301	78 201	_____	____
Total Expenses	$163 593	$122 812	_____	____
Net Income	$136 272	$264 394	_____	____

C. _____

_____

ANSWERS TO SECTION 8.2 EXERCISES (cont.)

Exercise 1 (cont.)

D. _____
_____
_____
_____
_____
_____
_____
_____
_____
_____
_____
_____
_____
_____
_____
_____

Exercise 2, p. 267

A.

	Year 1	Year 2	Year 3	Year 4	Year 5
Sales	$20 700	$22 356	$23 184	$23 805	$24 219
Per cent of Year 1	_____ %	_____ %	_____ %	_____ %	_____ %
Increase in Percentage		_____	_____	_____	_____

B. _____
_____
_____

Exercise 3, p. 267

A.

	Year 1	%*	Year 2	%	Year 3	%	Year 4	%	Year 5	%
Sales	$57 000	_____	$58 254	_____	$58 767	_____	$59 223	_____	$59 451	_____
Expenses	$35 000	_____	$36 050	_____	$36 575	_____	$36 785	_____	$37 520	_____
Net Income	$22 000	_____	$22 204	_____	$22 192	_____	$22 438	_____	$21 931	_____
* % of First Year										

B. _____
_____
_____
_____
_____

Name _____   Date _____

ANSWERS TO SECTION 8.2 EXERCISES (cont.)

Exercise 4, p. 267

A.

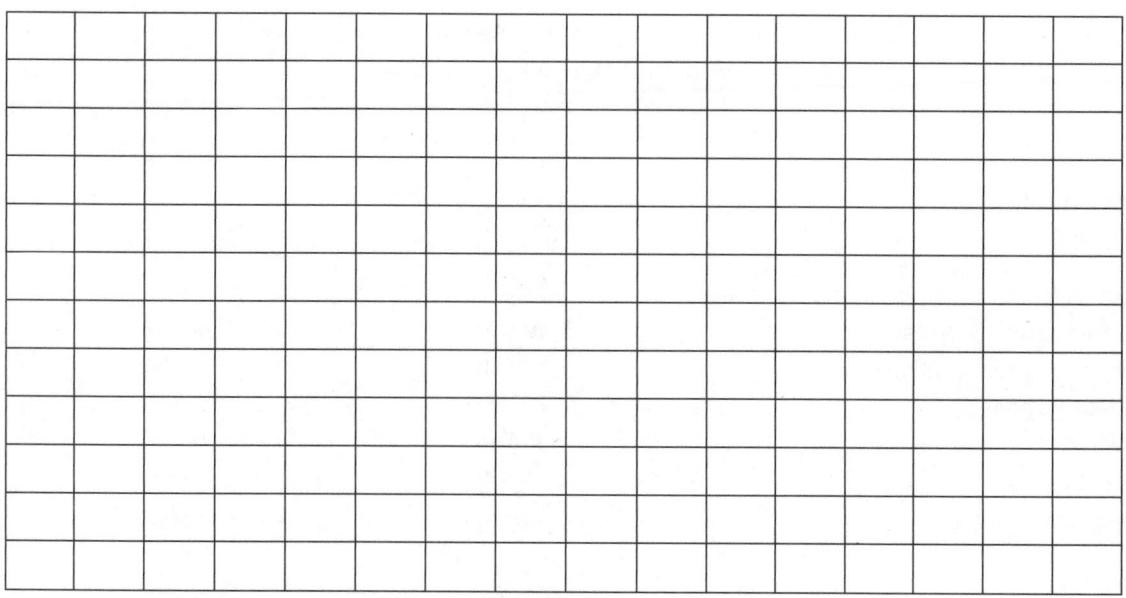

B. _____

_____

_____

Name _____   Date _____

ANSWERS TO SECTION 8.2 EXERCISES (cont.)

Exercise 5, p. 268

A.

Income Statements
Year End December 31, 20–

	Company A		Company B	
Revenue				
Sales	$197 000	_____ %	$421 000	_____ %
Expenses				
Automotive Expense	$ 40 200	_____ %	$ 80 270	_____ %
Bank Interest Expense	3 500	_____ %	27 050	_____ %
Rent Expense	12 000	_____ %	30 000	_____ %
Wages Expense	86 750	_____ %	214 860	_____ %
Other Expenses	1 800	_____ %	10 900	_____ %
Total Expenses	$144 250	_____ %	$363 080	_____ %
Net Income	$ 52 750	_____ %	$ 57 920	_____ %

B. _____

_____

_____

_____

_____

_____

_____

_____

_____

_____

_____

_____

ANSWERS TO SECTION 8.2 EXERCISES (cont.)

Exercise 6, p. 268

A.

Income Statements
Year End December 31, 20—

	Ace Cleaning			Tip Top Cleaners		
Revenues	$294 325	_____ %		$147 821	_____ %	
Operating Expenses						
Bank Charges Expense	$ 6 700	_____ %		$ 7 100	_____ %	
Car Expense	28 070	_____ %		11 190	_____ %	
Cleaning Supplies Expense	52 950	_____ %		36 960	_____ %	
Insurance Expense	2 800	_____ %		500	_____ %	
Utilities Expense	6 500	_____ %		2 100	_____ %	
Miscellaneous Expense	1 800	_____ %		750	_____ %	
Rent Expense	18 000	_____ %		12 000	_____ %	
Telephone Expense	3 721	_____ %		1 570	_____ %	
Wages Expense	100 971	_____ %		75 360	_____ %	
Total Expenses	$221 512	_____ %		$147 530	_____ %	
Net Income	$ 72 813	_____ %		$ 291	_____ %	

B. _____

_____

C. _____

_____

_____

_____

_____

_____

ANSWERS TO SECTION 8.3 REVIEW QUESTIONS (text p. 275)

How Accountants Use Balance Sheets

1. _____
2. _____
3. _____
4. _____
5. _____
_____

ANSWERS TO SECTION 8.3 REVIEW QUESTIONS (cont.)

6. _____

7. _____

8. _____

_____

9. _____

10. _____

11. _____

12. _____

13. _____

_____

ANSWERS TO SECTION 8.3 EXERCISES (text p. 276)

Exercise 1, p. 276

A. Current assets: _____

B. Fixed assets: _____

C. Current liabilities: _____

D. Long-term liabilities: _____

E. Working capital: _____

F. Mortgage payable: _____

Name _____   Date _____

ANSWERS TO SECTION 8.3 EXERCISES (cont.)

Exercise 2, p. 277

_____

_____

_____

ANSWERS TO SECTION 8.3 EXERCISES (cont.)

Exercise 3, p. 277

A., B.

Goodenough Company
Balance Sheet Data

	Year 1	%*	Year 2	%	Year 3	%	Year 4	%	Year 5	%
Current Assets	$50 000	___	$55 500	___	$59 500	___	$64 000	___	$68 500	___
Current Liabilities	35 000	___	38 000	___	40 000	___	42 500	___	45 000	___
Working Capital	___	___	___	___	___	___	___	___	___	___

* Calculate percent of Year 1 amount.

C.

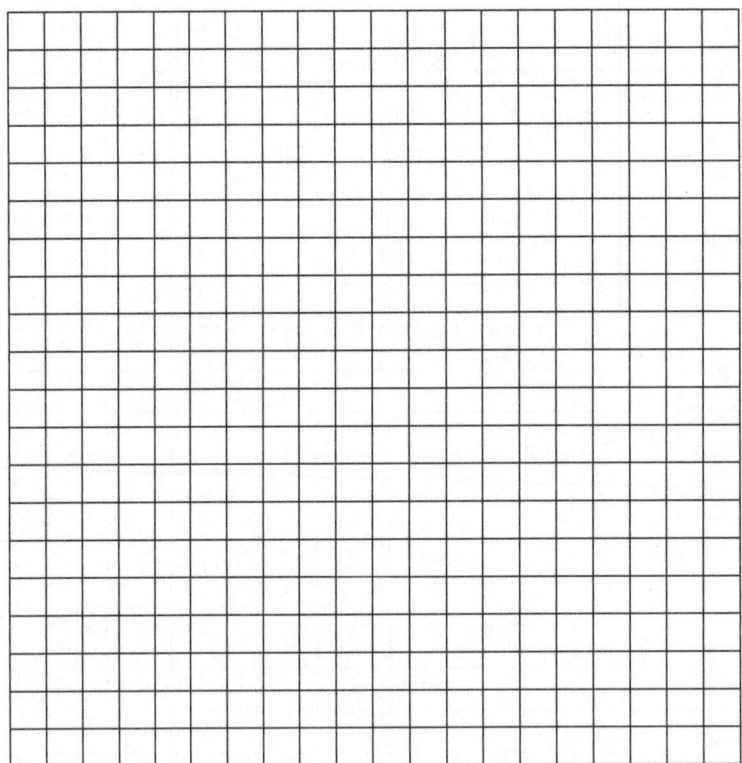

Name _____   Date _____

ANSWERS TO SECTION 8.3 EXERCISES (cont.)

Exercise 4, p. 278

A.

	Balance Sheets December 31, 20—				
	Neon Company		**Radon Company**		
Items	**$**	**%**	**$**	**%**	
Assets					
Bank	$ 3 000		$14 500		
Accounts Receivable	10 000		5 500		
Plant and Equipment	132 000		53 000		
Automobiles	38 000		26 000		
Total Assets	$183 000		$99 000		
Liabilities and Equity					
Accounts Payable	$ 19 000		$ 2 200		
Mortgage Payable	92 500		18 000		
Owner's Equity	71 500		78 800		
Total Liabilities and Equity	$183 000		$99 000		

B. _____
_____
_____
_____
_____
_____

C. _____
_____
_____
_____
_____
_____
_____
_____
_____

ANSWERS TO SECTION 8.3 EXERCISES (cont.)

Exercise 5, p. 278

A.

Items	Balance Sheets December 31, 20—			
	Leo Company		Capricorn Company	
	$	%	$	%
Assets				
Bank	$ 1 000		$ 31 000	
Accounts Receivable	25 000		–	
Plant and Equipment	150 000		160 000	
Automobiles	50 000		29 000	
Total Assets	$226 000		$220 000	
Liabilities and Equity				
Accounts Payable	$ 25 000		$ 11 000	
Loan Payable—Automobile	20 000		20 000	
Mortgage Payable	–		150 000	
Owner's Equity	181 000		39 000	
Total Liabilities and Equity	$226 000		$220 000	

B. _____

_____

_____

_____

_____

_____

_____

_____

_____

_____

_____

ANSWERS TO SECTION 8.3 EXERCISES (cont.)

Exercise 6, p. 279

A.

Playfair Company
Comparative Balance Sheet
December 31, 20-4 and 20-3

	20-4	20-3	Increase or Decrease (−)	% Change
Assets				
Current Assets				
Bank	$ 9 090	$ 5 500		
Accounts Receivable	65 220	35 700		
Supplies	70 636	45 600		
Total Current Assets	$144 946	$ 86 800		
Fixed Assets				
Land	$ 50 000	$ 50 000		
Buildings	135 000	138 000		
Equipment	141 000	160 000		
Automobilies	25 000	30 000		
Total Fixed Assets	$351 000	$378 000		
Total Assets	$495 946	$464 800		
Liabilities and Owner's Equity				
Current Liabilities				
Accounts Payable	$ 97 936	$ 52 750		
Bank Loan	50 000	50 000		
Total Current Liabilities	$147 936	$102 750		
Long-Term Liability				
Mortgage Payable	$ 70 000	$ 75 000		
Total Liabilities	$217 936	$177 750		
T. Jennings, Capital				
Capital, January 1	$287 050	$277 700		
Net Income	90 960	84 350		
	$378 010	$362 050		
Drawings	100 000	75 000		
Capital, December 31	$278 010	$287 050		
Total Liabilities & Equity	$495 946	$464 800		

Chapter 8 *The Work Sheet and Financial Statements*

ANSWERS TO SECTION 8.3 EXERCISES (cont.)

Exercise 6 (cont.)

B. _____
_____
_____
_____
_____
_____
_____
_____
_____
_____
_____

ANSWERS TO SECTION 8.4 REVIEW QUESTIONS (text p. 282)

Financial Statements and Accountability

1. _____
2. _____
_____
3. _____
_____
4. _____
5. _____
6. _____
_____
_____
7. _____
8. _____
_____
9. _____
_____
_____
10. _____
11. _____
_____
_____
_____
12. _____
13. _____
_____

ANSWERS TO SECTION 8.4 REVIEW QUESTIONS (cont.)

14. ———————————————————————————————————————

———————————————————————————————————————

———————————————————————————————————————

ANSWERS TO SECTION 8.4 EXERCISES (text p. 282)

Exercise 1, p. 282

A. ———————————————————————————————————————

B. ———————————————————————————————————————

———————————————————————————————————————

C.   a. ———————————————————————————————————

      b. ———————————————————————————————————

      c. ———————————————————————————————————

D. ———————————————————————————————————————

E. ———————————————————————————————————————

F. ———————————————————————————————————————

G. ———————————————————————————————————————

———————————————————————————————————————

———————————————————————————————————————

H. ———————————————————————————————————————

———————————————————————————————————————

———————————————————————————————————————

———————————————————————————————————————

I. ———————————————————————————————————————

J. ———————————————————————————————————————

K. ———————————————————————————————————————

L. ———————————————————————————————————————

ANSWERS TO SECTION 8.5 COMPUTER EXERCISES (text p. 290)

Using Software to Analyze Financial Statements

Exercise 1, p. 290

Use Simply Accounting and Microsoft Excel to complete this exercise.

ANSWERS TO SECTION 8.5 COMPUTER EXERCISES (cont.)

Challenge Exercise 2, p. 290

Use Microsoft Excel and Microsoft Word to complete this exercise.

ANSWERS TO CHAPTER 8 REVIEW EXERCISES (text p. 291)

Exercise 1, p. 291   Using Your Knowledge

A. _____
_____
_____
_____
_____
_____
_____
_____

B. _____
_____
_____
_____
_____
_____
_____

Exercise 2, p. 292

WORK SHEET

Ying Lo — Six Months Ended June 30, 20—

ACCOUNTS	TRIAL BALANCE DEBIT	TRIAL BALANCE CREDIT	INCOME STATEMENT DEBIT	INCOME STATEMENT CREDIT	BALANCE SHEET DEBIT	BALANCE SHEET CREDIT
Bank	5 1 6 20				5 1 6 20	
Accounts Receivable	9 2 5 5 50				9 2 5 5 50	
Office Supplies	1 5 2 5 —				1 5 2 5 —	
Office Equipment	10 3 5 6 —				10 3 5 6 —	
Automobile	19 2 5 5 65				19 2 5 5 65	
Professional Library	5 3 6 3 25				5 3 6 3 25	
Accounts Payable		2 6 1 8 25				2 6 1 8 25
GST Payable		6 5 0 —				6 5 0 —
GST Recoverable	4 1 0 —				4 1 0 —	
Ying Lo, Capital		34 0 2 4 81				34 0 2 4 81
Ying Lo, Drawings	20 0 0 0 —				20 0 0 0 —	
Fees Earned		55 2 8 5 —		55 0 8 5 —		
Car Expense	4 5 9 2 36		4 5 9 2 36			
Miscellaneous Expense	1 2 5 4 85		1 2 5 4 85			
Rent Expense	7 2 0 0 —		7 2 0 0 —			
Salaries Expense	9 2 3 5 —		9 2 3 5 —			
Telephone Expense	3 0 2 5 —		3 0 2 5 —			
Utilities Expense	5 8 9 25		5 8 9 25			
	92 5 7 8 06	92 5 7 8 06	25 8 9 6 46	55 2 8 5 —	66 6 8 1 60	37 2 9 3 06
			29 3 8 8 54			29 3 8 8 54
			55 2 8 5 —		66 6 8 1 60	

ANSWERS TO CHAPTER 8 REVIEW EXERCISES (cont.)

Exercise 2 (cont.)

Income Statement

Name _____   Date _____

ANSWERS TO CHAPTER 8 REVIEW EXERCISES (cont.)

Exercise 2 (cont.)

_____

_____

_____

ANSWERS TO CHAPTER 8 REVIEW EXERCISES (cont.)

Exercise 3, p. 293

WORK SHEET

Star Delivery

Year Ended December 31, 20—

ACCOUNTS	TRIAL BALANCE DEBIT	TRIAL BALANCE CREDIT	INCOME STATEMENT DEBIT	INCOME STATEMENT CREDIT	BALANCE SHEET DEBIT	BALANCE SHEET CREDIT
Bank	1 8 5 2 25					
Accounts Receivable	15 3 25 –					
Office Supplies	1 8 63 –					
Furniture and Equipment	7 2 5 8 36					
Land	45 5 0 0 –					
Buildings	52 3 6 5 50					
Automobile	9 2 5 5 65					
Trucks	36 2 5 2 95					
Accounts Payable		3 5 7 9 25				
GST Payable		7 3 0 –				
GST Recoverable	4 5 0 –					
Bank Loan		25 0 0 0 –				
Mortgage Payable		75 0 0 0 –				
Danielle Nowak, Capital		58 0 9 9 98				
Danielle Nowak, Drawings	32 0 0 0 –					
Fees Earned		125 2 5 4 –				
Gas and Oil Expense	26 2 1 5 24					
Insurance Expense	2 6 5 7 25					
Miscellaneous Expense	1 5 2 6 85					
Telephone Expense	9 6 5 32					
Truck Repairs Expense	4 2 4 0 65					
Utilities Expense	1 5 7 5 65					
Wages Expense	48 3 5 9 56					
	287 6 6 3 23	287 6 6 3 23				

ANSWERS TO CHAPTER 8 REVIEW EXERCISES (cont.)

Exercise 3 (cont.)

Name _____ Date _____

_____

_____

_____

ANSWERS TO CHAPTER 8 REVIEW EXERCISES (cont.)

Exercise 4, p. 293

For each of the following, check off the most appropriate response in the space provided.

A.   Financial statements are prepared:

    a. once a year.

    b. at the end of the fiscal period.

    c. whenever management requires them.

    d. all of the above.

    e. none of the above.

B.   A work sheet is:

    a. one of the books of account.

    b. one of the financial statements.

    c. used instead of the financial statements.

    d. all of the above.

    e. none of the above.

C.   Extending amounts on a work sheet means:

    a. adding to the amounts because of additional transactions.

    b. placing debit amounts in debit columns and credit amounts in credit columns.

    c. transferring amounts into the Balance Sheet section or the Income Statement section.

    d. all of the above.

    e. none of the above.

D.   The process of balancing the work sheet involves:

    a. totalling the four right-hand money columns.

    b. calculating the difference between the two money columns in each of the last two sections.

    c. ensuring that the differences in b) above are equal to each other.

    d. all of the above.

    e. none of the above.

E.   A work sheet will not balance if:

    a. the Telephone Expense amount is extended to the Balance Sheet section Debit column.

    b. the Drawings amount is extended to the Income Statement section Debit column.

    c. the Capital amount is extended to the Balance Sheet section Debit column.

    d. all of the above.

    e. none of the above.

ANSWERS TO CHAPTER 8 REVIEW EXERCISES (cont.)

Exercise 4 (cont.)

F. You can tell what the net income or net loss figure is by:

    a. looking at the balancing figure in the Balance Sheet section of the work sheet. ☐

    b. looking at the balancing figure in the Income Statement section of the work sheet. ☐

    c. looking at the equity section of the completed balance sheet. ☐

    d. all of the above. ☐

    e. none of the above. ☐

G. All of the following statements, except one, are false. Indicate which statement is true.

    a. The report form of balance sheet is the only style used in the real business world. ☐

    b. The report form of balance sheet is common because it uses standard-sized paper. ☐

    c. The report form of balance sheet is horizontal in form. ☐

    d. The style of the report form of balance sheet eliminates the need for "balancing" totals. ☐

    e. The report form of balance sheet is more difficult to understand. ☐

H. All of the following statements, except one, are false. Indicate the one that is true.

On a classified balance sheet:

    a. automobiles are not included in the Fixed Assets section because their value decreases over time. ☐

    b. a mortgage payable is deducted from the asset, Building. ☐

    c. supplies are not included as a current asset because they are normally converted into cash. ☐

    d. a bank loan is included in long-term liabilities. ☐

    e. the values shown for the fixed assets are not necessarily their true market value. ☐

I. All of the following statements, except one, are true. Indicate which statement is false.

    a. The data in the books of account are considered to be "raw" data. ☐

    b. Accountants are judged on the basis of the accounting statements and reports that they prepare. Therefore, their work should be first-class in form and content. ☐

    c. All of the data necessary for the financial statements can be found on the work sheet. ☐

    d. An overall decrease in capital can occur in two ways. An overall increase in capital can occur in only one way. Therefore, decreases in capital are more common. ☐

    e. The beginning balance in the equity section of the balance sheet is not always that of January 1. ☐

J. During a fiscal period, a business suffered a loss of $12 000, began the period with a capital balance of $20 000, and ended the period with a debit balance of $2 000. The drawings for the fiscal period were:

    a. $ 6 000 ☐

    b. $10 000 ☐

    c. $30 000 ☐

    d. $18 000 ☐

    e. $14 000 ☐

Name _____ Date _____

ANSWERS TO CHAPTER 8 REVIEW EXERCISES (cont.)

Exercise 5, p. 295

A.

	Fiesta Restaurant Income Statement Years Ended March 31, 20-4 and 20-3			
	20-4	20-3	Increase or Decrease (−)	% Change
Revenue				
Food and Dining	$163 595	$150 290	_____	_____ %
Liquor and Bar	197 492	181 410	_____	_____ %
Total Revenues	$361 087	$331 700	_____	_____ %
Operating Expenses				
Bank Charges Expense	$ 920	$ 1 520	_____	_____ %
Car Expense	3 516	3 725	_____	_____ %
Insurance Expense	1 800	1 800	_____	_____ %
Utilities Expense	1 610	1 570	_____	_____ %
Food and Liquor Expense	157 315	140 290	_____	_____ %
Miscellaneous Expense	920	950	_____	_____ %
Rent Expense	24 000	24 000	_____	_____ %
Telephone Expense	1 350	1 290	_____	_____ %
Wages Expense	49 316	51 374	_____	_____ %
Total Expenses	$240 747	$226 519	_____	_____ %
Net Income	$120 340	$105 181	_____	_____ %

ANSWERS TO CHAPTER 8 REVIEW EXERCISES (cont.)

Exercise 5 (cont.)

B.

Fiesta Restaurant
Income Statement
Years Ended March 31, 20-4 and 20-3

	20-4			20-3	
Revenue					
Food and Dining	$163 595	_____ %		$150 290	_____ %
Liquor and Bar	197 492	_____ %		181 410	_____ %
Total Revenues	$361 087	_____ %		$331 700	_____ %
Operating Expenses					
Bank Charges Expense	$ 920	_____ %		$ 1 520	_____ %
Car Expense	3 516	_____ %		3 725	_____ %
Insurance Expense	1 800	_____ %		1 800	_____ %
Utilities Expense	1 610	_____ %		1 570	_____ %
Food and Liquor Expense	157 315	_____ %		140 290	_____ %
Miscellaneous Expense	920	_____ %		950	_____ %
Rent Expense	24 000	_____ %		24 000	_____ %
Telephone Expense	1 350	_____ %		1 290	_____ %
Wages Expense	49 316	_____ %		51 374	_____ %
Total Expenses	$240 747	_____ %		$226 519	_____ %
Net Income	$120 340	_____		$105 181	_____

C. _____

_____

_____

_____

_____

_____

_____

_____

ANSWERS TO CHAPTER 8 REVIEW EXERCISES (cont.)

Questions for Further Thought, p. 295

1. _____
   _____
   _____
   _____
   _____
   _____
   _____

2. _____
   _____
   _____
   _____
   _____

3. _____
   _____
   _____
   _____
   _____

4. _____
   _____
   _____
   _____

5. _____
   _____
   _____
   _____
   _____

6. _____
   _____
   _____
   _____

7. _____
   _____
   _____
   _____

ANSWERS TO CHAPTER 8 REVIEW EXERCISES (cont.)

Questions for Further Thought (cont.)

8. _____

_____

_____

_____

_____

9. _____

_____

_____

_____

CASE STUDIES (text p. 296)

Case 1 *Can Net Income Be Increased?*, p. 296

1.

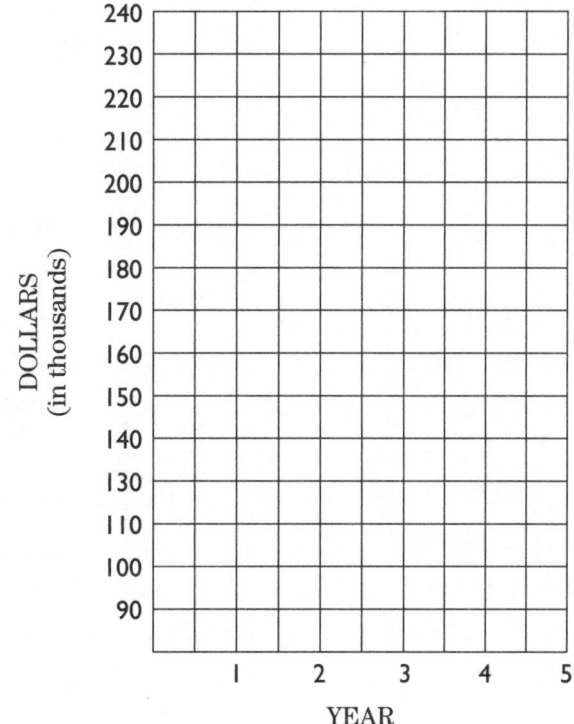

2. _____

3. _____

_____

4. _____

CASE STUDIES (cont.)

Case 1 (cont.)

5. _____

_____

_____

_____

_____

_____

_____

_____

_____

_____

_____

_____

_____

Case 2   *Analyzing Business Data*, p. 297

1 **a.** Increase in total assets

    b. Increase in A/P

       New mortgage

       Increase in equity

    c. The funds came from: trade creditors

                  the mortgage

                  retained profits

    d. Owner's drawings

       Net income for year $35 000

       Less amount retained in business

       Amount taken out by owner

2. **a.** Increase in total assets

    b. To make the mortgage payment

    c. The funds came from: increase in bank loan

                  retained profits

    d. Owner's drawings

       Net income for the year

       Less amount retained in business

       Amount taken out by owner

CASE STUDIES (cont.)

Case 2 (cont.)

3. a. Increase in total assets   _____

    b. To make the mortgage payment   _____

       To pay off the bank loan   _____

                                                       _____

    c. The funds came from: trade creditors   _____

                   retained profits   _____

                                                       _____

    d. Calculation of profit for Year 4

       Amount taken out by owner   _____

       Amount retained in business   _____

                                                       _____

Case 3 *Why Doesn't Net Income Equal Cash?*, p. 298

  1. _____

     _____

     _____

     _____

     _____

  2. _____

     _____

     _____

     _____

     _____

  3. _____

     _____

     _____

     _____

Case 4 *Interpreting Condensed Balance Sheets*, p. 299

  1. _____

  2. _____

  3. _____

  4. _____

     _____

     _____

CASE STUDIES (cont.)

Challenge Case 5   *Could You Get Student Council out of the Hole?*, p. 300

1. _____

2. _____

3. _____

CASE STUDIES (cont.)

Case 5 (cont.)

4. _____
   _____
   _____
   _____
   _____
   _____
   _____
   _____
   _____
   _____

Career   **LILIAN GOH/DIRECTOR, AUDIT OPERATIONS
OFFICE OF THE AUDITOR GENERAL OF CANADA**

ANSWERS TO RESEARCH QUESTIONS (text p. 302)

_____
_____
_____
_____
_____
_____
_____
_____
_____
_____
_____
_____
_____
_____
_____
_____
_____
_____
_____
_____
_____

Chapter 9 Completing the Accounting Cycle

ANSWERS TO SECTION 9.1 REVIEW QUESTIONS (text p. 307)

The Adjustment Process

1. _____

_____

_____

2. _____

_____

3. _____

_____

_____

4. _____

5. _____

_____

6. _____

_____

7. _____

_____

_____

_____

8. _____

9. _____

10. _____

11. _____

12. _____

_____

13. _____

_____

_____

_____

14. _____

_____

15. _____

_____

16. _____

_____

17. _____

ANSWERS TO SECTION 9.1 EXERCISES (text p. 308)

Exercise 1, p. 308

Complete the following schedule.

Supplies	Trial Balance Figure	Supplies Closing Inventory Figure	Supplies Expense Figure
1.	$300.00	$100.00	
2.	$1 400.00	$650.00	
3.		$175.00	$250.00
4.	$950.00		$740.00

Prepaid Insurance	Trial Balance Figure	Prepaid Insurance Final Calculation	Insurance Expense Figure
1. $875.00		$325.00	
2. $9 600.00		$800.00	
3. $925.00			$315.00
4.		$410.00	$375.00

Exercise 2, p. 308   *Infinity Ward*   COD   WW3 MW3

GENERAL JOURNAL   PAGE

DATE		PARTICULARS	P.R.	DEBIT	CREDIT
20-3 Dec	31	Supplies Expense		3 600 —	
		Supplies			3 600 —
July	1	Insurance Expense			
		Prepaid Insurance			
		Advertising Expens		10 000 —	
		A/P			10 000 —

J-Shore   Thurs/Jerse-day

ANSWERS TO SECTION 9.1 EXERCISES (cont.)

Exercise 3, p. 308

Using the following information, complete the inventory sheet and make the adjusting entry in the T-accounts.

Inventory Item	Quantity	Unit Price	Value	
Rubber bands	3 boxes	$ 1.50 per box		
Envelopes #8	10 boxes	32.00 per box		
Envelopes #10	4 1/2 boxes	36.00 per box		
Envelopes, manila	2 boxes	28.00 per box		
Printer cartridges	2 boxes	31.20 per box		
Letterhead	10M sheets	22.50 per M		
Copy paper	4M sheets	10.00 per M		
File folders	2 boxes	6.00 per box		
Paper clips	12 boxes	1.50 per box		
Staples	15 boxes	4.10 per box		
Pencils, regular	4 doz.	5.50 per doz.		
Pencils, red	2 doz.	6.10 per doz.		
		Total		

Supplies	Supplies Expense
2 018.00	

Exercise 4, p. 309

Year	Insurance Expense	Prepaid Insurance (Dec. 31)
20-1		
20-2		
	Total Expense $648	

Name _____   Date _____

ANSWERS TO SECTION 9.1 EXERCISES (cont.)

Exercise 5, p. 309

A.

	Total number of months of insurance used as of the designated year-end	Total number of months of insurance unused as of the designated year-end	Value of the prepaid insurance at the designated year-end
a.			
b.			
c.			
d.			
e.			
f.			

B.

GENERAL JOURNAL

PAGE

DATE	PARTICULARS	P.R.	DEBIT	CREDIT

ANSWERS TO SECTION 9.1 EXERCISES (cont.)

Exercise 6, p. 309

Prepaid Licences	Truck Licence Expense	Bank

ANSWERS TO SECTION 9.2 REVIEW QUESTIONS (text p. 319)

Adjusting Entries and the Work Sheet

1. _____

2. _____

3. _____
   _____
   _____
   _____
   _____
   _____

4. _____
   _____

5. _____
   _____

6. _____
   _____

Name Harraj Sdavnh   Date Dnv.

Exercise 1, p. 320

A.

WORK SHEET

P. Tang and Company   Year Ended December 31, 20-4

ACCOUNTS	TRIAL BALANCE		ADJUSTMENTS		INCOME STATEMENT		BALANCE SHEET	
	DEBIT	CREDIT	DEBIT	CREDIT	DEBIT	CREDIT	DEBIT	CREDIT
Bank	1 8 0 0 –							
Accounts Receivable	19 5 0 0 –							
Supplies	1 0 0 0 –							
Prepaid Insurance	1 7 5 0 –							
Equipment	22 0 0 0 –							
Automobile	21 0 0 0 –							
Accounts Payable		4 3 6 0 –						
P. Tang, Capital		54 0 4 0 –						
P. Tang, Drawings	15 0 0 0 –							
Fees Earned		60 3 0 0 –						
Car Expense	3 8 0 0 –							
General Expense	2 9 5 0 –							
Miscellaneous Expense	7 0 0 –							
Rent Expense	7 2 0 0 –							
Wages Expense	22 0 0 0 –							
	118 7 0 0 –	118 7 0 0 –						

ANSWERS TO SECTION 9.2 EXERCISES (cont.)

Exercise 1 (cont.)

B.

GENERAL JOURNAL   PAGE

DATE	PARTICULARS	P.R.	DEBIT	CREDIT
20-4				

C.

GENERAL LEDGER

Bank		Accounts Receivable		Supplies	
1 800		19 500		1 000	

Prepaid Insurance		Equipment		Automoblie	
1 750		22 000		21 000	

Accounts Payable		P. Tang, Capital		P. Tang, Drawings	
	4 360		54 040	15 000	

(Ledger continues on next page.)

ANSWERS TO SECTION 9.2 EXERCISES (cont.)

Exercise 1 (cont.)

C. (cont.)

Fees Earned		Car Expense		General Expense
	60 300	3 800		2 950

Miscellaneous Expense

700

P. Tang and Company
Adjusted Trial Balance
December 31, 20-4

ACCOUNTS	DEBIT	CREDIT

Rent Expense

7 200

Wages Expense

22 000

Supplies Expense

Insurance Expense

ANSWERS TO SECTION 9.2 EXERCISES (cont.)

Exercise 1 (cont.)

Optional

D.

P. Tang and Company

Income Statement

Year Ended December 31, 20-4

ANSWERS TO SECTION 9.2 EXERCISES (cont.)

Exercise 1 (cont.)

Optional

D. (cont.)

P. Tang and Company

Balance Sheet

December 31, 20-4

ANSWERS TO SECTION 9.2 EXERCISES (cont.)

Exercise 2, p. 320

A.

Mission Marketing

WORK SHEET

Year Ended December 31, 20-3

ACCOUNTS	TRIAL BALANCE DEBIT	TRIAL BALANCE CREDIT	ADJUSTMENTS DEBIT	ADJUSTMENTS CREDIT	INCOME STATEMENT DEBIT	INCOME STATEMENT CREDIT	BALANCE SHEET DEBIT	BALANCE SHEET CREDIT
Bank	2 4 9 0 —							
Accounts Receivable	21 6 0 0 —							
Supplies	4 2 5 0 —							
Prepaid Insurance	1 2 5 4 —							
Equipment	19 2 0 0 —							
Automobile	44 2 0 0 —							
Accounts Payable		6 5 6 5 —						
GST Payable		7 8 0 —						
GST Recoverable	5 1 0 —							
C.Ans, Capital		71 2 7 5 —						
C.Ans, Drawings	40 0 0 0 —							
Fees Earned		135 7 0 0 —						
Car Expense	13 2 1 4 —							
Miscellaneous Expense	1 5 6 3 —							
Rent Expense	18 0 0 0 —							
Utilities Expense	2 8 0 0 —							
Wages Expense	45 2 3 9 —							
	214 3 2 0 —	214 3 2 0 —						

ANSWERS TO SECTION 9.2 EXERCISES (cont.)

Exercise 2 (cont.)

B.

GENERAL JOURNAL   PAGE

DATE		PARTICULARS	P.R.	DEBIT	CREDIT

C.

GENERAL LEDGER

Bank	
2 490	

Accounts Receivable	
21 600	

Supplies	
4 250	

Prepaid Insurance	
1 254	

Equipment	
19 200	

Automobile	
44 200	

Accounts Payable	
	6 565

GST Payable	
	780

GST Recoverable	
510	

C. Ans, Capital	
	71 275

C. Ans, Drawings	
40 000	

Fees Earned	
	135 700

(Ledger continues on next page.)

ANSWERS TO SECTION 9.2 EXERCISES (cont.)

Exercise 2 (cont.)

C. (cont.)

Car Expense		Miscellaneous Expense		Rent Expense	
13 214		1 563		18 000	

Mission Marketing

Adjusted Trial Balance

December 31, 20-3

ACCOUNTS	DEBIT	CREDIT

Utilities Expense

2 800

Wages Expense

45 239

Supplies Expense

Insurance Expense

ANSWERS TO SECTION 9.2 EXERCISES (cont.)

Exercise 2 (cont.)

Optional

D.

Mission Marketing

Income Statement

Year Ended December 31, 20-3

ANSWERS TO SECTION 9.2 EXERCISES (cont.)

Exercise 2 (cont.)

Optional

D. (cont.)

Mission Marketing

Balance Sheet

December 31, 20-3

ANSWERS TO SECTION 9.3 REVIEW QUESTIONS (text p. 324)

Closing Entries Concepts

1. _____
   _____
   _____

2. _____
   _____

3. _____

4. _____
   _____

5. _____

6. _____

7. _____
   _____
   _____

8. _____

9. _____
   1. _____
   2. _____
   3. _____

10. _____
    1. _____
    2. _____
    3. _____

ANSWERS TO SECTION 9.3 EXERCISES (text p. 324)

Exercise 1, p. 324

_____
_____
_____
_____
_____
_____

ANSWERS TO SECTION 9.3 EXERCISES (cont.)

Exercise 2, p. 325 A., B.

GENERAL LEDGER

Bank		Bank Loan		S. Mosar, Capital		S. Mosar, Drawings	
100			300		740	750	

Accounts Receivable		Accounts Payable		Advertising Revenue		Sales Revenue	
200			150		1 750		450

Supplies				Bank Charges		Miscellaneous Expense	
50				20		5	

Equipment				Printing Expense		Rent Expense	
50				500		250	

				Telephone Expense		Utilities Expense	
				25		40	

						Wage Expense	
						400	

Name _____   Date _____

ANSWERS TO SECTION 9.3 EXERCISES (cont.)

Exercise 3, p. 325   (Workbook Exercise)

In the chart below, the steps in the accounting cycle are given in incorrect order.

Required: 1. **In the column headed Step No., enter the correct step number according to the sequence of steps given in the text on page 323.**

2. **In two of the remaining five columns, place check marks to indicate when the step is performed and by whom.**

Steps in the Accounting Cycle	Step No.	Done Daily	Done Monthly	Done at the End of the Fiscal Period	Done by Junior Personnel	Done by Senior Personnel
Journal entries posted to the ledger accounts.						
Adjusting and closing entries journalized and posted.						
Post-closing trial balance.						
Financial statements prepared.						
Ledger balanced by means of a trial balance.						
Accounting entries recorded in the journal.						
Work sheet prepared.						
Transactions occur.						

Exercise 4, p. 326

A. Accounting is _____ in nature.

B. The _____ states that financial reporting is done in equal periods of time.

C. Asset and liability accounts are considered to be _____ accounts.

D. _____ have their balances continue on into the succeeding fiscal period.

E. Revenue, expense, and drawings accounts are considered to be _____ accounts.

F. The balances in _____ do not continue into the _____ fiscal period.

G. Another name for a nominal account is a _____.

H. Nominal accounts begin each fiscal period with _____.

I. The process of removing the "old" balances from the nominal accounts is known as

_____ .

ANSWERS TO SECTION 9.3 EXERCISES (cont.)

Exercise 4 (cont.)

J. _____ means to cause it to have no balance.

K. During a fiscal period, the Capital account shows _____
_____ .

L. Changes in equity during a fiscal period (except for additional investments by the owner) are contained in _____ accounts.

M. At the end of the fiscal period, the ledger is brought up to date by _____
_____ .

N. One of the final steps in the accounting cycle is to bring the Capital account _____ and to _____ the nominal accounts.

O. The final step in the accounting cycle is _____ .

ANSWERS TO SECTION 9.4 REVIEW QUESTIONS (text p. 334)

Journalizing and Posting the Closing Entries

1. _____
2. _____
_____
_____
_____
_____
3. _____
_____
_____
_____
_____
4. _____
5. _____
6. _____
_____
_____
7. _____
_____
8. _____
_____
_____
_____
_____

ANSWERS TO SECTION 9.4 EXERCISES (text p. 334)

Exercise 1, p. 334

GENERAL JOURNAL   PAGE

DATE		PARTICULARS	P.R.	DEBIT	CREDIT

Name _H_____ Date _____

Exercise 2, p. 335

A.   There are two because one adjustment is for the increase in supplies and the other for a decrease in the supplies account.

B.

GENERAL JOURNAL   PAGE

DATE		PARTICULARS	P.R.	DEBIT	CREDIT
		Adjusting Entries			
Dec.	31	Supplies		800 —	
		Accounts Payable			800 —
	31	Supplies Used Expense		1055 —	
		Supplies			1055 —
	31	Insurance Expense		1625 —	
		Prepaid Insurance			1625 —
		Closing Entries			
	31	Revenue		98370 —	
		Income Summary			98370 —
	31	Income Summary		46682 —	
		Advertising Expense			1200 —
		Bank Charges Expense			96 —
		Supplies Used Expense			8005 —
		Miscellaneous Expense			1902 —
		Rent Expense			6000 —
		Utilities Expense			2104 —
		Wages Expense			25750 —
		Insurance Expense			1625 —
	31	Income Summary		9342 —	
		R. Tompko, Capital			9342 —
		R. Tompko, Capital		42000 —	
		R. Tompko, Drawings			42000 —

Copyright © 2002 Pearson Education Canada Inc., Toronto, Ontario

Name _____ Date _____

Exercise 2 (cont.)

C.

GENERAL LEDGER

Bank		Supplies		Prepaid Insurance	
790		2 755		2 450	

Equipment		Accounts Payable		GST Payable	
17 005			1 075		580

GST Recoverable		R. Tompko, Capital		R. Tompko, Drawings	
365			9 342	42 000	

Revenue		Advertising Expense		Bank Charges Expense	
	98 370	1 200		96	

Supplies Used Expense		Miscellaneous Expense		Rent Expense	
6 950		1 902		6 000	

Utilities Expense		Wages Expense		Insurance Expense	
2 104		25 750			

Income Summary	

ANSWERS TO SECTION 9.4 EXERCISES (cont.)

Exercise 2 (cont.)

D.

Golden Tresses Hair Stylists

Post-Closing Trial Balance

December 31, 20—

Exercise 3, p. 335

Indicate whether each of the following statements is true or false by placing a "T" or an "F" in the space indicated. Explain the reason for each "F" response.

a. Journalizing and posting the adjusting and closing entries is a routine task that can be done by any knowledgeable accounting clerk.

b. All of the data required to journalize the adjusting and closing entries can be found on the work sheet.

c. It can be assumed that all adjustments have been thought of once the work sheet is completed.

d. The adjusting entries must be journalized and posted to bring the ledger into agreement with the figures on the financial statements.

e. An explanation is needed for each individual adjusting entry being journalized.

f. The adjusting and closing entries in the journal are dated as of the end of the fiscal period.

g. The closing entries can be processed only by using the four-step method.

h. The figures for the first closing entry are taken from the income statement section, debit column, of the work sheet.

i. Because revenue accounts have debit balances, credit entries are needed to close them out.

j. The second closing entry transfers the balances in the expense accounts to the Income Summary account.

k. When the adjusting entries and the first two closing entries are journalized and posted, all but three of the accounts in the equity section of the ledger will have nil balances.

ANSWERS TO SECTION 9.4 EXERCISES (cont.)

Exercise 3 (cont.)

l. A loss has occurred if the Income Summary account has a credit balance before it is closed out. ☐

m. The first two entries in the Income Summary account are the same as the subtotals of the income statement section of the work sheet. ☐

n. The Income Summary account is not closed out if a loss occurs. ☐

Explanations for "F" Responses

_____

_____

_____

_____

_____

_____

_____

_____

_____

ANSWERS TO SECTION 9.5 REVIEW QUESTIONS (text p. 348)

Adjusting for Depreciation

1. _____

2. _____

3. _____

4. _____

5. _____

6. _____

7. _____

ANSWERS TO SECTION 9.5 REVIEW QUESTIONS (cont.)

8. _____
   _____

9. _____
   _____

10. _____
    _____
    _____

11. _____
    _____

12. _____
    _____

13. _____
    _____
    _____
    _____

ANSWERS TO SECTION 9.5 EXERCISES (text p. 348)

Exercise 1, p. 348

For each of the following situations, allocate the total cost to the proper fiscal periods. Assume the company commenced business on January 1, 20-1, and has a fiscal year-end of December 31.

1. A truck was purchased on January 1, 20-1, for $18 000. It was expected to last for five full years, at the end of which it would have a trade-in value of $3 000. Use the straight-line method of depreciation.

20-1	20-2	20-3	20-4	20-5

2. A used vehicle was bought on November 1, 20-1, for $5 800. It was expected to last for four full years, at the end of which it would have a resale value of $1 000. Use the straight-line method of depreciation.

20-1	20-2	20-3	20-4	20-5

ANSWERS TO SECTION 9.5 EXERCISES (cont.)

Exercise 1 (cont.)

3. A building was purchased on May 1, 20-2, for the sum of $113 000. It was expected to last for 25 years, at which time it would have a resale value of $5 000. Use the straight-line method of depreciation.

20-1	20-2	20-3	20-4	20-5

4. A new machine was bought on January 1, 20-1, for $54 000. It is depreciated using the declining-balance method at the rate of 20 per cent.

20-1	20-2	20-3	20-4	20-5

5. A new building was bought on July 1, 20-1, for $282 000. It is depreciated using the declining-balance method at a rate of 5 per cent.

20-1	20-2	20-3	20-4	20-5

Exercise 2, p. 349

A.

Year	Straight-line Depreciation	
	Depreciation	Balance
1		
2		
3		
4		
5		

ANSWERS TO SECTION 9.5 EXERCISES (cont.)

Exercise 2 (cont.)

B.

Year	Declining-balance Depreciation	
	Depreciation	Balance
1		
2		
3		
4		
5		

C.

_____

_____

Exercise 3, p. 349

A.

	20-1	20-2	20-3	20-4	20-5

ANSWERS TO SECTION 9.5 EXERCISES (cont.)

Exercise 3 (cont.)

B.

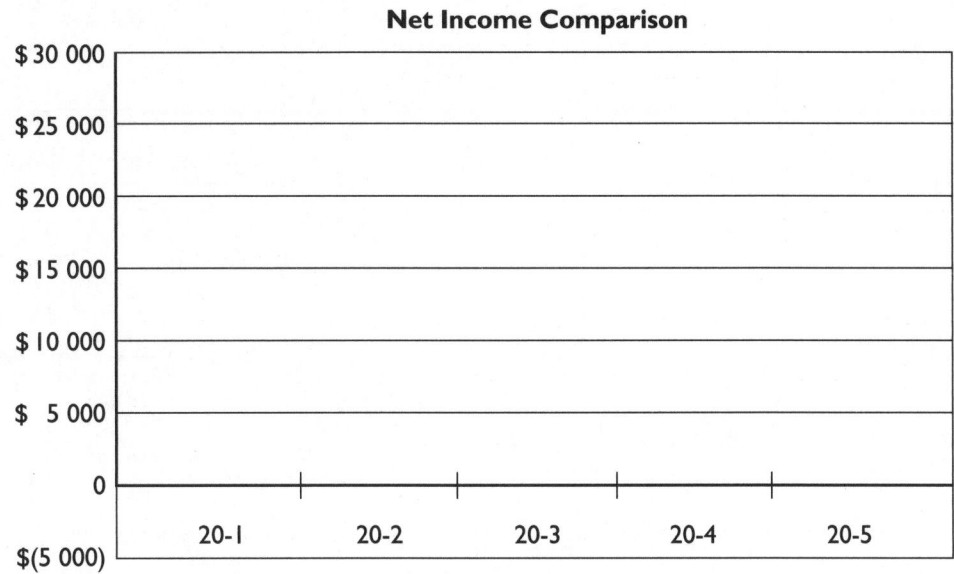

C. _____
_____
_____
_____
_____

Exercise 4, p. 350

The simplified general ledger of Shahid Company at the end of its annual fiscal period appears below.

A. **Using the additional information that is provided, record the year-end adjusting entries directly in the T-accounts.**

B. **Prepare an adjusted trial balance.**

A.

GENERAL LEDGER

Bank	Accounts Receivable	Supplies
400	8 285	1 900

(Ledger continues on next page.)

ANSWERS TO SECTION 9.5 EXERCISES (cont.)

Exercise 4 (cont.)

Prepaid Insurance		Land		Buildings	
1 800		50 000		70 000	

Accum. Depr.—Buildings		Equipment		Accum. Depr.—Equipment	
	6 750	96 500			24 000

Accounts Payable		J. Salk, Capital		J. Salk, Drawings	
	3 200		144 985	30 000	

Revenue		Bank Charges Expense		Delivery Expense	
	140 700	450		1 500	

Miscellaneous Expense		Telephone Expense		Utilities Expense	
490		390		1 300	

Wages Expense		Supplies Expense		Insurance Expense	
56 620					

Depreciation Exp.—Buildings		Depreciation Exp.—Equipment	

Additional Information

1. Inventory of supplies at the year-end is $850.

2. Unexpired insurance at the year-end is $625.

3. Depreciation is calculated on a straight-line basis. The building is expected to last 40 years, at which time it will be worth $25 000. The equipment is expected to last 15 years, after which it will be worth $6 500. Ignore the 50% rule.

ANSWERS TO SECTION 9.5 EXERCISES (cont.)

Exercise 4 (cont.)

B.

Shahid Company

Adjusted Trial Balance

— date —

ACCOUNTS	DEBIT	CREDIT

ANSWERS TO SECTION 9.5 EXERCISES (cont.)

Exercise 5, p. 351

WORK SHEET

Vieira Associates — *Year Ended December 31, 20—*

ACCOUNTS	TRIAL BALANCE DEBIT	TRIAL BALANCE CREDIT	ADJUSTMENTS DEBIT	ADJUSTMENTS CREDIT	INCOME STATEMENT DEBIT	INCOME STATEMENT CREDIT	BALANCE SHEET DEBIT	BALANCE SHEET CREDIT
Bank	5 0 8 0 20							
Accounts Receivable	1 7 4 9 1 —							
Supplies	2 6 3 5 —							
Prepaid Insurance	1 8 0 0 —							
Equipment	1 0 2 0 0 —							
Accum. Depr.—Equipment		6 0 2 2 08						
Automobiles	3 2 5 0 0 —							
Accum. Depr.—Automobiles		1 6 5 7 5 —						
Accounts Payable		4 8 0 2 50						
GST Payable		9 4 0 20						
GST Recoverable	5 1 6 80							
C. Vieira, Capital		2 1 8 2 1 04						
C. Vieira, Drawings	4 8 0 0 0 —							
Consulting Fees		1 5 4 3 2 6 —						
Automobile Expense	3 2 7 5 6 04							
General Expense	1 5 7 5 —							
Rent Expense	1 0 0 0 0 —							
Telephone Expense	1 5 6 7 —							
Wages Expense	4 0 3 6 5 78							
	2 0 4 4 8 6 82	2 0 4 4 8 6 82						

Name _____   Date _____

Exercise 6, p. 351

| | | GENERAL JOURNAL | | | PAGE |
| | | | | | |

DATE		PARTICULARS	P.R.	DEBIT	CREDIT

Exercise 7, p. 351   Workbook Exercise

Calculating Depreciation with the 50% Rule in Effect

If you ever find yourself in a position where you have to prepare income tax forms for a business, you could very well find the process confusing when it comes to dealing with depreciation. This exercise is designed to give you some experience in this respect.

Suppose that your business had the following accounts on December 31, 2001, the end of its first year of business.

	Dr	Cr
Buildings	$240 000	
Accumulated Depreciation—Buildings		$6 000
Automobile	$ 62 000	
Accumulated Depreciation—Automobile		$9 300

Canada Customs and Revenue Agency (the tax department) would view these accounts simply as:

Buildings—Class 3 Undepreciated Capital Cost	$234 000
Automobiles—Class 10 Undepreciated Capital Cost	$ 52 700

ANSWERS TO SECTION 9.5 EXERCISES (cont.)

Exercise 7 (cont.)   **Workbook Exercise**

A.   When it came time to prepare income tax returns for the second year of business, you would have to include a tax form for calculating capital cost allowances (depreciation). This form would be prepared as shown below. There were no acquisitions or disposals of equipment during the year.

1 Class number	2 Undepreciated capital cost at the beginning of the year	3 Cost of acquisitions during the year (new property must be available for use)	4 Adjustments (show negative amounts in brackets)	5 Proceeds of dispositions during the year (amount not to exceed the capital cost)	6 Undepreclated capital cost (column 2 plus column 3 plus or minus column 4 minus column 5)	7 50% rule (deduct 1/2 of the amount, if any, by which the net cost of acquisitions exceeds column 5)	8 Reduced undepreciated capital cost (column 6 minus column 7)	9 CCA rate %	10 Capital cost allowance (column 8 multiplied by column 9; or a lower amount)	11 Undepreciate d capital cost at the end of the year (column 6 minus column 10)
3	$234 000	Ø	Ø	Ø	$234 000	Ø	$234 000	5%	$11 700	$222 300
10	$ 52 700	Ø	Ø	Ø	$ 52 700	Ø	$ 52 700	30%	$15 810	$ 36 890
									Total	$27 510

Required

1.   Assuming that the business uses the above methods for calculating depreciation, make entries in the ledger accounts on pages 251 and 252 to bring the Accumulated Depreciation accounts up to date. Use the Particulars column to briefly explain each entry.

B.   In the third year of operation, the business traded in its 1999 BMW automobile and purchased a new one. The automobile dealership agreed to a trade-in value for the old BMW of $36 890, which was the "book value" shown in company accounts. The cost of the new BMW was $75 000, meaning the business had to pay $38 110 to complete the sale. The accounting entries to record the above transactions are given for you, as follows:

	Dr	Cr
Automobile	75 000	
Accounts Payable		75 000
Purchased a new car		
Accounts Payable	36 890	
Accumulated Depreciation—Automobile	25 110	
Automobile		62 000
Traded in old car		
Accounts Payable	38 110	
Bank		38 110
Paid balance on new car		

Name _____   Date _____

ANSWERS TO SECTION 9.5 EXERCISES (cont.)

Exercise 7 (cont.)   **Workbook Exercise**

Required

2. Post the above transactions in the accounts provided. Use the Particulars column to briefly explain each entry.

3. Show the calculation used to determine the book value of the 1999 BMW.

4. On page 252, complete the capital cost allowance form for the third business year. Note that in the third year, columns 3, 5, and 7 are used. Be careful to read the column headings carefully as you proceed.

5. Identify the column of the CCA form where the 50% rule affects your calculations.

6. In the ledger, bring the Accumulated Depreciation accounts up to date. Use the Particulars column to briefly explain each entry. Use the capital cost allowance figures from the CCA form.

7. From the accounts, calculate the net book values of the fixed assets and see that they agree with the undepreciated capital cost figures, column 11 on the tax form.

ACCOUNT *Bank*   No.

DATE	PARTICULARS	P.R.	DEBIT	CREDIT	DR/CR	BALANCE

ACCOUNT *Building*   No.

DATE	PARTICULARS	P.R.	DEBIT	CREDIT	DR/CR	BALANCE
2001	First year purchase		240 0 0 0 –		DR	240 0 0 0 –

ACCOUNT *Accumulated Depreciation—Building*   No.

DATE	PARTICULARS	P.R.	DEBIT	CREDIT	DR/CR	BALANCE
2001	Depr. Year 1 (50% rule)			6 0 0 0 –	CR	6 0 0 0 –

ANSWERS TO SECTION 9.5 EXERCISES (cont.)

Exercise 7 (cont.)   **Workbook Exercise**

ACCOUNT *Automobile*   No.

DATE		PARTICULARS	P.R.	DEBIT	CREDIT	DR/CR	BALANCE
2001		First year purchase		62 0 0 0 –		DR	62 0 0 0 –

ACCOUNT *Accumulated Depreciation—Automobile*   No.

DATE		PARTICULARS	P.R.	DEBIT	CREDIT	DR/CR	BALANCE
2001		Depr. Year 1 (50% rule)			9 3 0 0 –	CR	9 3 0 0 –

ACCOUNT *Accounts Payable*   No.

DATE		PARTICULARS	P.R.	DEBIT	CREDIT	DR/CR	BALANCE

1 Class number	2 Undepreciated capital cost at the beginning of the year	3 Cost of acquisitions during the year (new property must be available for use)	4 Adjustments (show negative amounts in brackets)	5 Proceeds of dispositions during the year (amount not to exceed the capital cost)	6 Undepreclated capital cost (column 2 plus column 3 plus or minus column 4 minus column 5)	7 50% rule (deduct 1/2 of the amount, if any, by which the net cost of acquisitions exceeds column 5)	8 Reduced undepreciated capital cost (column 6 minus column 7)	9 CCA rate %	10 Capital cost allowance (column 8 multiplied by column 9; or a lower amount)	11 Undepreciated capital cost at the end of the year (column 6 minus column 10)

Total

ANSWERS TO SECTION 9.5 EXERCISES (cont.)

Exercise 7 (cont.)   **Workbook Exercise**

_____

_____

_____

_____

_____

_____

_____

_____

_____

_____

_____

_____

ANSWERS TO CHAPTER 9.6 COMPUTER REVIEW QUESTIONS (text p. 355)

Adjusting and Closing Accounts with Simply Accounting

1. _____

2. _____

   _____

3. _____

   _____

   _____

   _____

4. _____

ANSWERS TO SECTION 9.6 COMPUTER EXERCISES (text p. 355)

Exercise 1, p. 355

ANSWERS TO SECTION 9.6 COMPUTER EXERCISES (text p. 355)

Exercise 2, p. 355   Challenge Exercise

Spreadsheet Exercise

Load the model named ANDREWS and enter May's trial balance figures, which are shown in Figure 1 below.

◇	A	B	C	D	E
1					
2		Andrews Landscaping			Work Sheet
3					
4				Trial Balance	
5				*Debit*	*Credit*
6		Bank		2 021.66	
7		Accounts Receivable		2 800.00	
8		Supplies		1 255.13	
9		Equipment		3 898.21	
10		Truck		6 000.00	
11		Bank Loan			5 000.00
12		Accounts Payable			2 741.36
13		GST Payable			3 018.29
14		GST Recoverable		709.51	
15		O. Andrews, Capital			14 969.27
16		O. Andrews, Drawings		9 600.00	
17		Fees Earned			43 118.46
18		Advertising Expense		7 022.47	
19		Bank Charges Expense		149.25	
20		General Expense		389.11	
21		Insurance Expense		1 485.00	
22		Rent Expense		4 800.00	
23		Telephone Expense		345.87	
24		Utilities Expense		702.53	
25		Wages Expense		27 668.64	
26				68 847.38	68 847.38
27		Net Income			

FIGURE I The trial balance of Andrews Landscaping for May

Change the heading at G2 to read Three Months Ended May 31, 20—. Save your work frequently.

The owner of the business, Olivia Andrews, is concerned that the profits are not high enough. She wants an updated net income figure for the first quarter of the year. Therefore, adjustments to account balances will have to be made in order to calculate the most accurate net income possible.

To insert the two columns needed for adjustments, move the cell pointer to column F and perform the insert commands of your spreadsheet. Type column headings, then enter SUM functions at F26 and G26. Your revised spreadsheet model should look like the partial one shown in Figure 2 on the next page.

ANSWERS TO SECTION 9.6 COMPUTER EXERCISES (cont.)

Exercise 2 (cont.)

◇	A	B	C	D	E	F	G
1							
2		Andrews Landscaping			Work Sheet		
3							
4				Trial Balance		Adjustments	
5				*Debit*	*Credit*	*Debit*	*Credit*
6		Bank		2 021.66			
7		Accounts Receivable		2 800.00			
8		Supplies		1 255.13			
9		Equipment		3 898.21			
10		Truck		6 000.00			
11		Bank Loan			5 000.00		
12		Accounts Payable			2 741.36		
13		GST Payable			3 018.29		
14		GST Recoverable		709.51			
15		O. Andrews, Capital			14 969.27		
16		O. Andrews, Drawings		9 600.00			
17		Fees Earned			43 118.46		
18		Advertising Expense		7 022.47			
19		Bank Charges Expense		149.25			
20		General Expense		389.11			
21		Insurance Expense		1 485.00			
22		Rent Expense		4 800.00			
23		Telephone Expense		345.87			
24		Utilities Expense		702.53			
25		Wages Expense		27 668.64			
26				68 847.38	68 847.38	0.00	0.00
27		Net Income					
28							

FIGURE 2 The work sheet with columns inserted for adjustments

Entering Adjustments

The following adjustments will affect the account balances of Andrews Landscaping:

1. A count revealed $602.35 of Supplies on hand.

2. An invoice for equipment purchased on May 29 was not received until early June. The equipment cost $912.60 and the GST paid was $63.88, for a total invoice amount of $976.48.

3. A 12-month insurance policy for $1 485 was bought on March 1. The entire amount was debited to Insurance Expense at that time. The owner wants the balance of this account reduced so it will reflect only the amount of insurance expired in the last three months.

Enter the adjustments in columns F and G of your spreadsheet model. Because rows may be inserted in a spreadsheet, new accounts can be listed in numerical order instead of beneath the other trial balance accounts. Assign appropriate account numbers for any new accounts you create.

ANSWERS TO SECTION 9.6 COMPUTER EXERCISES (cont.)

Exercise 2 (cont.)

Extending the Work Sheet

If you recorded the adjustments correctly, the totals in columns F and G should be $2 743.01. You should have added two additional accounts: Supplies Expense and Prepaid Insurance. If you did not obtain these totals or enter these accounts, ask you teacher for assistance before continuing.

Notice that, although you made the adjustment, the balances in the Income Statement and Balance Sheet columns are unchanged. The formulas in these cells must be modified so that they respond to the new figures in the Adjustments columns.

Move the cell pointer to J6, the Bank amount in the balance sheet section. This cell contains a cell reference (D6). In order for J6 to respond to any future changes in the Adjustments columns, a formula will have to be entered. At J6, type **D6 +F6 −G6**. This instruction will add debits and subtract credits on the work sheet. When this formula is entered, no change occurs in the Bank account balance because no adjustments were made.

Copy the formula at J6 down to all the balance sheet accounts that have debit amounts.

You must be careful when you extend accounts with credit balances. A slight change in the formula is needed. **Move the cell pointer to K12 (Bank Loan). Enter E12 −F12 +G12.** This will subtract debits and add credits. **Use your copy commands to complete the balance sheet section.**

Finish extending the work sheet by entering formulas to transfer the income statement amounts. Your finished model should look similar to Figure 3 on the next page.

ANSWERS TO SECTION 9.6 COMPUTER EXERCISES (cont.)

Exercise 2 (cont.)

◇	B	C	H	I	J	K
2	Andrews Landscaping				Month Ended May 31, 20—	
3						
4			Income Statement		Balance Sheet	
5			*Debit*	*Credit*	*Debit*	*Credit*
6	Bank				2 021.66	
7	Accounts Receivable				2 800.00	
8	Prepaid Insurance				1 113.75	
9	Supplies				602.35	
10	Equipment				4 810.81	
11	Truck				6 000.00	
12	Bank Loan					5 000.00
13	Accounts Payable					3 717.84
14	GST Payable					3 018.29
15	GST Recoverable				773.39	
16	O. Andrews, Capital					14 969.27
17	O. Andrews, Drawings				9 600.00	
18	Fees Earned			43 118.46		
19	Advertising Expense		7 022.47			
20	Bank Charges Expense		149.25			
21	General Expense		389.11			
22	Insurance Expense		371.25			
23	Rent Expense		4 800.00			
24	Supplies Expense		652.78			
25	Telephone Expense		345.87			
26	Utilities Expense		702.53			
27	Wages Expense		27 668.64			
28			42 101.90	43 118.46	27 721.96	26 705.40
29	Net Income		1 016.56			1 016.56
30			43 118.46	43 118.46	27 721.96	27 721.96
31						

FIGURE 3 The work sheet after adjustments are made and amounts are extended.

Improving the Spreadsheet Model

There are often ways to improve the performance of the spreadsheet models you are developing. For example, the model you developed for Andrews Landscaping allows you to complete work sheets and financial statements month after month with minimal effort. However, what if a net loss occurred? Could your model handle this situation without any further input on your part?

You may remember that the major change to the work sheet brought about by a net loss is the placement of the balancing figure. If there is a net income, the balancing figure is placed in the outer two of the last four columns. Conversely, if there is a net loss, the balancing figure is placed in the inner two of the last four columns.

The "finely tuned" spreadsheet model should be able to make a logical decision. It should be able to handle simple matters, such as, "If there is a net income, show the amount here," or "If there is a net loss, show the amount there." To accomplish this goal, we must use the IF function.

Name _____   Date _____

Exercise 2 (cont.)

The IF Function

The IF function is called a logical function because it can make simple decisions. The structure of the IF function is as follows:

prefix *FUNCTION NAME **(Condition, True Response, False Response)***

The prefix, function name, and parentheses are new. Let us examine how the IF function would be used at cell H29 of the Andrews Landscaping work sheet.

A logical statement for cell H29 could be expressed like this: If revenues are greater than expenses, calculate and show the net income. If revenues are not greater than expenses, show zero. The IF function dissected below will accomplish this logical procedure:

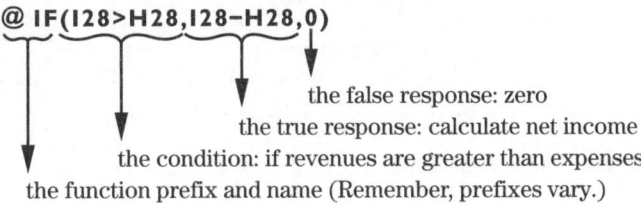

the false response: zero
the true response: calculate net income
the condition: if revenues are greater than expenses
the function prefix and name (Remember, prefixes vary.)

Using the function prefix for your spreadsheet software, enter the above function at cell H29.

When you press the Return key, you should notice no difference in your model because revenues are greater than expenses. Accordingly, the net income is calculated and shown in H29. **To test the function, reduce the Fees Earned amount in cell E18 to $118.46.** Now revenues are not greater than expenses, so 0.00 is shown at H29. **After testing, change the contents of E18 back to $43 118.46.**

Now that you understand how IF functions work, you should see that one is also needed at cell I29, the location where net losses are shown. **Enter the proper IF function at I29 and a cell reference at J29.**

Once again, test your model by changing Fees Earned at E18 to $118.46 and back again. Figures 4 and 5 below allow you to check you work.

◇	A	B	C		H	I	J	K
18		Fees Earned				43 118.46		
19		Advertising Expense			7 022.47			
20		Bank Charges Expense			149.25			
21		General Expense			389.11			
22		Insurance Expense			371.25			
23		Rent Expense			4 800.00			
24		Supplies Expense			652.78			
25		Telephone Expense			345.87			
26		Utilities Expense			702.53			
27		Wages Expense			27 668.64			
28					42 101.90	43 118.46	27 721.96	26 705.40
29		Net Income			1 016.56	-	-	1 016.56
30					43 118.46	43 118.46	27 721.96	27 721.96
31								

FIGURE 4 The response of the IF function when there is a net income

ANSWERS TO SECTION 9.6 COMPUTER EXERCISES (cont.)

Exercise 2 (cont.)

◇	A	B	C	H	I	J	K
18		Fees Earned			118.46		
19		Advertising Expense		7 022.47			
20		Bank Charges Expense		149.25			
21		General Expense		389.11			
22		Insurance Expense		371.25			
23		Rent Expense		4 800.00			
24		Supplies Expense		652.78			
25		Telephone Expense		345.87			
26		Utilities Expense		702.53			
27		Wages Expense		27 668.64			
28				42 101.90	118.46	27 721.96	26 705.40
29		Net Loss		–	41 983.44	41 983.44	–
30				42 101.90	42 101.90	69 705.40	26 705.40
31							

FIGURE 5 The response of the IF function when there is a net loss

You can change Net Income to Net Loss by typing a new label. However, some spreadsheet programs allow you to have *labels* as the true and false response of an IF function. An IF function that would work well at cell B29 is:

@IF(H29>0,"Net Income","Net Loss")

Note that when you want the IF function to display labels, they usually must be typed inside quotation marks.

You should now have some idea how useful the IF function can be. Accountants can be alerted to costs that are too high, sales projections that are too low, and many other kinds of management information by keying in IF functions at strategic points in their spreadsheets.

Percentage Analysis

Another way to improve this spreadsheet model is to have each expense shown on the income statement expressed as a percentage of total revenue. For Andrews Landscaping, this is accomplished by dividing each number by Fees Earned and expressing the answer in a per cent format. Refer to Figure 6 below for an example.

To get your model to look like Figure 6, do the following:

1. **Change the heading at M42 to** *Three Months Ended May 31, 20—.*

2. **Move the cell pointer to P45 and insert a column.**

3. **Type the** *Per Cent* **heading at P45.**

4. You will remember that a new account was added to the work sheet: Supplies Expense. **To have this account appear on the income statement, move the cell pointer M53 and insert a row. Then enter the account title and cell reference for its balance.** (Make sure that this cell reference comes from column H.)

Check your progress against Figure 6 to ensure that all expense account balances in column N match those in column H, from which they are derived.

Name _____ Date _____

Exercise 2 (cont.)

◇	L	M	N	O	P
39					
40		Andrews Landscaping			
41		Income Statement			
42		Three Months Ended May 31, 20—			
43					
44					
45	*Revenue*				Per Cent
46	Fees Earned			$ 43 118.46	100.00%
47	*Operating Expenses*				
48	Advertising Expense		$ 7 022.47		16.29%
49	Bank Charges Expense		149.25		0.35%
50	General Expense		389.11		0.90%
51	Insurance Expense		371.25		0.86%
52	Rent Expense		4 800.00		11.13%
53	Supplies Expense		652.78		1.51%
54	Telephone Expense		345.87		0.80%
55	Utilities Expense		702.53		1.63%
56	Wages Expense		27 668.64		64.17%
57	Total Expenses			42 101.90	97.64%
58	*Net Income*			$ 1 016.56	2.36%
59					

FIGURE 6 In column P, each income statement figure is expressed as a percentage of Fees Earned.

Copying with Absolute Cell References

Move the cell pointer to P48. Expressing the Advertising amount as a percentage of Fees Earned is a simple matter. **Divide cell N48 (Advertising) by O46 (Fees Earned) and apply a per cent format.**

Before using your copy commands, remember that cell references change when copied to new locations. In this case, you want the references to expense account balances to change, but not the reference to Fees Earned. You must convert the cell reference for Fees Earned into an *absolute cell reference*. An **absolute cell reference** is one that will not change when copied.

At P48, the formula is N48/O46. To change O46 to an absolute cell reference, dollar signs are entered in front of the row and the column references. (Most spreadsheets have shortcut commands to do this. At the very least, the dollar signs can be typed.) **At P48, enter N48/O46.**

Copy the new formula at P48 down to P56. To complete column P, also express Fees Earned, Total Expenses, and Net Income as percentages of Fees Earned.

Computer Review Questions

1. Why is the IF function called a "logical" function?

   _____

   _____

2. Within the parentheses of an IF function, what three items are separated by commas?

   _____

   _____

   _____

ANSWERS TO SECTION 9.6 COMPUTER EXERCISES (cont.)

Exercise 2 (cont.)

3. If labels are to be used as the true and false responses of an IF function, how must they be written? Give an example.

   _____

   _____

   _____

4. What are absolute cell references?

   _____

   _____

5. How would cell A62 be written as an absolute reference?

   _____

Computer Exercises

A. **Update the balance sheet section of your spreadsheet model for Andrews Landscaping.** You will have to put in a new date and make room for the Prepaid Insurance account.

B. A late invoice for advertising was discovered. It was for radio time on May 29 and 30, so it should be included in May's work sheet and statements. The total invoice amount was $1 546.15, which included $1 445 for advertising and $101.15 for GST.

   1. **Make the necessary changes in the adjustment columns of the work sheet (columns F and G).**

   2. The work sheet should balance automatically, but the financial statements will be wrong. **Correct all references to net income or net loss on the income statement and the balance sheet.**

C. You need to make sure that the financial statements will automatically respond to all future situations (i.e., net income or net loss). To accomplish this goal, enter appropriate IF functions on the balance sheet. Pay particular attention to calculations of capital. **Test your model under three conditions: net income greater than drawings, net income less than drawings, and net loss.** (Note: *To test your model, change Fees Earned and Bank by equal amounts in the trial balance section of the work sheet.*)

Note: page 269 follows next.

ANSWERS TO CHAPTER 9 REVIEW EXERCISES (text p. 356)

Exercise 1, p. 356

A. The clerk did do something wrong, he should have calculated

B.

Bank	Prepaid Insurance	Insurance Expense

Exercise 2, p. 357

ACCOUNT *Supplies*   No.

DATE	PARTICULARS	P.R.	DEBIT	CREDIT	DR/CR	BALANCE

ACCOUNT *Supplies Expense*   No.

DATE	PARTICULARS	P.R.	DEBIT	CREDIT	DR/CR	BALANCE

ANSWERS TO CHAPTER 9 REVIEW EXERCISES (text p. 356)

Exercise 3, p. 357

Prepaid Insurance	Insurance Expense

A. _____

B. _____

C. Insurance Expense _____

      Prepaid Insurance _____

D. _____

E. 1) _____

    2) _____

    3) _____

          Total _____

F. _____

G. Insurance Expense _____

    Prepaid Insurance _____

H. 1) National _____

          _____

    2) Regal _____

    3) Standard _____

          Total _____

ANSWERS TO CHAPTER 9 REVIEW EXERCISES (cont.)

Exercise 4, p. 358

A.

J. Soo and Associates

WORK SHEET — Year Ended December 31, 20-5

ACCOUNTS	TB Debit	TB Credit	Adj. Debit	Adj. Credit	IS Debit	IS Credit	BS Debit	BS Credit
Bank	2160 —						2160 —	
Accounts Receivable	11500 —						11500 —	
Supplies	1950 —			① 1310 —			640 —	
Prepaid Insurance	624 —			② 364 —			260 —	
Equipment	9200 —						9200 —	
Automobile	18350 —						18350 —	
Accounts Payable		5920 —		③ 115 —				6035 —
GST Payable		310 —						310 —
GST Recoverable	340 —						340 —	
J. Soo, Capital		36662 —						36662 —
J. Soo, Drawings	7500 —						7500 —	
Commissions		35650 —				35650 —		
Car Expense	3214 —		④ 50 —		3264 —			
Miscellaneous Expense	902 —		⑤ 65 —		967 —			
Rent Expense	6000 —				6000 —			
Utilities Expense	1563 —				1563 —			
Wages Expense	15239 —				15239 —			
	78542 —	78542 —						
Supplies Expense			① 1310 —		1310 —			
Insurance Expense			② 364 —		364 —			
			1789 —	1789 —	28707 —	35650 —	49950 —	43007 —
					6943 —			6943 —
					35650 —	35650 —	49950 —	49950 —

ANSWERS TO CHAPTER 9 REVIEW EXERCISES (cont.)

Exercise 4 (cont.)

B.

GENERAL JOURNAL
PAGE

DATE		PARTICULARS	P.R.	DEBIT	CREDIT

C.

GENERAL LEDGER

Bank		Accounts Receivable		Supplies	
2 160		11 500		1 950	

Prepaid Insurance		Equipment		Automobile	
624		9 200		18 350	

Accounts Payable		GST Payable		GST Recoverable	
	5 920		310	340	

J. Soo, Capital		J. Soo, Drawings		Commissions	
	36 662	7 500			35 650

(Ledger continues on next page.)

ANSWERS TO CHAPTER 9 REVIEW EXERCISES (cont.)

Exercise 4 (cont.)

C. (cont.)

Car Expense		Miscellaneous Expense		Rent Expense	
3 214		902		6 000	

Utilities Expense		Wages Expense		Supplies Expense		Insurance Expense	
1 563		15 239					

J. Soo & Associates

Adjusted Trial Balance

December 31, 20-5

ANSWERS TO CHAPTER 9 REVIEW EXERCISES (cont.)

Exercise 4 (cont.)

Optional

D.

J. Soo & Associates

Income Statement

Year Ended December 31, 20-5

ANSWERS TO CHAPTER 9 REVIEW EXERCISES (cont.)

Exercise 4 (cont.)

Optional

D. (cont.)

J. Soo & Associates

Balance Sheet

December 31, 20-5

ANSWERS TO CHAPTER 9 REVIEW EXERCISES (cont.)

Exercise 5, p. 359

WORK SHEET

Karen Millette, Real Estate — *Year Ended September 30, 20-4*

ACCOUNTS	TRIAL BALANCE DEBIT	TRIAL BALANCE CREDIT	ADJUSTMENTS DEBIT	ADJUSTMENTS CREDIT	INCOME STATEMENT DEBIT	INCOME STATEMENT CREDIT	BALANCE SHEET DEBIT	BALANCE SHEET CREDIT
Bank	3 8 0 0 -							
Accounts Receivable	10 9 0 0 -							
Supplies	5 0 0 -							
Prepaid Insurance	1 0 0 0 -							
Land	50 0 0 0 -							
Building	70 0 0 0 -							
Accum. Deprec.—Building		6 8 2 5 -						
Furniture and Equipment	15 0 0 0 -							
Accum. Deprec.—Furn. & Equip.		5 4 0 0 -						
Automotive Equipment	17 0 0 0 -							
Accum. Deprec.—Auto Equipment		8 6 7 0 -						
Accounts Payable		4 0 0 -						
Bank Loan		100 0 0 0 -						
Karen Millette, Capital		35 0 0 5 -						
Karen Millette, Drawings	30 0 0 0 -							
Commissions Revenue		96 6 0 0 -						
Advertising Expense	4 7 0 0 -							
Bank Charges	8 1 0 0 -							
Car Expense	8 0 0 0 -							
Commissions Expense	18 0 0 0 -							
Miscellaneous Expense	2 0 0 -							
Postage Expense	6 0 0 -							
Telephone Expense	9 0 0 -							
Utilities Expense	2 2 0 0 -							
Wages Expense	12 0 0 0 -							
	252 9 0 0 -	252 9 0 0 -						

ANSWERS TO CHAPTER 9 REVIEW EXERCISES (cont.)

Exercise 6, p. 360

Tom's Plastering

WORK SHEET

Year Ended October 31, 20-1

ACCOUNTS	TRIAL BALANCE DEBIT	TRIAL BALANCE CREDIT	ADJUSTMENTS DEBIT	ADJUSTMENTS CREDIT	INCOME STATEMENT DEBIT	INCOME STATEMENT CREDIT	BALANCE SHEET DEBIT	BALANCE SHEET CREDIT
Bank	1412 01							
Accounts Receivable	7545 —							
Supplies	1416 70							
Small Tools	1903 —							
Prepaid Insurance	2107 80							
Equipment	9500 —							
Accum. Deprec.—Equipment		3200 —						
Truck	19500 —							
Accum. Deprec.—Truck		8000 —						
Accounts Payable		2407 35						
GST Payable		702 —						
GST Recoverable	480 —							
Bank Loan		10000 —						
Tom Michaud, Capital		17510 28						
Tom Michaud, Drawings	35534 —							
Revenue		120365 —						
Bank Interest and Charges	1325 15							
Materials Used	25369 20							
Miscellaneous Expense	756 32							
Rent Expense	6000 —							
Telephone Expense	864 32							
Truck Expense	8325 40							
Utilities Expense	4563 26							
Wages Expense	35582 47							
	162184 63	162184 63						

Name _____ Date _____

Exercise 6 (cont.)

_____

Income Statement
_____
_____

ANSWERS TO CHAPTER 9 REVIEW EXERCISES (cont.)

Exercise 6 (cont.)

Balance Sheet

ANSWERS TO CHAPTER 9 REVIEW EXERCISES (cont.)

Exercise 1, p. 361   Comprehensive Exercise

Oakville Journal

WORK SHEET

Year Ended December 31, 20-8

ACCOUNTS	TRIAL BALANCE DEBIT	TRIAL BALANCE CREDIT	ADJUSTMENTS DEBIT	ADJUSTMENTS CREDIT	INCOME STATEMENT DEBIT	INCOME STATEMENT CREDIT	BALANCE SHEET DEBIT	BALANCE SHEET CREDIT
Bank	2 0 0 0 -							
Accounts Receivable	15 3 1 7 20							
Supplies and Materials	23 7 9 5 16							
Prepaid Insurance	4 2 0 0 -							
Land	75 0 0 0 -							
Buildings	105 0 0 0 -							
Accum. Dep.—Buildings		7 5 0 0 -						
Equipment	95 7 0 0 -							
Accum. Dep.—Equipment		22 7 1 0 -						
Automotive Equipment	75 3 2 5 -							
Accum. Dep.—Auto. Equipment		30 0 0 0 -						
Accounts Payable		9 2 1 6 42						
GST Payable		1 2 8 0 -						
GST Recoverable	7 5 0 -							
Bank Loan		100 0 0 0 -						
Mortgage Payable		110 0 0 0 -						
R. Lucht, Capital		61 1 4 8 91						
R. Lucht, Drawings	50 0 0 0 -							
Revenue—Advertising		218 9 4 6 -						
Revenue—Circulation		91 3 1 5 -						
Bank Interest and Charges	12 1 5 0 -							
Bldg. Maintenance Expense	3 2 2 0 -							
Car Expense	4 9 6 0 50							
Miscellaneous Expense	5 9 4 0 13							
Mortgage Interest Expense	5 5 0 0 -							
Postage Expense	1 2 4 0 -							
Office Salaries Expense	34 3 1 9 15							
Sales Promotion Expense	2 7 5 0 -							
Telephone Expense	2 9 4 6 -							
Truck Expense	26 3 3 4 19							
Utilities Expense	11 3 5 0 -							
Wages Expense	94 3 1 9 -							
	652 1 1 6 33	652 1 1 6 33						

Name _____   Date _____

ANSWERS TO CHAPTER 9 REVIEW EXERCISES (cont.)

Exercise 1 (cont.)   **Comprehensive Exercise**

B.

_____

Income Statement

_____

ANSWERS TO CHAPTER 9 REVIEW EXERCISES (cont.)

Exercise 1 (cont.)   **Comprehensive Exercise**

B. (cont.)

_____

Balance Sheet

_____

Name _____ Date _____

ANSWERS TO CHAPTER 9 REVIEW EXERCISES (cont.)

Exercise 1 (cont.) **Comprehensive Exercise**

C.

GENERAL JOURNAL   PAGE

DATE		PARTICULARS	P.R.	DEBIT	CREDIT
		Adjusting Entries			

ANSWERS TO CHAPTER 9 REVIEW EXERCISES (cont.)

Exercise 1 (cont.)   **Comprehensive Exercise**

C. (cont.)

GENERAL JOURNAL   PAGE

DATE		PARTICULARS	P.R.	DEBIT	CREDIT
		Closing Entries			

ANSWERS TO CHAPTER 9 REVIEW EXERCISES (cont.)

Exercise 1 (cont.) **Comprehensive Exercise**

D.

GENERAL LEDGER

Bank		Accounts Receivable		Supplies & Materials	
2 000		15 317.20		23 795.16	

Prepaid Insurance		Land		Buildings	
4 200		75 000		105 000	

Accum. Dep.—Buildings		Equipment		Accum. Dep.—Equipment	
	7 500	95 700			22 710

Automotive Equipment		Accum. Dep.—Auto. Equip.	
75 325			30 000

Accounts Payable		GST Payable		GST Recoverable	
	9 216.42		1 280	750	

Bank Loan		Mortgage Payable		R. Lucht, Capital	
	100 000		110 000		61 148.91

R. Lucht, Drawings		Revenue — Advertising		Revenue — Circulation	
50 000			218 946		91 315

(Ledger continues on next page.)

Name _____ Date _____

Exercise 1 (cont.)   **Comprehensive Exercise**

D. (cont.)

Bank Interest & Charges		Building Maintenance Expense		Car Expense	
12 150		3 220		4 960.50	

Miscellaneous Expense		Mortgage Interest Expense		Office Salaries Expense	
5 940.13		5 500		34 319.15	

Postage Expense		Sales Promotion Expense		Telephone Expense	
1 240		2 750		2 946	

Truck Expense		Utilities Expense		Wages Expense	
26 334.19		11 350		94 319	

Depreciation Expense—Buildings		Depreciation Expense—Equipment		Depreciation Expense—Automotive Equipment	

Supplies and Materials Expense		Insurance Expense		Income Summary	

ANSWERS TO CHAPTER 9 REVIEW EXERCISES (cont.)

Exercise 1 (cont.)　　　**Comprehensive Exercise**

E.

Post-Closing Trial Balance

ACCOUNTS	DEBIT	CREDIT

Name _____ Date _____

Exercise 2, p. 362   Comprehensive Exercise

GENERAL JOURNAL   PAGE

DATE		PARTICULARS	P.R.	DEBIT	CREDIT

Questions for Further Thought, p. 363

1. _____
   _____
   _____
   _____
   _____
   _____

2. _____
   _____
   _____
   _____

3. _____
   _____

ANSWERS TO CHAPTER 9 REVIEW EXERCISES (cont.)

Questions for Further Thought (cont.)

4. _____
_____
_____
_____
_____
_____
_____
_____

5. _____
_____

6. _____
_____

7. _____
_____

8. _____
_____

CASE STUDIES (text p. 364)

Case 1   *A Balancing Act*, p. 364

1. _____
_____

2. _____

3. _____
_____
_____
_____
_____
_____

Case 2   *A Mix-Up in Year-End Accounting*, p. 365

1. _____
_____
_____

2. _____
_____
_____

CASE STUDIES (cont.)

Case 2 (cont.)

3. _____

_____

4. _____

5. _____

_____

_____

_____

_____

_____

_____

_____

_____

_____

6. _____

_____

_____

_____

_____

_____

_____

_____

_____

_____

_____

_____

_____

_____

_____

_____

_____

CASE STUDIES (cont.)
Challenge Case 3 *Can you Meet This Deadline?*, p. 369

WORK SHEET

Stetsko and Company

Six Months Ended June 30, 20—

ACCOUNTS	TRIAL BALANCE		ADJUSTMENTS		INCOME STATEMENT		BALANCE SHEET	
	DEBIT	CREDIT	DEBIT	CREDIT	DEBIT	CREDIT	DEBIT	CREDIT

Name _____ Date _____

CASE STUDIES (cont.)

Co-operative Learning

Case 4 *A Better Way of Depreciating a Truck?*, p. 370

1. The comparative depreciation schedule is shown below:

Year	Distance Travelled	Depreciation Straight-line	Depreciation Km travelled
1	*21 468*	*3 937.50*	*2 546.96*
2	*35 698*	*3 937.50*	*4 235.21*
3	*42 654*	*3 937.30*	*5 060.47*
4	*45 965*	*3 937.50*	*5 453.29*
5	*40 365*	*3 937.50*	*4 788.90*
6	*35 632*	*3 937.50*	*4 227.38*
7	*27 526*	*3 937.50*	*3 265.68*
8	*16 201*	*3 937.50*	*1 922.09*
Totals	*265.509*	*31 500.00*	*31 499.98*

2. _____

_____

_____

_____

_____

_____

_____

_____

_____

_____

Career   **DAVID YAN/BANK AND INVESTMENT TEAM MANAGER**

ANSWERS TO DISCUSSION QUESTIONS (text p. 371)

1. _____
_____
_____
_____
_____
_____

2. _____
_____
_____
_____
_____
_____

3. _____
_____
_____
_____
_____
_____
_____
_____
_____

4. _____
_____
_____

5. _____
_____
_____

Chapter 10 | Cash Control and Banking

ANSWERS TO SECTION 10.1 REVIEW QUESTIONS (text p. 378)

Payment Systems

1. _____

2. _____

3. _____

4. _____

5. _____

6. _____

7. _____

8. _____

9. _____

10. _____

11. _____

12. _____

13. _____

14. _____

15. _____

Name _____   Date _____

ANSWERS TO SECTION 10.1 EXERCISES (text p. 379)

Exercise 1, p. 379

A.   Three things I already know about debit and credit cards:

_____

_____

_____

B.   Three things I would like to know about debit and credit cards:

_____

_____

_____

C.   Three things my partner already knows about debit and credit cards:

_____

_____

_____

Three things my partner would like to know about debit and credit cards:

_____

_____

_____

Exercise 2, p. 379

2.   **Complete each of the following statements by writing the appropriate word or phrase from the list on textbook page 379. A word or phrase may be used once, more than once, or not at all.**

A.   _____ usually consists of dollar bills and coins.

B.   Of the payment systems covered in the text, _____ take the longest time to transfer money from one party to another.

C.   To overcome the lack of portability of cash, _____ are used.

D.   Websites must be _____ to ensure payment information remains private.

E.   A pre-set limit for the amount a person can purchase is a feature of _____.

F.   The _____ symbol indicates that debit cards may used for purchases.

G.   Transactions with _____ are made frequently but typically have small dollar values.

H.   Of the three most common non-cash payment systems, _____ are experiencing the most rapid growth in use.

I.   Using _____ is the payment system that provides the greatest annual dollar value.

J.   When making a payment with _____, you need not provide personal identification.

K.   Monthly mortgage payments are examples of _____.

L.   The number of debit and credit card transactions are close to the frequency of _____.

ANSWERS TO SECTION 10.1 EXERCISES (cont.)

Exercise 3, p. 380

Part A

a. _____
_____

b. _____

c. _____
_____

d. _____
_____

e. _____
_____
_____

f. _____
_____
_____

Part B

a. _____
_____
_____
_____
_____
_____
_____

ANSWERS TO SECTION 10.1 EXERCISES (cont.)

Exercise 4, p. 380

```
○ ○ ○                        New Message                              ⬭

Send  Attach  Address  Fonts  Colors  Save As Draft

       To: [                                                        ]
       Cc: [                                                        ]
  Subject: [                                                        ]
  Account: [                              ▾]
```

ANSWERS TO SECTION 10.2 REVIEW QUESTIONS (text p. 387)

Accounting for Cash Receipts

1. _____
   _____

2. _____
   _____

3. _____
   _____
   _____
   _____

4. _____
   _____

5. _____
   _____

ANSWERS TO SECTION 10.2 REVIEW QUESTIONS (cont.)

6. _____

7. _____
_____
_____
_____

8. _____
_____
_____
_____

9. _____

10. _____

11. _____

12. _____

13. _____
_____

14. _____
_____

ANSWERS TO SECTION 10.2 EXERCISES (text p. 388)

Exercise 1, p. 388

Use the list on page 388 of the textbook to complete the sentences below.

A. The _____ of a business represent the money taken in from business operations.

B. It is customary for a business that _____ to receive payment from its customers by way of cheques through the mail.

C. Cheques received in the mail are _____ by the mail clerk before being deposited in the bank.

D. Sales slips are _____ to ensure that all slips are accounted for.

E. At the end of a business day, cash register receipts are _____ in the business's bank account.

F. An electronic cash register that is connected to a central computer is known as a
_____ .

G. A small quantity of money used to start the cash register activity for the day is known as a
_____ .

H. An overage produces a _____ in the Cash Short and Over account.

I. A shortage produces a _____ in the Cash Short and Over account.

J. Cash _____ are more common than cash _____ .

K. Businesses are required by the banks to use a _____ .

L. Cheques received by a business are endorsed _____ before being deposited.

ANSWERS TO SECTION 10.2 EXERCISES (cont.)

Exercise 2, p. 388

a.

Cash Proof

Date _____

Cash Register Tape Totals

Cash Sales		
PST		
GST		
Receipts per tape		

Cash Received

Cash Count		
Less: Change Fund		
Actual Cash Received		

CASH SHORT OR OVER $ [   ]

Cash Proof

Date _____

Cash Register Tape Totals

Cash Sales		
PST		
GST		
Receipts per tape		

Cash Received

Cash Count		
Less: Change Fund		
Actual Cash Received		

CASH SHORT OR OVER $ [   ]

GENERAL JOURNAL   PAGE

DATE		PARTICULARS	P.R.	DEBIT	CREDIT

b.

Cash Short or Over
_____ | _____
_____ | _____
_____ | _____
_____ | _____

ANSWERS TO SECTION 10.2 EXERCISES (cont.)

Exercise 3, p. 389

A. **Note:** The charge sales in this exercise refer to sales on account, not credit card transactions.

CASH PROOF AND SALES SUMMARY   DATE

PART 1. CHARGE SLIPS	SALES	GST	PST	ACCOUNTS RECEIVABLE	CASH
Charge Sales Slips					
Less: Credit Slips					
Net Charge Sales					
PART 2. CASH SALES					
Cash Sales Slips					
Less: Refunds					
Net Cash Sales					
CASH SHORT OR OVER ☐ ☐					
COLUMN TOTALS					

B.

GENERAL JOURNAL   PAGE

DATE	PARTICULARS	P.R.	DEBIT	CREDIT

Exercise 4, p. 389

a. _____   c. _____

b. _____   d. _____

ANSWERS TO SECTION 10.2 EXERCISES (cont.)

Exercise 5, p. 390

Cheques

CREDIT ACCOUNT NO.	DATE
NAME	

PARTICULARS	AMOUNT
TOTAL CHEQUES (CARRY FORWARD)	

CURRENT ACCOUNT DEPOSIT

Commercial Bank

CREDIT ACCOUNT NO.	DATE
NAME	
DEPOSITED BY	

× $ 5		
× $ 10		
× $ 20		
× $ 50		
× $100		
×		
×		
COINS		
SUB-TOTAL TELLER		
VISA		
U.S. CHEQUES		
U.S. CASH		
TOTAL CHEQUES (BROUGHT FORWARD)		
SUB-TOTAL		
U.S. EXCHANGE (PLUS/MINUS)		
TOTAL DEPOSIT		

CURRENT ACCOUNT DEPOSIT

ANSWERS TO SECTION 10.3 REVIEW QUESTIONS (text p. 395)

Accounting for Cash Payments

1. _____
2. _____
   _____
3. _____
   _____
4. _____
5. _____
   _____
6. _____
   _____
7. _____
   _____
8. _____
9. _____

ANSWERS TO SECTION 10.3 EXERCISES (text p. 395)

Exercise 1, p. 395

GENERAL JOURNAL   PAGE 1

DATE		PARTICULARS	P.R.	DEBIT	CREDIT
20– Jan	15	Petty Cash		200 —	
		Bank			200 —
		Establishing a petty cash fund			

Exercise 2, p. 395

GENERAL JOURNAL   PAGE 1

DATE		PARTICULARS	P.R.	DEBIT	CREDIT
20– Feb	20	Petty Cash		50 —	
		Bank			50 —
		Increase the petty cash fund			

Name _Harra____ Date _____

Exercise 3, p. 395

A.

SUMMARY OF CHARGES

ACCOUNTS	GST		AMOUNTS	
Supplies		70	10 —	1 0 70
Miscellaneous Expens		94	13 49	18 43
Sales Promotion		60	8 50	9 10
Building Maintenance		59	22 66	24 25
C. Parker Drawings		—	12 —	12 —
Car Expense		57	8 17	8 74
Postage	1 23		17 50	18 73
	5 63		92 32	97 95

B.

GENERAL JOURNAL   PAGE

DATE	PARTICULARS	P.R.	DEBIT	CREDIT
2011 March 16	Supplies		10 —	
	Miscellaneous Expense		13 49	
	Sales Promotion		8 50	
	Building Maintenance		22 66	
	C. Parker, Drawings		12 —	
	Car Expense		8 17	
	Postage		17 50	
	GST Recoverable		5 63	
	Bank			97 95

ANSWERS TO SECTION 10.3 EXERCISES (cont.)

Exercise 4, p. 396

A.

SUMMARY OF CHARGES

ACCOUNTS	GST	AMOUNTS

B.

GENERAL JOURNAL   PAGE

DATE	PARTICULARS	P.R.	DEBIT	CREDIT

ANSWERS TO SECTION 10.3 EXERCISES (cont.)

Exercise 5, p. 396

Indicate whether each of the following statements is true or false by placing a "T" or an "F" in the space indicated. Explain the reason for each "F" response in the space provided.

A.   The Petty Cash account in the general ledger must never change.

B.   A petty cash voucher must be prepared for every payment out of the fund.

C.   The petty cash fund is used for the purpose of cutting down on the number of cheques issued.

D.   The accounting entry to replenish the petty cash fund is made by the keeper of the fund.

E.   The petty cash box is locked and put away in a safe place outside business hours.

F.   The keeper of the petty cash fund must never borrow from it.

G.   The petty cash summary is organized by general ledger accounts.

H.   A payment out of petty cash can only be charged to an expense account or an asset account.

I.   If an auditor were to check the petty cash fund, the procedure would be to total all of the cash and vouchers in the box and check this total against the balance in the Petty Cash account.

Explanations for "F" Responses:

_____

_____

_____

_____

_____

_____

ANSWERS TO SECTION 10.4 REVIEW QUESTIONS (text p. 404)

Accounting Controls for Cash

1.   _____

_____

_____

2.   _____

3.   _____

_____

4.   _____

_____

ANSWERS TO SECTION 10.4 REVIEW QUESTIONS (cont.)

5. _____
_____

6. _____
_____

7. _____

8. _____
_____

9. _____
_____

10. _____
_____

11. _____
_____

12. _____
_____

13. _____
_____
_____

14. _____
_____
_____

15. _____
_____

ANSWERS TO SECTION 10.4 EXERCISES (text p. 404)

Exercise 1, p. 404

A. _____
_____
_____
_____
_____

B. _____
_____
_____

ANSWERS TO SECTION 10.4 EXERCISES (cont.)

Exercise 1 (cont.)

C. _____

_____

_____

_____

_____

_____

_____

D. _____

_____

_____

E. _____

_____

_____

_____

F. _____

_____

_____

_____

_____

_____

_____

_____

G. _____

_____

_____

_____

_____

H. _____

_____

_____

_____

_____

_____

_____

ANSWERS TO SECTION 10.4 EXERCISES (cont.)

Exercise 1 (cont.)

I. _____

_____

_____

_____

_____

_____

J. _____

_____

_____

_____

_____

_____

_____

K. _____

_____

_____

_____

L. _____

_____

_____

_____

Exercise 2, p. 405

a. _____

_____

_____

ANSWERS TO SECTION 10.4 EXERCISES (cont.)

Exercise 2 (cont.)

b. 1. _____

_____

2. _____

_____

Exercise 3, p. 407

a. _____

b. _____

c. _____

d. _____

e. _____

f. _____

Exercise 4, p. 408

_____

_____

_____

ANSWERS TO SECTION 10.4 EXERCISES (cont.)

Exercise 4 (cont.)

GENERAL JOURNAL   PAGE

DATE		PARTICULARS	P.R.	DEBIT	CREDIT

ANSWERS TO SECTION 10.5 COMPUTER REVIEW QUESTIONS (text p. 411)

Using Computers for Bank Reconciliation

1. _____
   _____
   _____
   _____
   _____
   _____

2. _____
   _____
   _____
   _____

3. _____
   _____
   _____
   _____
   _____

Name ______________________________ Date ______________________________

ANSWERS TO SECTION 10.5 COMPUTER EXERCISES (text p. 411)

1. **Use the spreadsheet model reconcile.xls to complete this exercise.**

This page is left blank intentionally.

Note: page 314 follows next.

ANSWERS TO SECTION 10.5 COMPUTER EXERCISES (cont.)

Communicate It (text p. 411)

List the main points of your letter before keying it in a word-processing program.

_____

_____

_____

_____

_____

ANSWERS TO CHAPTER 10 REVIEW EXERCISES (text p. 413)

Exercise 1, p. 413   Using Your Knowledge

Rough Work

SUMMARY

ANSWERS TO CHAPTER 10 REVIEW EXERCISES (cont.)

Exercise 2, p. 414

Proctor & Kemp
Bank Reconciliation Statement
July 31, 20-

Bank					1 8 0 8 64	Ledger					4 4 9 64
Add:						Add:					
Deduct:						Deduct:					
Outstanding Cheques						Missing Cheques					
852		1 2 3 50									
881		3 3 60									
889		6 0 —									
903		1 6 41									
910											

ANSWERS TO CHAPTER 10 REVIEW EXERCISES (cont.)

Exercise 2 (cont.)

GENERAL JOURNAL   PAGE

DATE		PARTICULARS	P.R.	DEBIT	CREDIT

ANSWERS TO CHAPTER 10 REVIEW EXERCISES (cont.)

Exercise 3, p. 416 (Workbook Exercise)

From the following records, prepare the bank reconciliation statement for Madison Company as of October 31, 20—. Record the necessary accounting entries in the books of the business.

a. Previous bank reconciliation statement

Madison Company

Bank Reconciliation Statement

September 30, 20—

Balance per Bank Statement		$2	1	0	2	69	Balance per General Ledger		$1	6 5 2	95
Deduct: Outstanding Cheques							Deduct: Service Charge	$12.50			
#519	$ 20.00						Loan Interest	36.25		4 8	75
#526	37.50										
#528	105.00										
#529	2.70										
#531	5.19										
#532	74.10										
#533	112.02										
#534	56.94										
#535	85.04		4	9	8	49					
True Balance		$1	6	0	4	20	True Balance		$1	6 0 4	20

ANSWERS TO CHAPTER 10 REVIEW EXERCISES (cont.)

Exercise 3 (cont.)

b. Partial cash payments journal   **c.** Partial cash receipts journal

PAGE 174

DATE		CH. NO.	BANK CR			
20— Oct.	1	536		1	9	05
	1	537	1	6	4	02
	2	538		7	3	74
	3	539		2	7	60
	3	540			1	95
	4	541	3	6	5	12
	5	542		9	2	06
	8	543		7	4	09
	8	544		1	9	65
	10	545		7	4	02
	11	546		7	6	75
	12	547		5	6	21
	12	548		4	2	96
	15	549		3	3	21
	17	550		2	4	02
	19	551		8	8	61
	22	552		5	8	36
	22	553		1	9	05
	23	554		9	1	50
	24	555		1	3	30
	24	556		1	7	50
	26	557			8	61
	29	558	1 0	4	7	65
	29	559	3	1	9	02
	30	560			1	75
	31	561			2	50
	31	562		1	9	41
			2 8	3	1	71

PAGE 147

DATE		BANK DR				AMOUNT OF DEPOSIT			
20— Oct.	3		1	6	50				
	3		2	5	02				
	3	5	1	6	95		5	5 8	47
	8	1	0	4	20				
	8	7	5	6	12				
	8		5	6	12				
	8		9	6	02	1	0	1 2	46
	11		3	3	40			3 3	40
	15		1	7	50				
	15		1	2	09			2 9	59
	22		1	9	06				
	22	5	0	2	00		5	2 1	06
	24		1	2	06				
	24		1	3	50				
	24		9	1	02				
	24		1	6	51		1	3 3	09
	29		5	6	93				
	29		8	3	16				
	29	1	0	2	52				
	29	1	2	7	06				
	29		3	1	50		4	0 1	17
	31	1	6	7	75				
	31	1	3	8	44		3	0 6	19
		2	9	9	5 43	2	9	9 5	43

ANSWERS TO CHAPTER 10 REVIEW EXERCISES (cont.)

Exercise 3 (cont.)

d. October general journal entry affecting Bank

GENERAL JOURNAL

PAGE 64

DATE		PARTICULARS	P.R.	DEBIT	CREDIT
20— Oct.	4	Bank Charges	540	1 2 50	
		Bank Interest	565	3 6 25	
		Bank	101		4 8 75
		To record charges picked up from September			
		bank statement			

e. Bank statement for October

Cheques				Deposits	Date	Balance
					Sept. 30	2 102.69
37.50	(526)				Oct. 30	2 065.19
				558.47	3	2 623.66
2.70	(529)	85.04	(535)		4	2 535.92
19.05	(536)				5	2 516.87
74.10	(532)	105.00	(528)		8	2 337.77
73.74	(538)			1 012.46	9	3 276.49
5.19	(531)	27.60	(539)		10	3 243.70
56.94	(534)				11	3 186.76
74.09	(543)	112.02	(533)	33.40	15	3 034.05
96.02	(N.S.F. cheque of J. Marble)				15	2 938.03
164.02	(537)				16	2 774.01
33.21	(549)	19.65	(544)	29.59	17	2 750.74
365.12	(541)				18	2 385.62
76.75	(546)			521.06	22	2 829.93
1.95	(540)	58.36	(552)		23	2 769.62
42.96	(548)				24	2 726.66
				133.09	25	2 859.75
88.61	(551)				26	2 771.14
91.50	(554)				29	2 679.64
13.30	(555)			401.17	30	3 067.51
8.61	(557)	1 047.65	(558)		31	2 011.25
15.20	(Interest)	30.20 (Service Charges)			31	1 965.85
43.50	(Discount Fee)				31	1 922.35

ANSWERS TO CHAPTER 10 REVIEW EXERCISES (cont.)

Exercise 3 (cont.)

f. General ledger account showing October figures

ACCOUNT *Bank*   No. *101*

DATE		PARTICULARS	P.R.	DEBIT	CREDIT	DR/CR	BALANCE
20— Sep.	30		—			DR	1 6 5 2 95
Oct.	4		J64		4 8 75		
	31		CP174		2 8 3 1 71		
	31		CR147	2 9 9 5 43		DR	1 7 6 7 92

Madison Company

Bank Reconciliation Statement

October 31, 20—

Bank						Ledger								

Name _____   Date _____

ANSWERS TO CHAPTER 10 REVIEW EXERCISES (cont.)

Exercise 3 (cont.)

GENERAL JOURNAL   PAGE _____

DATE		PARTICULARS	P.R.	DEBIT	CREDIT

Cases for Further Thought p. 417

1. _____
   _____
   _____
   _____
   _____
   _____
   _____

2. _____
   _____

3. _____
   _____

4. _____
   _____

5. _____
   _____
   _____
   _____
   _____

6. _____
   _____

7. _____
   _____

Name _____ Date _____

CASE STUDIES (text p. 418)

Case 1 *Cola Profits Go Flat,* p. 418

1. _____

    a. _____

    b. _____

        _____

    c. _____

        _____

        _____

    d. _____

        _____

2. _____

3. _____

       _____

       _____

       _____

Case 2 *Service Charges: Are They Always Fair?,* p. 418

1. _____

       _____

       _____

2. _____

       _____

       _____

       _____

3. _____

4. _____

       _____

       _____

5. _____

CASE STUDIES (cont.)

Challenge Case 3 *Trials of a Young Entrepreneur*, p. 419

1. _____

2. _____

3. _____
   _____
   _____
   _____

4. _____
   _____
   _____
   _____
   _____

5. _____
   _____
   _____
   _____

6. _____
   _____
   _____
   _____

7. _____
   _____
   _____

8. _____
   _____
   _____
   _____
   _____
   _____

Name _____ Date _____

CASE STUDIES (cont.)

Group Discussion Case   *The Good Life on Plastic Money,* p. 421

1. _____
   _____
   _____
   _____
   _____
   _____

2. _____

3. _____

4. _____
   _____
   _____
   _____
   _____
   _____

5. _____

Career   JANICE FUKAKUSA/EXECUTIVE VICE PRESIDENT, PERSONAL & COMMERCIAL BANKING, ROYAL BANK

ANSWERS TO DISCUSSION QUESTIONS (text p. 422)

1. _____

2. _____
   _____
   _____

3. _____
   _____
   _____

4. _____

Name _____ Date _____

ANSWERS TO SECTION 11.1 REVIEW QUESTIONS (text p. 428)

The Merchandising Business

and sells to the public

1. A business that sell a service, not a product

2. A business that buys goods to resell them at a profit

3. Wholesaler - Merchandising business that buys goods from manufacturers and sells to retailers
Retailer - Merchandising business that buys goods from wholesalers and manufactures

4. The merchandise inventory of a drug store consists of various health related items and medicine

5. stock-in-trade

6.

7. Current asset

8. The cost of all of the items sold is usually the biggest expense figure for a merchandising business.

9.

10.

11.

12.

  1.

  2.

  3.

  4.

13.

14.

15.

ANSWERS TO SECTION 11.1 EXERCISES (text p. 428)

Exercise 1, p. 428 (Workbook Exercise)

Complete the chart by filling in the blank spaces.

	Selling price	Cost price	Gross profit	Cost of goods sold as a % of selling price	Gross profit sold as a % of selling price
Easy	$250	$	$100	%	%
	$	$ 85	$ 40	%	%
	$ 80	$ 56	$	%	%
	$	$ 75	$ 75	%	%
	$300	$195	$	%	%
	$225	$	$ 63	%	%
More difficult	$	$ 54	$	%	40%
	$500	$	$	70%	%
	$200	$	$	65%	%
	$	$120	$	%	52%

Exercise 2, p. 429

A.

	Year 1	Year 2	Year 3
Beginning inventory	100 units	300 units	200 units
Merchandise purchased	700 units	900 units	650 units
Goods available for sale	800 units	1200 units	850 units
Merchandise sold	500 units	1 000 units	800 units
Ending inventory	300 units	200 units	50 units

ANSWERS TO SECTION 11.1 EXERCISES (text p. 428)

Exercise 2 (cont.)

B. On the income statement for Year 3:

Cost of Goods Sold

Beginning Inventory _____

Purchases _____

Goods Available for Sale _____

Deduct: Ending Inventory _____

Cost of Goods Sold _____

Exercise 3, p. 429

	Sales	Beginning Inventory	Purchases	Ending Inventory	Cost of Goods Goods Sold	Gross Profit Profit
1.	$125 000	$32 000	$74 250	$33 500		
2.	750 585	85 600	410 360	88 300		
3.	288 635	65 550	110 357	60 548		
4.	174 000	33 800	82 640	33 500		
5.	255 324	48 500	150 650	50 300		

Exercise 4, p. 429

Cost of Goods Sold Calculation

Beginning Inventory _____

Purchases _____

Total Merchandise Available for Sale _____

Deduct: Ending Inventory _____

Cost of Goods Sold _____

Exercise 5, p. 430

1. Beginning Inventory Figure _____
2. Selling Price of the Goods Sold _____
3. Beginning Inventory _____

Purchases _____

Cost of Merchandise Available for Sale _____

Deduct: Ending Inventory _____

Cost of Goods Sold _____

PMW

ANSWERS TO SECTION 11.1 EXERCISES (cont.)

Exercise 5 (cont.)

4. Gross Profit   _____

5. Total Operating Expenses   _____

6. Net Income   _____

ANSWERS TO SECTION 11.2 REVIEW QUESTIONS (text p. 433)

Accounting Procedures for a Merchandising Business

1. _____
   _____
   _____

2. _____

3. _____
     1. _____
     2. _____

4. _____
   _____
   _____

5. _____

6. _____

7. _____
   _____
   _____
   _____
   _____

8. _____
   _____
   _____
   _____
   _____
   _____

9. _____

10. _____
    _____
    _____

11. _____

ANSWERS TO SECTION 11.2 EXERCISES (text p. 433)

Exercise 1, p. 433

GENERAL JOURNAL   PAGE

DATE		PARTICULARS	P.R.	DEBIT	CREDIT
20-Dec.	1	Purchases		3 045 -	
		GST Recoverable		213 15	
		A/P- Paramount Manufacturing			3 258 15
		Purchase Invoice No. 435			
	2	Freight in		435 -	
		GST Recoverable		30 45	
		A/P- Murray Transport			465 45
		Purchase Invoice No. 616 for delivery of P.Inv #435			
	3	Supplies		236 -	
		GST Recoverable		16 52	
		A/P- Swiss Stationers			252 52
		P. Inv No. 7042			
	4	A/R - W. Purbhoo		479 55	
		Sales			417 -
		GST Payable			29 19
		PST Payable			33 36
		Sales Inv. # 789			
	5	Bank		105 80	
		Sales			92 -
		GST Payable			6 44
		PST Payable			7 36
		Cash Sales Slip No. 143			
	6	Purchases		2 678 -	
		GST Recoverable		187 46	
		A/P- Haniko Electric			2 865 46
		P. Inv. No. 902			

   Chapter 11 *Accounting for a Merchandising Business*   **329**

ANSWERS TO SECTION 11.2 EXERCISES (cont.)

Exercise 2, p. 434

A. The final inventory figure appears on the _balance sheet_ and on the _income statement_.

B. Neither the _____ nor the _____ is known during the accounting period.

C. The cost of goods sold figure is _calculated_ using a _formula_.

D. Merchandise inventory is kept in two accounts. These are the _merchandise_ _inventory_ and the _purchases_.

E. The _____ normally shows the merchandise inventory figure as of the _beginning of the fiscal period_.

F. At the fiscal year-end, the inventory is counted and valued at _____.

G. The Merchandise Inventory account is adjusted _____.

H. The _____ is the only accounting entry made to the Merchandise Inventory account.

I. Merchandise purchased during the fiscal period is debited to the _____.

J. The "Purchases" account is a short form of _____.

K. If merchandise is purchased on account, the account debited is _____.

L. If a tire company purchases office supplies, the account debited is _____.

M. For a merchandising business, the sales account is the _____.

N. When a business using the periodic inventory system sells goods, there is no accounting entry to record the _____.

O. The Freight-in account is used to accumulate the _____ _____.

Exercise 3, p. 434

Opening Inventory	Purchases	Freight-in	Closing Inventory	Cost of Goods Sold
$20 000	$40 000	$5 000	$25 000	
29 000	50 000	1 000	30 000	
12 000		1 000	15 000	50 000
	90 000	8 000	39 000	101 000
50 000	100 000		60 000	100 000
75 000	200 000	5 000		200 000

Name _____ Date _____

ANSWERS TO SECTION 11.3 REVIEW QUESTIONS (text p. 440)

Work Sheet for a Merchandising Business

1. _____
   _____
   _____

2. _____
   _____

3. _____
   _____

4. _____

5. _____
   _____
   _____
   _____
   _____
   _____

6. _____

7. _____

8. _____
   _____

9. _____
   _____

10. _____
    _____

11. _____

12. _____
    _____
    _____

13. _____

14. _____
    _____
    _____

ANSWERS TO SECTION 11.3 EXERCISES (text p. 441)

Exercise 1, p. 441

A.

WORK SHEET

Bok Trading Company — Year Ended Dec. 31, 20—

ACCOUNTS	TRIAL BALANCE DEBIT	TRIAL BALANCE CREDIT	ADJUSTMENTS DEBIT	ADJUSTMENTS CREDIT	INCOME STATEMENT DEBIT	INCOME STATEMENT CREDIT	BALANCE SHEET DEBIT	BALANCE SHEET CREDIT
Bank	500 —							
Accounts Receivable	17 910 —							
Merchandise Inventory	39 600 —							
Supplies	2 500 —			② 1 200 —				
Prepaid Insurance	1 800 —			③ 1 150 —				
Equipment	27 850 —							
Accum. Deprec.— Equipment		5 200 —		④ 2 600 —				
Accounts Payable		7 400 —		① 350 —				
GST Payable		550 —						
GST Recoverable	390 —							
PST Payable		628 —						
R. Bok, Capital		63 712 —						
R. Bok, Drawings	10 000 —							
Sales		94 310 —						
Purchases	41 500 —		① 300 —					
Freight-in	950 —							
Miscellaneous Expense	350 —		① 50 —					
Rent Expense	4 800 —							
Telephone Expense	1 500 —							
Utilities Expense	2 750 —							
Wages Expense	19 400 —							
	171 800 —	171 800 —						
Supplies Expense			② 1 200 —					
Insurance Expense			③ 1 150 —					
Depreciation—Equipment			④ 2 600 —					

ANSWERS TO SECTION 11.3 EXERCISES (cont.)

Exercise 1 (cont.)

B.

Bok Trading Company

Income Statement

Year Ended December 31, 20—

ANSWERS TO SECTION 11.3 EXERCISES (cont.)

Exercise 1 (cont.)

C.

Bok Trading Company

Balance Sheet

December 31, 20—

ANSWERS TO SECTION 11.3 EXERCISES (cont.)

Exercise 1 (cont.)

D.

GENERAL JOURNAL

PAGE

DATE	PARTICULARS	P.R.	DEBIT	CREDIT

ANSWERS TO SECTION 11.3 EXERCISES (cont.)

Exercise 2, p. 442

A.

Small Engine Sales and Service

WORKSHEET

Year Ended December 31, 20—

ACCOUNTS	TRIAL BALANCE DEBIT	TRIAL BALANCE CREDIT	ADJUSTMENTS DEBIT	ADJUSTMENTS CREDIT	INCOME STATEMENT DEBIT	INCOME STATEMENT CREDIT	BALANCE SHEET DEBIT	BALANCE SHEET CREDIT
Bank	5 2 0 —							
Accounts Receivable	12 2 6 0 —							
Merchandise Inventory	36 0 5 0 —							
Supplies	1 9 7 5 —							
Parts and Materials	10 3 5 0 —							
Prepaid Insurance	1 1 5 0 —							
Equipment	18 6 0 0 —							
Accum. Deprec. — Equipment		12 5 0 5 —						
Truck	18 0 0 0 —							
Accum. Deprec. — Truck		14 9 7 5 —						
Accounts Payable		5 3 6 0 —						
GST Payable		8 5 0 —						
GST Recoverable	4 2 0 —							
PST Payable		9 8 0 —						
H. Rohr, Capital		29 0 1 0 —						
H. Rohr, Drawings	25 0 0 0 —							
Revenue — Sales		80 3 6 2 —						
Revenue — Service		66 2 1 5 —						
Bank Charges	4 1 0 —							
Freight-in	8 6 2 —							
Miscellaneous Expense	6 5 0 —							
Purchases	52 7 9 5 —							
Rent Expense	3 6 0 0 —							
Telephone Expense	1 2 5 0 —							
Truck Expense	5 8 2 5 —							
Utilities Expense	2 2 4 0 —							
Wages Expense	18 3 0 0 —							
	210 2 5 7 —	210 2 5 7 —						

ANSWERS TO SECTION 11.3 EXERCISES (cont.)

Exercise 2 (cont.)

B.

Small Engine Sales and Service

Income Statement

Year Ended December 31, 20—

ANSWERS TO SECTION 11.3 EXERCISES (cont.)

Exercise 2 (cont.)

C.

Small Engine Sales and Service

Balance Sheet

December 31, 20—

ANSWERS TO SECTION 11.3 EXERCISES (cont.)

Exercise 2 (cont.)

D.

GENERAL JOURNAL

PAGE

DATE	PARTICULARS	P.R.	DEBIT	CREDIT

ANSWERS TO SECTION 11.3 EXERCISES (cont.)

Exercise 2 (cont.)

D. (cont.)

GENERAL JOURNAL   PAGE

DATE		PARTICULARS	P.R.	DEBIT	CREDIT

ANSWERS TO SECTION 11.3 EXERCISES (cont.)

Exercise 2 (cont.)

E.

GENERAL LEDGER

Bank	Accounts Receivable	Merchandise Inventory
520	12 260	36 050

Supplies	Parts and Materials	Prepaid Insurance
1 975	10 350	1 150

Equipment	Acc. Deprec. — Equip.	Truck
18 600	12 505	18 000

Acc. Deprec. — Truck	Accounts Payable	GST Payable
14 975	5 360	850

GST Recoverable	PST Payable	H. Rohr, Capital
420	980	29 010

H. Rohr, Drawings	Revenue — Sales	Revenue — Service
25 000	80 362	66 215

(Ledger continues on next page.)

ANSWERS TO SECTION 11.3 EXERCISES (cont.)

Exercise 2 (cont.)

E. (cont.)

Bank Charges		Freight-in		Miscellaneous Expense	
410		862		650	

Purchases		Rent Expense		Telephone Expense	
52 795		3 600		1 250	

Truck Expense		Utilities Expense		Wages Expense	
5 825		2 240		18 300	

Supplies Expense		Parts and Materials Expense		Insurance Expense	

Depreciation — Equipment		Depreciation — Truck		Income Summary	

ANSWERS TO SECTION 11.3 EXERCISES (cont.)

Exercise 2 (cont.)

F.

Small Engine Sales and Service

Post-Closing Trial Balance

December 31, 20—

ACCOUNTS	DEBIT	CREDIT

ANSWERS TO SECTION 11.3 EXERCISES (cont.)

Exercise 3, p. 443

A.

GENERAL JOURNAL   PAGE _____

DATE		PARTICULARS	P.R.	DEBIT	CREDIT

ANSWERS TO SECTION 11.3 EXERCISES (cont.)

Exercise 3 (cont.)

A. (cont.)

GENERAL JOURNAL   PAGE

DATE	PARTICULARS	P.R.	DEBIT	CREDIT

ANSWERS TO SECTION 11.3 EXERCISES (cont.)

Exercise 3 (cont.)

B.

GENERAL LEDGER

Bank	Accounts Receivable	Merchandise Inventory
3 250.00	33 930.10	43 700.00

Supplies	Prepaid Insurance	Land
3 400.50	2 090.00	35 000.00

Building	Accum. Deprec. — Building	Equipment
95 000.00	17 620.00	53 400.00

Accum. Deprec. — Equip.	Trucks	Accum. Deprec. — Trucks
31 527.00	76 000.00	57 752.00

Accounts Payable	GST Payable	GST Recoverable
40 820.20	1 350.00	720.00

(Ledger continues on next page.)

ANSWERS TO SECTION 11.3 EXERCISES (cont.)

Exercise 3 (cont.)

B. (cont.)

PST Payable		T. Barbini, Capital		T. Barbini, Drawings	
	1 560.00		159 180.05	36 000.00	

Sales		Advertising Expense		Freight-in	
	232 250.00	2 570.00		3 705.00	

Miscellaneous Expense		Purchases		Telephone Expense	
1 750.00		80 702.50		1 250.00	

Utilities Expense		Wages Expense		Supplies Expense	
12 316.00		57 275.15			

Insurance Expense		Depreciation — Building		Depreciation — Equipment	

Depreciation — Trucks		Income Summary			

ANSWERS TO SECTION 11.3 EXERCISES (cont.)

Exercise 3 (cont.)

C.

Barbini Stone Products

Post-Closing Trial Balance

December 31, 20—

ACCOUNTS	DEBIT	CREDIT

ANSWERS TO SECTION 11.4 REVIEW QUESTION (text p. 451)

Merchandise Returns and Allowances

1. _____

2. _____

3. _____
   _____

4. _____

5. _____
   _____

6. _____

ANSWERS TO SECTION 11.4 REVIEW QUESTION (cont.)

7. _____
   1. _____
   2. _____
   3. _____
   _____

8. _____
   _____
   _____
   _____
   _____

9. _____
10. _____
   _____
   _____
   _____

11. _____
   _____

12. _____
   _____
   _____
   _____
   _____

13. _____
   _____
   _____

14. _____
   _____
   _____

15. _____
   _____

ANSWERS TO SECTION 11.4 EXERCISES (text p. 451)

Exercise 1, p. 451

A. _____
B. _____
C. _____
D. _____
E. _____

ANSWERS TO SECTION 11.4 EXERCISES (cont.)

Exercise 1 (cont.)

F., G.

GENERAL JOURNAL   PAGE

DATE		PARTICULARS	P.R.	DEBIT	CREDIT

Exercise 2, p. 452

GENERAL JOURNAL   PAGE

DATE		PARTICULARS	P.R.	DEBIT	CREDIT

ANSWERS TO SECTION 11.4 EXERCISES (cont.)

Exercise 3, p. 453

A. _____   B. _____   C. _____

D. _____   E. _____   F. _____

G. _____

_____

_____

_____

_____

_____

_____

Exercise 4, p. 453

_____

_____

_____

_____

_____

_____

_____

_____

Exercise 5, p. 454

C.
                        Island Traders
                   Partial Income Statement
                 Year Ended December 31, 20—

ANSWERS TO SECTION 11.5 REVIEW QUESTIONS (text p. 459)

Sales Discounts

1. Cash discount - a reduction of the amount of a bill if payment is made on or before the discount date stated on the bill.

2. Terms of sale - arrangements made with customers as to when the goods or services are to be paid for and whether a cash discount is offered.

3. _____

4. _____

5. _____

6. _____

7. _____

8. _____

9. _____

10. _____

11. _____

12. _____

13. _____

14. _____

15. _____

16. _____

ANSWERS TO SECTION 11.5 EXERCISES (text p. 459)

Exercise 1, p. 459

1. Calculate the amount of the payment that is necessary in each case. Where credit notes are involved, assume the discount period is adjusted to start from the date on the credit note.

Date of Invoice	Total of Invoice	Terms of Sale	Amount of Credit Note	Date of Credit Note	Date Payment Is Made	Amount of Payment Required
Mar. 12	$ 52.50	2/10,n/30	–	–	Mar. 20	
May 18	47.25	Net 30	–	–	May 27	
Sep. 4	115.50	3/15,n/60	–	–	Oct. 10	
Feb. 6	1 050.00	1/20,n/60	$126.00	Feb. 18	Mar. 6	
Oct. 19	588.00	2/10,n/30	42.00	Nov. 5	Nov. 27	
Aug. 27	882.00	2/15,n/60	168.00	Sep. 7	Sep. 10	

Exercise 2, p. 460

2. Complete the following schedule by calculating the date that payment is required to pick up the discount, and the amount of the payment required.

Date of Invoice	Total of Invoice	Terms of Sale	Amount of Credit Note	Date of Credit Note	Date Payment Is Made	Amount of Payment Required
May 14	$147.00	2/10,n/30	–	–		
Apr. 15	315.00	3/20,n/60	$42.00	May 1		
Jun. 3	220.05	2/10,n/60	78.75	Jun. 20		
Nov. 20	59.25	2/15,n/60	36.75	Dec. 2		

ANSWERS TO SECTION 11.5 EXERCISES (cont.)

Exercise 3, p. 460

A., B.

GENERAL JOURNAL   PAGE

DATE		PARTICULARS	P.R.	DEBIT	CREDIT

C.

GENERAL JOURNAL   PAGE

DATE		PARTICULARS	P.R.	DEBIT	CREDIT

ANSWERS TO SECTION 11.5 EXERCISES (cont.)

Exercise 4, p. 461

A., B.

GENERAL JOURNAL

PAGE

DATE		PARTICULARS	P.R.	DEBIT	CREDIT

C., D.

GENERAL JOURNAL

PAGE

DATE		PARTICULARS	P.R.	DEBIT	CREDIT

ANSWERS TO SECTION 11.6 REVIEW QUESTIONS (text p. 465)

Perpetual Inventory

1. _____
   _____
2. _____
3. _____
   _____
4. _____
5. _____
6. _____
   _____
   _____
7. _____
   _____
   _____
   _____
   _____
   _____
   _____
8. _____
   _____
9. _____
   _____
   _____
   _____
   _____
10. _____
    _____
11. _____
    _____

ANSWERS TO SECTION 11.6 EXERCISES (text p. 465)

Exercise 1, p. 465

A. Additions to inventory are usually made from copies of _____.

B. _____ forces department stores to use the perpetual inventory system.

C. In a computer inventory system, each inventory item is given a _____.

D. The _____ inventory system produces up-to-the-minute information that cannot be produced by the _____ inventory system.

ANSWERS TO SECTION 11.6 EXERCISES (cont.)

Exercise 1 (cont.)

E. Deductions from inventory are usually made from copies of _____ or through _____ in a modern store.

F. Any differences between the _____ figures and the actual figures require an _____ to the book figures.

G. Even in a computer inventory system, a _____ of the stock is necessary.

H. A journal entry for a sale under the perpetual inventory system includes a debit to _____ and a credit to _____.

I. When buying inventory, the _____ account is not used with the perpetual inventory system.

J. Spoiled merchandise forces a debit to the _____ account.

Exercise 2, p. 466

A.

INVENTORY CONTROL CARD

Stock Number: 730-0320
Description: SCHAEFER CHEEK BLOCK
Location: Row 16 Bin 3
Maximum: 30
Minimum: 10

Date	Reference		Unit Cost	Quantity Received	Quantity Shipped	Balance on Hand
Feb. 20	Forward		15.50			28
26	S.O.	904			5	23

INVENTORY CONTROL CARD

Stock Number: 713-3011
Description: BARTON CAM CLEAT
Location: Row 20 Bin 14
Maximum: 50
Minimum: 20

Date	Reference		Unit Cost	Quantity Received	Quantity Shipped	Balance on Hand
Feb. 24	Forward		9.20			37
26	S.O.	910			10	27

ANSWERS TO SECTION 11.6 EXERCISES (cont.)

Exercise 2 (cont.)

B.   Inventory values at cost:

#730–0320   _____

#713–3011   _____

Exercise 3, p. 467

Shown below are some of the accounts (in T-account form) from the ledger of Master Security Systems. Master Security Systems has a computer accounting system and is able to keep its inventory and cost of goods accounts up to the minute. There is no account for Purchases. Assume that the bank account has a balance of $40 000.

Bank		Sales	
40 000			

Merchandise Inventory		Cost of Goods Sold	
50 000			

Record the journal entries for the following transactions directly into the ledger accounts above. Ignore freight-in, GST, and PST. When you finish recording the entries, calculate the balance of each account.

Transactions

1. Purchased merchandise for cash at a cost of $10 000.

2. Sold goods for cash. The goods, recorded in the inventory at $6 000, are sold for $11 000. *(Note: There are two aspects of this transaction to record.)*

3. Sold goods for cash. The goods, recorded in the inventory at $9 000, are sold for $15 000. *(Note: There are two aspects of this transaction to record.)*

4. Purchased merchandise for cash at a cost of $3 000.

ANSWERS TO SECTION 11.6 EXERCISES (cont.)

Exercise 4, p. 468

A. THE BOOKS OF FLEET FOOT RUNNERS

GENERAL JOURNAL   PAGE

DATE	PARTICULARS	P.R.	DEBIT	CREDIT

Chapter 11 *Accounting for a Merchandising Business* **359**

ANSWERS TO SECTION 11.6 EXERCISES (cont.)

Exercise 4 (cont.)

B.   IN THE BOOKS OF LAU'S SPORTS WAREHOUSE

Note: The running shoes cost Lau's Sports Warehouse $19.95 per pair.

GENERAL JOURNAL   PAGE

DATE		PARTICULARS	P.R.	DEBIT	CREDIT

ANSWERS TO SECTION 11.7 COMPUTER REVIEW QUESTIONS (text p. 473)

Simply Accounting Inventory Applications

1. _____
   _____
   _____
   _____
   _____
   _____
   _____
   _____
   _____

2. _____
   _____

3. _____
   _____

4. _____
   _____
   _____

5. _____
   _____

6. _____
   _____

ANSWERS TO SECTION 11.7 COMPUTER EXERCISES (text p. 473)

Exercise 1, p. 473

Exercise 2, p. 473

Name _____ Date _____

ANSWERS TO SECTION 11.8 REVIEW QUESTIONS (text p. 477)

Manufacturing Businesses — A Comparison

1. _____

2. _____
   _____
   _____
   _____

3. _____
   _____
   _____
   _____

4. _____
   _____
   _____

5. _____
   _____

6. _____
   _____

7. _____
   _____

8. _____
   _____
   _____
   _____

9. _____
   _____
   _____

10. _____

11. _____
   _____
   _____
   _____
   _____

12. _____
   _____

13. _____
   _____
   _____
   _____

ANSWERS TO SECTION 11.8 EXERCISES (text p. 477)

Exercise 1, p. 477

Exercise 2, p. 478

Cull's Novelties
Manufacturing Statement
Year Ended December 31, 20—

Raw materials			
Opening inventory of raw materials		$ 42 500	
Raw materials purchased	$89 600		
Freight charges	6 900		
Cost of raw materials purchased	(1) _____		
Raw materials available for use	(2) $ _____		
Less: Ending inventory of raw materials	(3) _____		
Raw materials used			$ 125 300
Direct labour			109 800
Factory overhead			
Indirect labour		$ 37 000	
Factory supplies used		11 600	
Property taxes		11 800	
Depreciation of factory and equipment		18 900	
Utilities		19 500	
Maintenance		8 000	
Total factory overhead costs		(4) _____	
Total manufacturing costs		(5) $ _____	
Add: Goods in process inventory, January 1			22 000
Total goods in process during the year		(6) $ _____	
Deduct: Goods in process inventory, December 31		(7) _____	
Cost of goods manufactured			$ 318 400

ANSWERS TO SECTION 11.8 EXERCISES (cont.)

Exercise 3, p. 478

_____

_____

_____

Name _Harraj_   Date _Mon./Dec. 5/2011_

Exercise 1, p. 480   **Using Your Knowledge**

GENERAL JOURNAL   PAGE

DATE		PARTICULARS	P.R.	DEBIT	CREDIT
20– May	1	A/R – Hewitt Construction		701 92	
		GST Payable		45 92	45 92
		Sales			656 –
		Sales Invoice No. 501			
	5	Purchases		1072 14	
		GST Recoverable		75 05	
		A/P – EMJ Steel			1147 19
		Purchase Invoice No. 702			
	8	A/P – Great Lakes Wood Products		625 95	
		Purchases Returns & Allowances			585 –
		GST Recoverable			40 95
		Credit Inv. Received			
	9	A/R – Northern Contracting		905 22	
		GST Payable			59 22
		Sales			846 –
		Sales Inv. 502			
	15	Sales Returns & Allowances		642 –	
		GST Payable		42 –	
		A/R			600 –
		Credit Inv. Issued			
	19	Bank		109 68	
		GST Payable			7 18
		Sales			102 50
		Cash Sales Slip			
	26	Freight-in		896 50	
		GST Recoverable		62 76	
		A/P – Pacific Transport			959 26
		P. Inv. No. 371			

ANSWERS TO CHAPTER 11 REVIEW EXERCISES (cont.)

Exercise 2, p. 480

GENERAL JOURNAL   PAGE

DATE		PARTICULARS	P.R.	DEBIT	CREDIT

ANSWERS TO CHAPTER 11 REVIEW EXERCISES (cont.)

Exercise 2 (cont.)

GENERAL JOURNAL   PAGE

DATE		PARTICULARS	P.R.	DEBIT	CREDIT

Exercise 3, p. 481

Indicate whether each of the following statements is true or false by placing a "T" or an "F" in the box indicated. Explain the reason for each "F" response in the space provided at the end of the exercise.

A. A "wholesaler" is a "merchandiser." Therefore, a "merchandiser" is a "wholesaler."

B. Some of the goods found in the inventory of a hardware store are also goods found in the inventory of a building supply store.

C. Merchandise inventory is on the balance sheet under Prepaid Expenses.

D. The cost of goods sold figure normally includes the cost of goods that are lost, stolen, or broken.

E. The merchandise inventory of a drug store is calculated by counting all of the goods on hand and multiplying by the selling prices marked on the goods.

F. An item that cost $40 and sold for $80 produced a gross profit of 50 per cent of the selling price.

G. The difference between the selling price and the cost price of the goods for a fiscal period is also the net income figure before any operating expenses are deducted.

H. The goods not sold represent the ending inventory.

I. The goods sold at selling prices represent the revenue figure.

J. The perpetual inventory system has not been commonly used because of the amount of work required to keep track of the many individual items in the inventory.

K. A used car business could easily use the perpetual inventory system because the number of items in its inventory is quite small.

ANSWERS TO CHAPTER 11 REVIEW EXERCISES (cont.)

Exercise 3 (cont.)

L. XYZ department store uses the periodic inventory system. It must take a physical inventory at least once a year.

M. A perpetual inventory results in a "calculated" inventory figure. The inventory quantities shown on a perpetual inventory listing should be checked by actually inspecting the inventory from time to time. This would make clear whether or not any goods had been stolen.

N. If the beginning inventory was 10 000 units and the ending inventory was 12 000 units, the business sold more units than it purchased.

O. The merchandise inventory figures can be found during the fiscal period from the Merchandise Inventory account.

P. The Purchases account is used to accumulate all purchases during the period.

Q. When a business that uses the periodic system sells goods, no accounting entry is made to reduce the merchandise inventory. If it were made, this entry would be: Debit Cost of Goods Sold and Credit Merchandise Inventory.

R. The Freight-in account is used to accumulate all transportation charges during the fiscal period.

S. Freight-in is considered to be a cost of the goods acquired.

T. On the work sheet, the Purchases figure in the trial balance is extended to the Income Statement section, Debit column.

U. On the work sheet, the Merchandise Inventory figure in the trial balance is extended to the Balance Sheet section, Debit column.

V. Both the beginning and the ending inventory figures are shown on the income statement of a merchandising company.

W. The Merchandise Inventory account is automatically adjusted by the closing entries.

X. A credit invoice is issued by the vendor and received by the buyer.

Y. The accounting entry for a credit note issued is either:

		DR	CR
a.	Accounts Receivable	$$$$	
	Sales		$$$$
	or		
b.	Accounts Receivable	$$$$	
	Sales Returns and Allowances		$$$$

Z. The best match for Merchandise Inventory on a balance sheet of a manufacturing company is Raw Materials Inventory.

ANSWERS TO CHAPTER 11 REVIEW EXERCISES (cont.)

Exercise 3 (cont.)

Explanations for "F" Responses:

_____

_____

_____

_____

_____

_____

_____

_____

_____

_____

_____

_____

_____

_____

_____

_____

_____

_____

_____

_____

Name _____ Date _____

Exercise 4, p. 482

Master Security Systems

Income Statement

Year Ended December 31, 20—

Copyright © 2002 Pearson Education Canada Inc., Toronto, Ontario

Name _____   Date _____

ANSWERS TO CHAPTER 11 REVIEW EXERCISES (cont.)

Exercise 5, p. 483

A.   Fill in the blanks to complete the statement.

Green's Garden Centre
Income Statement
Years Ended December 31, 20–1 and 20–2

	20-1	20-2
Sales	$100 000	$120 000
Costs of Goods Sold		
Opening Inventory	$ 20 000	$ 25 000
Purchases		
Goods Available for Sale	$	$ 63 000
Less Closing Inventory	25 000	
Cost of Goods Sold	$	$
Gross Profit	$ 65 000	$
Expenses	$	$ 37 000
Net Income	$ 33 000	$ 42 000

B.   a. _____

_____

   b. _____

_____

C.   _____

_____

Exercise 6, p. 483

	#460	#911
A. Quantity on hand to start	_____	_____
Receipts and shipments	_____	_____
	_____	_____
	_____	_____
	_____	_____
	_____	_____
Quantity on hand at end	_____	_____

B.   Inventory value for item #460

_____

ANSWERS TO CHAPTER 11 REVIEW EXERCISES (cont.)

Exercise 7, p. 483

(Note: The key to this exercise is that the gross profit figure is 40 per cent of the sales figure.)

Sutton Hardware Store

Estimated Income Statement

Month Ended January 31, 20—

Exercise 8, p. 484

Unaudited Net Income _____

A. Add cost of new equipment _____

    Deduct depreciation on new equipment _____

B. No change

C. Add overcharge on repairs to auto _____

D. Deduct supplies used _____

E. Deduct inventory deduction _____

Adjusted Net Income figure _____

ANSWERS TO CHAPTER 11 REVIEW EXERCISES (cont.)

Exercise 9, p. 485

A. _____

B. _____

C. _____

D. _____
_____

E. _____
_____

F. _____
_____

G. _____
_____

Exercise 10, p. 485

GENERAL JOURNAL   PAGE

DATE		PARTICULARS	P.R.	DEBIT	CREDIT

ANSWERS TO CHAPTER 11 REVIEW EXERCISES (cont.)

Exercise 11, p. 486

Superior Trading Company
Income Statement
Year Ended December 31, 20—

Revenue:			
Sales		207 245 50	
Sales Returns and Allowances		4 102 —	
Net Sales			203 1 52 50
Cost of Goods Sold:			
Beginning Merchandise Inventory		44 232 40	
Purchases	73 219 20		
Less Purchases Returns & Allowances	5 625 —		
Net Purchases		67 594 20	67 594 20
Freight-in		1 501 —	
COGAFS		113 418 60	
Ending Merchandise Inventory		43 750 —	
COGS			69 668 60
Gross Profit			133 483 90
Operating Expenses			
Advertising Expense			
Bank Charges Expense			
Car Expense			
Delivery Expense			
Depreciation Exp. – Automobiles			
Dep. Exp. — Equipment			

Name _____   Date _____

ANSWERS TO CHAPTER 11 REVIEW EXERCISES (cont.)

Questions for Further Thought, p. 487

1. _____
   _____
   _____
   _____
   _____
   _____

2. _____
   _____
   _____
   _____
   _____
   _____
   _____
   _____
   _____

3. _____
   _____

4. _____
   _____
   _____

5. _____
   _____
   _____
   _____
   _____
   _____
   _____
   _____

6. _____
   _____
   _____

7. _____
   _____

8. _____

9. _____
   _____
   _____

10. _____
    _____
    _____

11. _____

ANSWERS TO CHAPTER 11 REVIEW EXERCISES (cont.)

Questions for Further Thought (cont.)

12. _____
_____
_____
_____

13. _____
_____

14. _____
_____

15. _____
_____

16. _____

17. _____
_____

18. _____

A Case for Further Thought, p. 487

1. _____
_____
_____

CASE STUDIES (text p. 488)

Case 1 *Analyzing Income Statements for Two Merchandising Companies*, p. 488

1. _____
_____
_____
_____
_____

2. _____

3. a. _____

   b. _____

Case 2 *Why Have Gross Profits Declined?*, p. 489

1. _____

2. _____
_____
_____

CASE STUDIES (cont.)

Case 2 (cont.)

3. _____
   _____
   _____
   _____
   _____
   _____

4. _____
   _____
   _____
   _____
   _____
   _____
   _____
   _____

Case 3   *Squeeze Play?*, p. 490

1. _____
   _____
   _____
   _____

2. _____
   _____
   _____
   _____

3. _____
4. _____
   _____
   _____
   _____
   _____
   _____
   _____
   _____
   _____

CASE STUDIES (cont.)

Case 3 (cont.)

5. _____

Challenge Case 4   *A Scheme To Save Income Tax?*, p. 491

1. _____

2. _____

3. _____

4. _____

CASE STUDIES (cont.)

Challenge Case 5 *Budgeting — How Many Doughnuts Will the Grade 12s Eat?*, p. 492

This page is left blank intentionally.

Note: page 382 follows next.

Chapter 12 Modifying Accounting Systems

ANSWERS TO SECTION 12.1 REVIEW QUESTIONS (text p. 516)

Subsidiary Ledger Systems

1. _____
2. _____
   _____
   _____
   _____
3. _____
   _____
   _____
   _____
4. _____
   _____
5. _____
6. _____
7. _____
8. _____
9. _____
   _____
10. _____
    _____
11. _____
    1. _____
    2. _____
    3. _____
12. _____
    _____
13. _____
    _____
14. _____
    _____
15. _____
    _____
16. _____
    _____
17. _____
18. _____
    _____

ANSWERS TO SECTION 12.1 REVIEW QUESTIONS (cont.)

19. _____

20. _____

21. _____

    1. _____

    2. _____

22. _____
    _____
    _____
    _____

23. _____
    _____

24. _____
    _____

25. _____
    _____

ANSWERS TO SECTION 12.1 EXERCISES (text p. 517)

Exercise 1, p. 517

Subsidiary Ledger Features and Requirements	Manual System	Simply Accounting
a. Customers and vendors are removed from the general ledger.	✔	✔
b. Copies of source documents are sent to the general ledger clerk.	✔	✗
c. Control accounts are required.		
d. Totals in the subsidiary ledgers must be balanced with general ledger accounts at the end of each month.		
e. Two source documents affect Accounts Receivable.		
f. Produces a report that also indicates the age of invoices.		
g. The general ledger clerk and subsidiary ledger clerks work with copies of the same source document.		
h. Produces reports showing customer and vendor balances.		
i. A journal entry by a subsidiary ledger clerk automatically updates accounts in the general ledger.		
j. Totals in the subsidiary ledgers always balance with the general ledger control accounts.		

Name _____ Date _____

ANSWERS TO SECTION 12.1 EXERCISES (cont.)

Exercise 2, p. 518

A. The total value of the accounts receivable accounts is _____.

B. The total value of the accounts payable accounts is _____.

C. a.

Proctor's Pet Store

General Ledger Trial Balance

June 30, 20—

ACCOUNTS	DEBIT	CREDIT

C. b.

Proctor's Pet Store

Accounts Receivable Listing

June 30, 20—

ANSWERS TO SECTION 12.1 EXERCISES (cont.)

Exercise 2 (cont.)

C. c.

Proctor's Pet Store

Accounts Payable Listing

June 30, 20—

Exercise 3, p. 518

A. _____

B. _____

C. _____
_____

D. _____
_____

E. _____
_____
_____
_____
_____

F. _____
_____
_____

G. _____
_____
_____

ANSWERS TO SECTION 12.1 EXERCISES (cont.)

Exercise 4, p. 519

A., B.

ACCOUNTS RECEIVABLE LEDGER

ACCOUNT *Adams Bros., 12 Mountain Avenue*

DATE		PARTICULARS	P.R.	DEBIT	CREDIT	DR/CR	BALANCE
20— Jun.	30	Inv. No. 480		6 7 20		DR	6 7 20
	30	507		9 4 20		DR	1 6 1 40

ACCOUNT *Cozo & Son, 620 Main Street*

DATE		PARTICULARS	P.R.	DEBIT	CREDIT	DR/CR	BALANCE
20— Jun.	30	Inv. No. 512		7 5 65		DR	7 5 65

ACCOUNT *A. G. Farmer, 120A Blackwell Court*

DATE		PARTICULARS	P.R.	DEBIT	CREDIT	DR/CR	BALANCE
20— Jun.	30	Inv. No. 514		3 1 5 62		DR	3 1 5 62

ACCOUNT *S. P. Handy Ltd., 75 Porter Road*

DATE		PARTICULARS	P.R.	DEBIT	CREDIT	DR/CR	BALANCE
20— Jun.	30	Inv. No. 484		2 1 6 25		DR	2 1 6 25
	30	511		2 0 0 22	2 1 6 25	DR	4 1 6 47

ANSWERS TO SECTION 12.1 EXERCISES (cont.)

Exercise 4 (cont.)

A., B. (cont.)

ACCOUNT *R. Mortimer, 60 Hawley Crescent*

DATE		PARTICULARS	P.R.	DEBIT				CREDIT				DR/CR	BALANCE			
20— Jun.	30	Inv. No. 470		5	1	6	25					DR	5	1	6	25
	30	496		6	2	1	90					DR	1 1	3	8	15
	30	505		6	0	8	36					DR	1 7	4	6	51

ACCOUNT *Renforth Sales, 192 Dale Place*

DATE		PARTICULARS	P.R.	DEBIT				CREDIT				DR/CR	BALANCE			
20— Jun.	30	Inv. No. 510		1	3	7	62					DR	1	3	7	62

ACCOUNT *Vista Limited, 2001 Central Ave.*

DATE		PARTICULARS	P.R.	DEBIT				CREDIT				DR/CR	BALANCE			
20— Jun.	30	Inv. No. 515			5	0	–					DR		5	0	–

ACCOUNT

DATE		PARTICULARS	P.R.	DEBIT				CREDIT				DR/CR	BALANCE			

ANSWERS TO SECTION 12.1 EXERCISES (cont.)

Exercise 4 (cont.)

C.

Valley Distribution

Accounts Receivable Trial Balance

July 6, 20—

Exercise 5, p. 520

A., B.

ACCOUNTS PAYABLE LEDGER

ACCOUNT *Daiton Enterprises, 106 Fleet Street, Bathurst*   No.

DATE		PARTICULARS	P.R.	DEBIT	CREDIT	DR/CR	BALANCE
20— Sep.	30	Purchase Inv. No. 516			4 3 0 74	CR	4 3 0 74

ACCOUNT *Gordon & Associates, 700 King Street, Oakville*   No.

DATE		PARTICULARS	P.R.	DEBIT	CREDIT	DR/CR	BALANCE
20— Sep.	30	Purchase Inv. No. B7407			2 1 6 92	CR	2 1 6 92

ANSWERS TO SECTION 12.1 EXERCISES (cont.)

Exercise 5 (cont.)

A., B. (cont.)

ACCOUNT *Henderson Associates, Box 65, Welland*

DATE		PARTICULARS	P.R.	DEBIT	CREDIT	DR/CR	BALANCE
20— Sep.	30	Purchase Inv. No. 16421			5 0 7 –	CR	5 0 7 –
	30	16907			6 1 5 –	CR	1 1 2 2 –

ACCOUNT *Kohler, R. M., 141 Nixon Avenue, Bathurst*

DATE		PARTICULARS	P.R.	DEBIT	CREDIT	DR/CR	BALANCE
20— Sep.	30	Purchase Inv. No. 615			1 0 4 70	CR	1 0 4 70

ACCOUNT *North Shore Packaging, 1500 Middle Road, Leduc*

DATE		PARTICULARS	P.R.	DEBIT	CREDIT	DR/CR	BALANCE
20— Sep.	30	Purchase Inv. No. 901			7 4 87	CR	7 4 87

ACCOUNT *Orenson & Company, 560 The Eastway, Dauphin*

DATE		PARTICULARS	P.R.	DEBIT	CREDIT	DR/CR	BALANCE
20— Sep.	30	Purchase Inv. No. 1604			1 0 4 6 26	CR	1 0 4 6 26
	30	1809			5 1 6 15	CR	1 5 6 2 41

ANSWERS TO SECTION 12.1 EXERCISES (cont.)

Exercise 5 (cont.)

A., B. (cont.)

ACCOUNT Riggs, J. B., 75 Baxter Road, Enfield

DATE		PARTICULARS	P.R.	DEBIT	CREDIT	DR/CR	BALANCE
20— Sep.	30	Purchase Inv. No. 74621			5 0 2 –	CR	5 0 2 –

ACCOUNT Smithers, P. R., 106 Farr Street, Woodstock

DATE		PARTICULARS	P.R.	DEBIT	CREDIT	DR/CR	BALANCE
20— Sep.	30	Purchase Inv. No. 74			5 7 05	CR	5 7 05

ACCOUNT Union Advertising, 7900 Primeau Avenue, Markham

DATE		PARTICULARS	P.R.	DEBIT	CREDIT	DR/CR	BALANCE
20— Sep.	30	Purchase Inv. No. 16352			4 3 6 21	CR	4 3 6 21
	30	17201			7 0 2 16	CR	1 1 3 8 37
	30	17306			5 1 8 90	CR	1 6 5 7 27

ACCOUNT

DATE		PARTICULARS	P.R.	DEBIT	CREDIT	DR/CR	BALANCE

ANSWERS TO SECTION 12.1 EXERCISES (cont.)

Exercise 5 (cont.)

C.

	Magnetic Controls Company

Accounts Payable Trial Balance

October 7, 20—

Exercise 6, p. 522

A.

Blue Bell Company

Accounts Receivable Trial Balance

— at beginning —

Name _____ Date _____

ANSWERS TO SECTION 12.1 EXERCISES (cont.)

Exercise 6 (cont.)

A. (cont.)

Blue Bell Company

Accounts Payable Trial Balance

— at beginning —

B., C., D.

ACCOUNTS RECEIVABLE LEDGER

Crozier	Elyk	Isola
200	150	500

Lim	Perrier	Tams
300	300	250

ACCOUNTS PAYABLE LEDGER

Ace Co.	Delta Supplies	Galaxy Co.
225	150	75

Metro Hardware	Sun Inc.	Pace Equipment
300	400	300

ANSWERS TO SECTION 12.1 EXERCISES (cont.)

Exercise 6 (cont.)

B., C., D. (cont.)

GENERAL LEDGER

Bank		Accounts Receivable		Supplies	
500		1 700		70	

Equipment		Automobiles		Bank Loan	
4 000		10 000			1 000

Accounts Payable		C. Chen, Capital		C. Chen, Drawings	
	1 450		14 550	200	

Revenue		Advertising Expense		General Expense	
	12 400	500		130	

Rent Expense		Utilities Expense		Wages Expense	
1 800		1 500		9 000	

ANSWERS TO SECTION 12.1 EXERCISES (cont.)

Exercise 6 (cont.)

D.

GENERAL JOURNAL   PAGE

DATE		PARTICULARS	P.R.	DEBIT	CREDIT

ANSWERS TO SECTION 12.1 EXERCISES (cont.)

Exercise 6 (cont.)

D. (cont.)

GENERAL JOURNAL   PAGE ____

DATE		PARTICULARS	P.R.	DEBIT	CREDIT

ANSWERS TO SECTION 12.1 EXERCISES (cont.)

Exercise 6 (cont.)

E.

Blue Bell Company

Accounts Receivable Trial Balance

— at end —

Blue Bell Company

Accounts Payable Trial Balance

— at end —

ANSWERS TO SECTION 10.2 EXERCISES (cont.)

Exercise 6 (cont.)

E. (cont.)

Blue Bell Company

General Ledger Trial Balance

— at end —

ACCOUNTS	DEBIT	CREDIT

ANSWERS TO SECTION 12.2 REVIEW QUESTIONS (text p. 536)

The Synoptic Journal

1. _____

2. _____

3. _____

4. _____
   _____

5. _____
   _____
   _____

6. _____

ANSWERS TO SECTION 12.2 REVIEW QUESTIONS (text p. 536)

7. _____
   _____
   _____

8. _____
   _____
   _____

9. _____
   _____

10. _____
    _____
    _____
    _____

11. _____
    _____
    _____

12. _____
    _____
    _____

13. _____
    _____

ANSWERS TO SECTION 12.2 EXERCISES (text p. 537)

Exercise 1, p. 537

Indicate whether each of the following statements is true or false by placing a "T" or "F" in the box provided. Explain the reason for each "F" response in the space provided.

a. A non-routine transaction is one that is out of the ordinary.

b. The synoptic journal is ideally suited to a large company.

c. A synoptic journal is a multi-columnar journal.

d. In the synoptic journal, there would be a special column for Sales Tax Payable because it is a frequently occurring item.

e. The headings in a synoptic journal are always the same as those shown in the textbook.

f. The main advantage of the synoptic journal is time saved in journalizing transactions.

g. An advantage of the synoptic journal is that it is not necessary to balance the accounting entry for every transaction.

h. The synoptic journal is balanced at the end of every month and at the end of every page.

i. The accuracy of the synoptic journal is checked by cross-balancing.

ANSWERS TO SECTION 12.2 EXERCISES (cont.)

Exercise 1 (cont.)

j. The synoptic journal should be cross-balanced before the final totals are inked in and the journal ruled off. ☐

k. It is customary to forward the totals from one page of the synoptic journal to the next. ☐

l. The total of the Other Accounts debit section is posted as a debit to the general ledger. ☐

m. The postings from the synoptic journal are dated the last day of the month. ☐

n. No cross-referencing is necessary when using a synoptic journal. ☐

o. A two-journal system provides a different route for non-routine transactions. ☐

p. A debit amount can be entered in a credit column if it is circled. ☐

q. Every entry in the synoptic journal takes only one line. ☐

Explanation for "F" responses:

_____

_____

_____

_____

_____

_____

_____

_____

_____

_____

_____

ANSWERS TO SECTION 12.2 EXERCISES (cont.)

Exercise 2, p. 537

A.   **SYNOPTIC JOURNAL**

DATE		CUSTOMER / SUPPLIER	NO.	BANK DEBIT	BANK CREDIT	ACCOUNTS RECEIVABLE DEBIT	ACCOUNTS RECEIVABLE CREDIT	
								1
								2
								3
								4
								5
								6
								7
								8
								9
								10
								11
								12
								13
								14
								15
								16
								17
								18
								19
								20
								21
								22
								23
								24
								25
								26
								27
								28
								29
								30
								31
								32
								33
								34

Name _____ Date _____

Exercise 2 (cont.)

MONTH OF _____   PAGE *19*

	ACCOUNTS PAYABLE		SALES OR REVENUE CREDIT	PURCHASES DEBIT	PST PAYABLE CREDIT	OTHER ACCOUNTS			
	DEBIT	CREDIT				ACCOUNT	P.R.	DEBIT	CREDIT
1									
2									
3									
4									
5									
6									
7									
8									
9									
10									
11									
12									
13									
14									
15									
16									
17									
18									
19									
20									
21									
22									
23									
24									
25									
26									
27									
28									
29									
30									
31									
32									
33									
34									

ANSWERS TO SECTION 12.2 EXERCISES (cont.)

Exercise 2 (cont.)

B.

SYNOPTIC JOURNAL POSTING SUMMARY

ACCOUNTS	DEBIT	CREDIT

Exercise 3, p. 539

Shown on the next page, in condensed form, are the synoptic journal and the T-account general ledger of Plastic Products, owned by Jean Webb.

A. Post the synoptic journal to the general ledger. Ignore dates and cross-references. Use check marks to indicate that postings are completed.

B. Take off a general ledger trial balance.

ANSWERS TO SECTION 12.2 EXERCISES (cont.)

Exercise 3 (cont.)

A.

SYNOPTIC JOURNAL　　　　　**MONTH OF JUNE 20—**　　　　　**PAGE** *16*

DATE		PARTICULARS	BANK		ACCOUNTS RECEIVABLE		ACCOUNTS PAYABLE		SALES	PURCH.	PST PAYBL.	OTHER ACCOUNTS			
			DEBIT	CREDIT	DEBIT	CREDIT	DEBIT	CREDIT	CREDIT	DEBIT	CREDIT	ACCOUNT	P.R.	DEBIT	CREDIT
Jun.	20	Forwarded	1800	1450	2150	1970	1270	1350	1750	1460	160				
	23	Laine	55						50		5				
	23	Moors		60								Rent		60	
	24	Park			110				100		10				
	25	Reid	80			80									
	25	Ruel		250			250								
	25	Sacerty		20								Telephone		20	
	26	Bass						150		150					
	26	Clayton						300		300					
	27	Delski		40								Wages		40	
	27	Eady						90				Car Exp.		90	
	27	Green		70								Freight-in		70	
	27	Hock	400			400									
	30	Klaus		230			230								
	30	McCoy	88						80		8				
	30	Nagy			77				70		7				
	30	Perry			44				40		4				
			2423	2120	2381	2450	1750	1890	2090	1910	194			280	

ANSWERS TO SECTION 12.2 EXERCISES (cont.)

Exercise 3 (cont.)

A. (cont.)

GENERAL LEDGER

Bank	
70	

Accounts Receivable	
350	

Merchandise Inventory	
900	

Supplies	
100	

Equipment	
2 000	

Bank Loan	
	1 000

Accounts Payable	
	150

PST Payable	
	300

J. Webb, Capital	
	3 020

J. Webb, Drawings	
500	

Sales	
	4 500

Bank Charges	
40	

Car Expense	
500	

Freight-in	
100	

General Expense	
90	

Purchases	
2 000	

Rent Expense	
300	

Telephone Expense	
50	

Utilities Expense	
1 220	

Wages Expense	
750	

ANSWERS TO SECTION 12.2 EXERCISES (cont.)

Exercise 3 (cont.)

B.

_____

_____

_____

ACCOUNTS	DEBIT	CREDIT

ANSWERS TO SECTION 12.2 EXERCISES (cont.)

Exercise 4, p. 541   Comprehensive Exercise

A., C.   **SYNOPTIC JOURNAL**

DATE		CUSTOMER / SUPPLIER	NO.	BANK		ACCOUNTS RECEIVABLE		
				DEBIT	CREDIT	DEBIT	CREDIT	
								1
								2
								3
								4
								5
								6
								7
								8
								9
								10
								11
								12
								13
								14
								15
								16
								17
								18
								19
								20
								21
								22
								23
								24
								25
								26
								27
								28
								29
								30
								31
								32
								33
								34
								35
								36
								37

Name _____   Date _____

A., C.   **MONTH OF**   PAGE **73**

	ACCOUNTS PAYABLE		SALES OR REVENUE CREDIT	PURCHASES DEBIT	PST PAYABLE CREDIT	OTHER ACCOUNTS			
	DEBIT	CREDIT				ACCOUNT	P.R.	DEBIT	CREDIT

Name _____   Date _____

Exercise 4 (cont.)

B.

ACCOUNTS RECEIVABLE LEDGER

ACCOUNT *R. Lai*

DATE		PARTICULARS	P.R.	DEBIT	CREDIT	DR/CR	BALANCE
20— Jun.	30	Forwarded #1407				DR	2 0 7 2 15

ACCOUNT *G. Langford*

DATE		PARTICULARS	P.R.	DEBIT	CREDIT	DR/CR	BALANCE
20— Jun.	30	Forwarded #1431				DR	3 1 6 20

ACCOUNT *R. Potts*

DATE		PARTICULARS	P.R.	DEBIT	CREDIT	DR/CR	BALANCE
20— Jun.	30	Forwarded #1436				DR	2 9 7 6 90

ACCOUNTS PAYABLE LEDGER

ACCOUNT *City Hardware Supply*

DATE		PARTICULARS	P.R.	DEBIT	CREDIT	DR/CR	BALANCE
20— Jun.	30	Forwarded #1742				CR	2 7 4 2 10

ANSWERS TO SECTION 12.2 EXERCISES (cont.)

Exercise 4 (cont.)

B. (cont.)

ACCOUNT *Clix Oil Company*

DATE		PARTICULARS	P.R.	DEBIT	CREDIT	DR/CR	BALANCE

ACCOUNT *Joe Jay Transport*

DATE		PARTICULARS	P.R.	DEBIT	CREDIT	DR/CR	BALANCE

ACCOUNT *Special Steel Products*

DATE		PARTICULARS	P.R.	DEBIT	CREDIT	DR/CR	BALANCE
20— Jun.	30	Forwarded #147				CR	3 5 2 3 25

D.

GENERAL LEDGER

ACCOUNT *Bank*   No. *101*

DATE		PARTICULARS	P.R.	DEBIT	CREDIT	DR/CR	BALANCE
20— Jun.	30	Forwarded				DR	12 4 0 0 –

ACCOUNT *Accounts Receivable*   No. *105*

DATE		PARTICULARS	P.R.	DEBIT	CREDIT	DR/CR	BALANCE
20— Jun.	30	Forwarded				DR	5 3 6 5 25

ANSWERS TO SECTION 12.2 EXERCISES (cont.)

Exercise 4 (cont.)

D. (cont.)

ACCOUNT *Merchandise Inventory*   No. *110*

DATE		PARTICULARS	P.R.	DEBIT	CREDIT	DR/CR	BALANCE
20— Jun.	30	Forwarded				DR	46 0 9 0 20

ACCOUNT *Supplies*   No. *115*

DATE		PARTICULARS	P.R.	DEBIT	CREDIT	DR/CR	BALANCE
20— Jun.	30	Forwarded				DR	1 3 9 5 —

ACCOUNT *Store Equipment*   No. *120*

DATE		PARTICULARS	P.R.	DEBIT	CREDIT	DR/CR	BALANCE
20— Jun.	30	Forwarded				DR	40 9 0 6 —

ACCOUNT *Accumulated Depreciation — Store Equipment*   No. *121*

DATE		PARTICULARS	P.R.	DEBIT	CREDIT	DR/CR	BALANCE
20— Jun.	30	Forwarded				CR	14 7 2 6 —

ACCOUNT *Delivery Equipment*   No. *130*

DATE		PARTICULARS	P.R.	DEBIT	CREDIT	DR/CR	BALANCE
20— Jun.	30	Forwarded				DR	39 5 0 0 —

ACCOUNT *Accumulated Depreciaition — Delivery Equipment*   No. *131*

DATE		PARTICULARS	P.R.	DEBIT	CREDIT	DR/CR	BALANCE
20— Jun.	30	Forwarded				CR	20 1 4 5 —

ANSWERS TO SECTION 12.2 EXERCISES (cont.)

Exercise 4 (cont.)

D. (cont.)

ACCOUNT *Accounts Payable* No. *201*

DATE		PARTICULARS	P.R.	DEBIT	CREDIT	DR/CR	BALANCE
20— Jun.	30	Forwarded				CR	6 2 6 5 35

ACCOUNT *PST Payable* No. *205*

DATE		PARTICULARS	P.R.	DEBIT	CREDIT	DR/CR	BALANCE
20— Jun.	30	Forwarded				CR	2 4 0 –

ACCOUNT *Loan Payable — Federal Finance* No. *210*

DATE		PARTICULARS	P.R.	DEBIT	CREDIT	DR/CR	BALANCE
20— Jun.	30	Forwarded				CR	8 5 5 0 85

ACCOUNT *F. Dunn, Capital* No. *301*

DATE		PARTICULARS	P.R.	DEBIT	CREDIT	DR/CR	BALANCE
20— Jun.	30	Forwarded				CR	87 9 5 2 08

ACCOUNT *F. Dunn, Drawings* No. *302*

DATE		PARTICULARS	P.R.	DEBIT	CREDIT	DR/CR	BALANCE
20— Jun.	30	Forwarded				DR	6 0 0 0 –

ANSWERS TO SECTION 12.2 EXERCISES (cont.)

Exercise 4 (cont.)

D. (cont.)

ACCOUNT *Sales*   No. *401*

DATE		PARTICULARS	P.R.	DEBIT	CREDIT	DR/CR	BALANCE
20— Jun.	30	Forwarded				CR	53 7 1 4 50

ACCOUNT *Delivery Expense*   No. *505*

DATE		PARTICULARS	P.R.	DEBIT	CREDIT	DR/CR	BALANCE
20— Jun.	30	Forwarded				DR	5 2 5 8 –

ACCOUNT *Freight–in*   No. *510*

DATE		PARTICULARS	P.R.	DEBIT	CREDIT	DR/CR	BALANCE
20— Jun.	30	Forwarded				DR	9 5 6 23

ACCOUNT *General Expense*   No. *515*

DATE		PARTICULARS	P.R.	DEBIT	CREDIT	DR/CR	BALANCE
20— Jun.	30	Forwarded				DR	2 9 5 3 10

ACCOUNT *Purchases*   No. *520*

DATE		PARTICULARS	P.R.	DEBIT	CREDIT	DR/CR	BALANCE
20— Jun.	30	Forwarded				DR	14 1 2 0 –

ANSWERS TO SECTION 12.2 EXERCISES (cont.)

Exercise 4 (cont.)

D. (cont.)

ACCOUNT *Rent Expense*   No. *525*

DATE		PARTICULARS	P.R.	DEBIT	CREDIT	DR/CR	BALANCE
20— Jun.	30	Forwarded				DR	2 4 0 0 –

ACCOUNT *Wages Expense*   No. *530*

DATE		PARTICULARS	P.R.	DEBIT	CREDIT	DR/CR	BALANCE
20— Jun.	30	Forwarded				DR	14 2 5 0 –

ANSWERS TO SECTION 12.2 EXERCISES (cont.)

Exercise 4 (cont.)

E.

_____

_____

_____

ACCOUNTS	DEBIT	CREDIT

Name _____ Date _____

ANSWERS TO SECTION 12.2 EXERCISES (cont.)

Exercise 4 (cont.)

F.

Crest Hardware

Accounts Receivable Trial Balance

July 31, 20—

Crest Hardware

Accounts Payable Trial Balance

July 31, 20—

ANSWERS TO SECTION 12.3 REVIEW QUESTIONS (text p. 549)

The Five-Journal System

1. _____
   _____
   _____

2. _____
   _____
   _____

3. _____
   1. _____
   2. _____
   _____

4. _____
   _____
   _____
   _____

5. _____
   _____

6. _____

7. _____
   _____
   _____
   _____
   _____

8. _____

9. _____

10. _____

11. _____

12. _____
    _____
    _____
    _____
    _____

13. _____

ANSWERS TO SECTION 12.3 EXERCISES (text p. 550)

Exercise 1, p. 550

CASH PAYMENTS JOURNAL   MONTH OF   PAGE

| DATE | PARTICULARS | OTHER ACCOUNTS DEBIT | | | WAGES DEBIT | PURCHASES DEBIT | ACCOUNTS PAYABLE DEBIT | REF. NO. | BANK CREDIT |
		ACCOUNT	P.R.	AMOUNT					

Name _____ Date _____

ANSWERS TO SECTION 12.3 EXERCISES (cont.)

Exercise 2, p. 551

a. _____ g. _____ m. _____

b. _____ h. _____ n. _____

c. _____ i. _____ o. _____

d. _____ j. _____ p. _____

e. _____ k. _____ q. _____

f. _____ l. _____ r. _____

Exercise 3, p. 551

A., B.

SALES JOURNAL   MONTH OF May 2 20—   PAGE 18

DATE	PARTICULARS	GST PAYABLE CREDIT	PST PAYABLE CREDIT	SALES CREDIT	REF. NO.	ACCOUNTS RECEIVABLE DEBIT
May 8	C. Perry	15 05	17 20	215 —	317	247 25
10	Mercer Company	13 30	15 20	190 —	318	218 50

ANSWERS TO SECTION 12.3 EXERCISES (cont.)

Exercise 3 (cont.)

A., B. (cont.)

CASH RECEIPTS JOURNAL MONTH OF May 2017 PAGE 27

DATE	PARTICULARS	OTHER ACCOUNTS CREDIT ACCOUNT	P.R.	AMOUNT	GST PAYABLE CREDIT	PST PAYABLE CREDIT	SALES CREDIT	ACCOUNTS RECEIVABLE CREDIT	REF. NO.	BANK DEBIT
May 2	R. Jones							436 80		436 80
4	A. Racicot				4 90	5 60	70 —		97	80 50
9	S. Storey							95 —		95 —
11	R. Russell							200 —		200 —

ANSWERS TO SECTION 12.3 EXERCISES (cont.)

Exercise 3 (cont.)

A., B. (cont.)

CASH PAYMENTS JOURNAL

MONTH OF   PAGE 36

DATE	PARTICULARS	OTHER ACCOUNTS DEBIT ACCOUNT	P.R.	AMOUNT	WAGES DEBIT	GST RECOV. DEBIT	SUPPLIES DEBIT	ACCOUNTS PAYABLE DEBIT	REF. NO.	BANK CREDIT
May 1	Morris Company					29 75		425 -	75	454 75
5	P. Fobert				275 -				76	275 -
9	A. Popov							300 -	77	300 -

ANSWERS TO SECTION 12.3 EXERCISES (cont.)

Exercise 3 (cont.)

A., B. (cont.)

PURCHASES JOURNAL

MONTH OF _____ PAGE 14

DATE	PARTICULARS	OTHER ACCOUNTS DEBIT ACCOUNT	P.R.	AMOUNT	DELIVERY EXPENSE DEBIT	GST RECOVERABLE DEBIT	PURCHASES DEBIT	SUPPLIES DEBIT	REF. NO.	ACCOUNTS PAYABLE CREDIT
May 2	Gramelco			371 -		26 46	378 -			404 46
9	Wonder Mfg.					7 72		110 95		117 97
10	Presse Fittings					30 50	435 75			466 25
12	Newbay Supplies					14 70	810 -			324 70

ANSWERS TO SECTION 12.3 EXERCISES (cont.)

Exercise 3 (cont.)

A., B. (cont.)

GENERAL JOURNAL

PAGE 17

DATE		PARTICULARS	P.R.	DEBIT	CREDIT
20— May	4	Supplies~~ral Expense~~		30 —	
		General Expense			30 —
		Fixing an error (information memo)			

Exercise 4, p. 552   Workbook Exercise

Husky Hardware is owned by J. Jolley. The accounting system for this business contains five journals and three ledgers. The subsidiary ledgers are posted daily directly from the source documents. There is PST of 8 per cent on all sales.

Husky Hardware
General Ledger Trial Balance
June 30, 20—

101	Bank	$ 26 142.00	
105	Accounts Receivable	4 212.00	
110	Merchandise Inventory	40 951.20	
115	Supplies	3 000.00	
120	Store Equipment	26 750.00	
121	Accumulated Depreciation —Store Equipment		$ 5 000.00
125	Delivery Equipment	35 000.00	
126	Accumulated Depreciation — Delivery Equipment		12 000.00
201	Accounts Payable		50 639.40
205	PST Payable		1 085.20
301	J. Jolley, Capital		61 643.60
305	J. Jolley, Drawings	58 763.40	
401	Sales		198 000.00
501	Purchases	95 000.00	
505	Miscellaneous Expense	2 077.10	
510	Rent	18 000.00	
515	Wages	18 472.50	
		$328 368.20	$328 368.20

ANSWERS TO SECTION 12.3 EXERCISES (cont.)

Exercise 4 (cont.)

Husky Hardware
Accounts Receivable Trial Balance
June 30, 20—

J. Berkley, 260 Waters Avenue	No. 490	$950.40	
	No. 496	151.20	
	No. 503	615.60	$1 717.20
T. Fong, 300 Centre Street	No. 501		577.80
S. Harvey, 466 Keele Street	No. 502		783.00
R. Taylor, 588 Four Winds Drive	No. 498		1 134.00
			$4 212.00

Husky Hardware
Accounts Payable Trial Balance
June 30, 20—

Household Utensils Company, 487 Hope Avenue	No. 52	$10 675.00
J. & A. Hardware Supply, 600 Olde Street	No. 596	5 052.50
Learner Bros., 501 Leduc Avenue	No. 141	30 672.00
Specialty Manufacturing Co., Utopia	No. 163	4 239.90
		$50 639.40

A. **Journalize the transactions listed below in the five journals of Husky Hardware. Ignore GST.**

Transactions

July

2   *Cheque Copy*
No. 187 to D.C. Harper for the rent for the month, $3 000.00.

Purchase Invoice
From Household Utensils Company, No. 87 for the purchase of merchandise, $1 845.00.

3   *Sales Invoices*
No. 504 to S. Harvey, $500.00 plus PST.

No. 505 to R. Taylor, $260.00 plus PST.

No. 506 to T. Fong, $420.00 plus PST.

No. 507 to J. Berkley, $640.00 plus PST.

4   *Cash Receipt*
From the owner, J. Jolley, to increase his investment in the company, $10 000.00.

ANSWERS TO SECTION 12.3 EXERCISES (cont.)

Exercise 4 (cont.)

A. (cont.)

5   *Purchase Invoice*
From Learner Bros., No. 206 for supplies, $356.00.

Cheque Copy
No. 188 to Supply House for the cash purchase of merchandise, $1 470.00.

Cash Register Slips
Cash sales for the week, $8 221.00 plus PST.

8   *Cash Receipt*
From T. Fong to pay Invoice No. 501, $577.80.

9   *Sales Invoices*
No. 508 to L. Peck, $410.00 plus PST.

No. 509 to S. Harvey, $180.00 plus PST.

No. 510 to T. Fong, $250.00 plus PST.

10   *Purchase Invoice*
From J. & A. Hardware Supply, No. 612 for a shipment of hammers, saws, and other tools, $3 150.00.

12   *Cash Register Slips*
Cash sales for the week, $9 360.00 plus PST.

Bank Debit Memo
From Sovereign Bank, bank account decrease for service charge, $102.00.

Cheque Copy
No. 189 to Modern Manufacturing Co. for the cash purchase of merchandise, $2 730.00.

13   *Cash Receipts*
From S. Harvey to pay Invoices No. 502 and No. 504, $1 323.00.

From J. Berkley to pay Invoices No. 490 and No. 496, $1 101.60.

15   *Cheque Copies*
No. 190 to Learner Bros. on account, $15 000.00.

No. 191 to Household Utensils Company on account, $5 000.00.

No. 192 to B. Wiley, wages for the first half of the month, $1 250.00.

No. 193 to W. Brown, wages for the first half of the month, $1 500.00.

No. 194 to J. Jolley, withdrawal by owner, $2 000.00.

No. 195 to the Provincial Government to remit PST for the previous month, $1 085.20.

17   *Sales Invoices*
No. 511 to V. Pucci, $750.00 plus PST.

No. 512 to L. Peck, $450.00 plus PST.

No. 513 to S. Harvey, $190.00 plus PST.

ANSWERS TO SECTION 12.3 EXERCISES (cont.)

Exercise 4 (cont.)

A. (cont.)

17 *Cash Receipt*
From R. Taylor to pay Invoice No. 498, $1 134.00.

18 *Non-Routine Transaction*
Bills amounting to $240.80 representing miscellaneous expenses paid out of the owner's pocket. Credit the owner's Drawings account.

19 *Cash Register Slips*
Cash sales for the week, $8 560.00 plus PST.

Cash Receipts
From S. Harvey to pay account in full, $399.60.

From T. Fong to pay Invoice No. 506, $453.60.

From L. Peck to pay Invoice No. 508, $442.80.

22 *Purchase Invoice*
From Maple Feed Company, No. 996 for the purchase of merchandise, $6 037.50.

23 *Purchase Invoice*
From Household Utensils Company, No. 156 for the purchase of merchandise, $4 126.50.

26 *Cash Register Slips*
Cash sales for the week, $10 650.00 plus PST.

Cheque Copy
No. 196 to Learner Bros. for the cash purchase of merchandise, $2 625.00.

29 *Cheque Copies*
No. 197 to Household Utensils Company to pay Invoice No. 52, $5 675.00.

No. 198 to J. & A. Hardware Supply to pay Invoice No. 596, $5 052.50.

No. 199 to Specialty Manufacturing Company to pay Invoice No. 163, $4 239.90.

31 *Cheque Copies*
No. 200 to B. Wiley, wages for the last half of the month, $1 250.00.

No. 201 to W. Brown, wages for the last half of the month, $1 500.00.

No. 202 to J. Jolley for personal use, $800.00.

B.   **Balance and post the journals to the general ledger.**

C.   **Balance the general ledger.**

D.   **Balance the subsidiary ledgers.**

ANSWERS TO SECTION 12.3 EXERCISES (cont.)

Exercise 4 (cont.)

A. (cont.)

SALES JOURNAL   **MONTH OF**   **PAGE** 56

DATE	PARTICULARS	SALES TAX PAYABLE CREDIT	SALES CREDIT	INV. NO.	ACCOUNTS RECEIVABLE DEBIT

ANSWERS TO SECTION 12.3 EXERCISES (cont.)

Exercise 4 (cont.)

A. (cont.)

PURCHASES JOURNAL

MONTH OF _____　　　　　　　　　　　**PAGE 85**

DATE	PARTICULARS	OTHER ACCOUNTS DEBIT			PURCHASES DEBIT	SUPPLIES DEBIT	REF. NO.	ACCOUNTS PAYABLE CREDIT
		ACCOUNT	P.R.	AMOUNT				

GENERAL JOURNAL　　　　　　　　　　**PAGE 16**

DATE	PARTICULARS	P.R.	DEBIT	CREDIT

Name _____ Date _____

Exercise 4 (cont.)

A. (cont.)

CASH PAYMENTS JOURNAL   **MONTH OF**   **PAGE 93**

| DATE | PARTICULARS | OTHER ACCOUNTS DEBIT | | | WAGES DEBIT | PURCHASES DEBIT | ACCOUNTS PAYABLE DEBIT | CHQ. NO. | BANK CREDIT |
		ACCOUNT	P.R.	AMOUNT					

ANSWERS TO SECTION 12.3 EXERCISES (cont.)

Exercise 4 (cont.)

A. (cont.)

CASH RECEIPTS JOURNAL   **MONTH OF**   **PAGE 42**

DATE	PARTICULARS	OTHER ACCOUNTS CREDIT			ACCOUNTS RECEIVABLE CREDIT	SALES TAX PAYABLE CREDIT	SALES CREDIT	REF. NO.	BANK DEBIT
		ACCOUNT	P.R.	AMOUNT					

ANSWERS TO SECTION 12.3 EXERCISES (cont.)

Exercise 4 (cont.)

B.

GENERAL LEDGER

ACCOUNT *Bank*   No. *101*

DATE		PARTICULARS	P.R.	DEBIT	CREDIT	DR/CR	BALANCE
20— Jun.	30	Forwarded	–			DR	26 1 4 2 –

ACCOUNT *Accounts Receivable*   No. *105*

DATE		PARTICULARS	P.R.	DEBIT	CREDIT	DR/CR	BALANCE
20— Jun.	30	Forwarded	–			DR	4 2 1 2 –

ACCOUNT *Merchandise Inventory*   No. *110*

DATE		PARTICULARS	P.R.	DEBIT	CREDIT	DR/CR	BALANCE
20— Jun.	30	Forwarded	–			DR	40 9 5 1 20

ACCOUNT *Supplies*   No. *115*

DATE		PARTICULARS	P.R.	DEBIT	CREDIT	DR/CR	BALANCE
20— Jun.	30	Forwarded	–			DR	3 0 0 0 –

ACCOUNT *Store Equipment*   No. *120*

DATE		PARTICULARS	P.R.	DEBIT	CREDIT	DR/CR	BALANCE
20— Jun.	30	Forwarded	–			DR	26 7 5 0 –

ANSWERS TO SECTION 12.3 EXERCISES (cont.)

Exercise 4 (cont.)

B. (cont.)

ACCOUNT *Accumulated Depreciation — Store Equipment*   No. *121*

DATE		PARTICULARS	P.R.	DEBIT	CREDIT	DR/CR	BALANCE
20—Jun.	30	Forwarded	–			CR	5 0 0 0 –

ACCOUNT *Delivery Equipment*   No. *125*

DATE		PARTICULARS	P.R.	DEBIT	CREDIT	DR/CR	BALANCE
20—Jun.	30	Forwarded	–			DR	35 0 0 0 –

ACCOUNT *Accumulated Depreciation — Delivery Equipment*   No. *126*

DATE		PARTICULARS	P.R.	DEBIT	CREDIT	DR/CR	BALANCE
20—Jun.	30	Forwarded	–			CR	12 0 0 0 –

ACCOUNT *Accounts Payable*   No. *201*

DATE		PARTICULARS	P.R.	DEBIT	CREDIT	DR/CR	BALANCE
20—Jun.	30	Forwarded	–			CR	50 6 3 9 40

ACCOUNT *PST Payable*   No. *205*

DATE		PARTICULARS	P.R.	DEBIT	CREDIT	DR/CR	BALANCE
20—Jun.	30	Forwarded	–			CR	1 0 8 5 20

ANSWERS TO SECTION 12.3 EXERCISES (cont.)

Exercise 4 (cont.)

B. (cont.)

ACCOUNT *J. Jolley, Capital*   No. *301*

DATE		PARTICULARS	P.R.	DEBIT	CREDIT	DR/CR	BALANCE
20— Jun.	30	Forwarded	–			CR	61 6 4 3 60

ACCOUNT *J. Jolley, Drawings*   No. *305*

DATE		PARTICULARS	P.R.	DEBIT	CREDIT	DR/CR	BALANCE
20— Jun.	30	Forwarded	–			DR	58 7 6 3 40

ACCOUNT *Sales*   No. *401*

DATE		PARTICULARS	P.R.	DEBIT	CREDIT	DR/CR	BALANCE
20— Jun.	30	Forwarded	–			CR	198 0 0 0 –

ACCOUNT *Purchases*   No. *501*

DATE		PARTICULARS	P.R.	DEBIT	CREDIT	DR/CR	BALANCE
20— Jun.	30	Forwarded	–			DR	95 0 0 0 –

ANSWERS TO SECTION 12.3 EXERCISES (cont.)

Exercise 4 (cont.)

B. (cont.)

ACCOUNT *Miscellaneous Expense*   No. *505*

DATE		PARTICULARS	P.R.	DEBIT	CREDIT	DR/CR	BALANCE
20— Jun.	30	Forwarded	–			DR	2 0 7 7 10

ACCOUNT *Rent Expense*   No. *510*

DATE		PARTICULARS	P.R.	DEBIT	CREDIT	DR/CR	BALANCE
20— Jun.	30	Forwarded	–			DR	18 0 0 0 –

ACCOUNT *Wages Expense*   No. *515*

DATE		PARTICULARS	P.R.	DEBIT	CREDIT	DR/CR	BALANCE
20— Jun.	30	Forwarded	–			DR	18 4 7 2 50

ACCOUNTS RECEIVABLE LEDGER

ACCOUNT *J. Berkley*   *260 Waters Avenue*

DATE		PARTICULARS			P.R.	DEBIT	CREDIT	DR/CR	BALANCE
20— Jun.	30	Forwarded	#490	950.40					
			#496	151.20					
			#503	615.60	–			DR	1 7 1 7 20

Name _____ Date _____

ANSWERS TO SECTION 12.3 EXERCISES (cont.)

Exercise 4 (cont.)

B. (cont.)

ACCOUNT T. Fong   300 Centre Road

DATE		PARTICULARS	P.R.	DEBIT	CREDIT	DR/CR	BALANCE
20— Jun.	30	Forwarded #501	–			DR	5 7 7 80

ACCOUNT S. Harvey   466 Keele Street

DATE		PARTICULARS	P.R.	DEBIT	CREDIT	DR/CR	BALANCE
20— Jun.	30	Forwarded #502	–			DR	7 8 3 –

ACCOUNT L. Peck   12 Semore St.

DATE	PARTICULARS	P.R.	DEBIT	CREDIT	DR/CR	BALANCE

ACCOUNT V. Pucci   466 Altavista Road

DATE	PARTICULARS	P.R.	DEBIT	CREDIT	DR/CR	BALANCE

ANSWERS TO SECTION 12.3 EXERCISES (cont.)

Exercise 4 (cont.)

B. (cont.)

ACCOUNT R. Taylor   588 Four Winds Drive

DATE		PARTICULARS	P.R.	DEBIT	CREDIT	DR/CR	BALANCE
20— Jun.	30	Forwarded #498	–			DR	1 1 3 4 –

ACCOUNTS PAYABLE LEDGER

ACCOUNT Household Utensils Company   487 Hope Avenue

DATE		PARTICULARS	P.R.	DEBIT	CREDIT	DR/CR	BALANCE
20— Jun.	30	Forwarded #52	–			CR	10 6 7 5 –

ACCOUNT J. & A. Hardware Supply   600 Olde Street

DATE		PARTICULARS	P.R.	DEBIT	CREDIT	DR/CR	BALANCE
20— Jun.	30	Forwarded #596	–			CR	5 0 5 2 50

ACCOUNT Learner Bros.   5012 Leduc Avenue

DATE		PARTICULARS	P.R.	DEBIT	CREDIT	DR/CR	BALANCE
20— Jun.	30	Forwarded #141	–			CR	30 6 7 2 –

ANSWERS TO SECTION 12.3 EXERCISES (cont.)

Exercise 4 (cont.)

B. (cont.)

ACCOUNT *Maple Feed Company*   *Maple*

DATE		PARTICULARS	P.R.	DEBIT	CREDIT	DR/CR	BALANCE

ACCOUNT *Specialty Manufacturing*   *Utopia*

DATE		PARTICULARS	P.R.	DEBIT	CREDIT	DR/CR	BALANCE
20— Jun.	30	Forwarded #163	–			CR	4 2 3 9 90

ANSWERS TO SECTION 12.3 EXERCISES (cont.)

Exercise 4 (cont.)

C.

Husky Hardware

General Ledger Trial Balance

July 31, 20—

ACCOUNTS	DEBIT	CREDIT

ANSWERS TO SECTION 12.3 EXERCISES (cont.)

Exercise 4 (cont.)

D.

Husky Hardware
Accounts Receivable Trial Balance
July 31, 20—

Husky Hardware
Accounts Payable Trial Balance
July 31, 20—

ANSWERS TO SECTION 12.4 COMPUTER REVIEW QUESTIONS (text p. 555)

Computer Accounting Systems

1. _____

2. _____

3. _____

4. _____

5. _____

6. _____

7. _____

8. _____

ANSWERS TO SECTION 12.4 COMPUTER EXERCISES (text p. 556)

Exercise 1, p. 556

A.

General Ledger Data Entry Form
G/L Journal Entry
Single Currency

		Date
Prepared by		
Approved by		

Batch Number _____ **Batch Description** _____ (Max. of 30 characters)

Date _____ Period _____ Year _____ Source _____

Detail Reference	Entry Description (Max. of 30 characters)	Account	Debit	Credit
	Totals:			

Entry Comment (Max. of 30 characters)

General Ledger Data Entry Form 9 of 10   Filename: GL-JESC.RET

ANSWERS TO SECTION 12.4 COMPUTER EXERCISES (cont.)

Exercise 1 (cont.)

A. (cont.)

General Ledger Data Entry Form
G/L Journal Entry
Single Currency

		Date
Prepared by		
Approved by		

Batch Number _____   **Batch Description** _____ (Max. of 30 characters)

Date _____   Period _____   Year _____   Source _____

Detail Reference	Entry Description (Max. of 30 characters)	Account	Debit	Credit

Totals:

Entry Comment (Max. of 30 characters)

General Ledger Data Entry Form 9 of 10   Filename: GL-JESC.RET

ANSWERS TO SECTION 12.4 COMPUTER EXERCISES (cont.)

Exercise 1 (cont.)

A. (cont.)

				Date
General Ledger Data Entry Form			Prepared by	
G/L Journal Entry			Approved by	
Single Currency				

Batch Number ———— **Batch Description** ——————————————————— (Max. of 30 characters)

Date ————————— Period ——————————— Year ——————— Source ———————

Detail Reference	Entry Description (Max. of 30 characters)	Account	Debit	Credit
————	—————————————	————	————	————
————	—————————————	————	————	————
————	—————————————	————	————	————
————	—————————————	————	————	————
————	—————————————	————	————	————
————	—————————————	————	————	————
————	—————————————	————	————	————
————	—————————————	————	————	————
————	—————————————	————	————	————
————	—————————————	————	————	————
————	—————————————	————	————	————
————	—————————————	————	————	————
————	—————————————	————	————	————

Totals:

Entry Comment (Max. of 30 characters)

———————————————————————————————————

———————————————————————————————————

General Ledger Data Entry Form 9 of 10   Filename: GL-JESC.RET

ANSWERS TO SECTION 12.4 COMPUTER EXERCISES (cont.)

Exercise 1 (cont.)

A. (cont.)

General Ledger Data Entry Form
G/L Journal Entry
Single Currency

		Date
Prepared by		
Approved by		

Batch Number _____ **Batch Description** _____ (Max. of 30 characters)

Date _____ Period _____ Year _____ Source _____

Detail Reference	Entry Description (Max. of 30 characters)	Account	Debit	Credit
_____	_____	_____	_____	_____
_____	_____	_____	_____	_____
_____	_____	_____	_____	_____
_____	_____	_____	_____	_____
_____	_____	_____	_____	_____
_____	_____	_____	_____	_____
_____	_____	_____	_____	_____
_____	_____	_____	_____	_____
_____	_____	_____	_____	_____
_____	_____	_____	_____	_____
_____	_____	_____	_____	_____
_____	_____	_____	_____	_____

Totals: _____ _____

Entry Comment (Max. of 30 characters)

_____
_____
_____

General Ledger Data Entry Form 9 of 10

Filename: GL-JESC.RET

Name _____ Date _____

ANSWERS TO SECTION 12.4 COMPUTER EXERCISES (cont.)

Exercise 1 (cont.)

A. (cont.)

General Ledger Data Entry Form
G/L Journal Entry
Single Currency

		Date
Prepared by		
Approved by		

Batch Number _____ **Batch Description** _____ (Max. of 30 characters)

Date _____ Period _____ Year _____ Source _____

Detail Reference	Entry Description (Max. of 30 characters)	Account	Debit	Credit
_____	_____	_____	_____	_____
_____	_____	_____	_____	_____
_____	_____	_____	_____	_____
_____	_____	_____	_____	_____
_____	_____	_____	_____	_____
_____	_____	_____	_____	_____
_____	_____	_____	_____	_____
_____	_____	_____	_____	_____
_____	_____	_____	_____	_____
_____	_____	_____	_____	_____
_____	_____	_____	_____	_____
_____	_____	_____	_____	_____

Totals: _____ _____

Entry Comment (Max. of 30 characters)
_____
_____
_____

General Ledger Data Entry Form 9 of 10   Filename: GL-JESC.RET

Note: page 446 follows next.

ANSWERS TO SECTION 12.4 COMPUTER EXERCISES (cont.)

This page is left blank intentionally.

ANSWERS TO SECTION 12.5 CASE APPLICATION: MODIFYING ACCOUNTING SYSTEMS (text p. 558)

PAGE 1

CASH RECEIPTS JOURNAL

NAMES:

DATE	EXPLANATION	BANK DEBIT	RENT REVENUE CREDIT	GOV'T GRANT CREDIT	SPECIAL REVENUE CREDIT	OTHER ACCOUNTS			
						TITLE	P.R.	DEBIT	CREDIT

ANSWERS TO SECTION 12.5 CASE APPLICATION:
MODIFYING ACCOUNTING SYSTEMS (cont.)

PAGE 1

CASH PAYMENTS JOURNAL

NAMES:

DATE	EXPLANATION	BANK CREDIT	RENT EXPENSE DEBIT	SPECIAL ASSESS. DEBIT	LAND DEBIT	OTHER ACCOUNTS TITLE	P.R.	DEBIT	CREDIT

ANSWERS TO SECTION 12.5 CASE APPLICATION: MODIFYING ACCOUNTING SYSTEMS (cont.)

5 a.

CASH PROOF	Day 1
Opening Cash Balance (DR.)	_____
Add: Cash Debits for Day 1	_____
Total Cash Debits	_____
Less: Cash Credits for Day 1	_____
Cash Balance from journals	_____
Actual Cash Count	_____
Cash Short or Over	_____

CASH PROOF	Day 2
Opening Cash Balance (DR.)	_____
Add: Cash Debits for Day 2	_____
Total Cash Debits	_____
Less: Cash Credits for Day 2	_____
Cash Balance from journals	_____
Actual Cash Count	_____
Cash Short or Over	_____

6.

ASSETS

ACCOUNT Bank   No. 101

DATE	PARTICULARS	P.R.	DEBIT	CREDIT	DR/CR	BALANCE

ACCOUNT Land   No. 150

DATE	PARTICULARS	P.R.	DEBIT	CREDIT	DR/CR	BALANCE

ANSWERS TO SECTION 12.5 CASE APPLICATION: MODIFYING ACCOUNTING SYSTEMS (cont.)

6. (cont.)

ACCOUNT *Houses*   No. *155*

DATE	PARTICULARS	P.R.	DEBIT	CREDIT	DR/CR	BALANCE

ACCOUNT *Railroads*   No. *165*

DATE	PARTICULARS	P.R.	DEBIT	CREDIT	DR/CR	BALANCE

ACCOUNT *Utilities*   No. *170*

DATE	PARTICULARS	P.R.	DEBIT	CREDIT	DR/CR	BALANCE

LIABILITIES

ACCOUNT *Mortgage Payable*   No. *250*

DATE	PARTICULARS	P.R.	DEBIT	CREDIT	DR/CR	BALANCE

PARTNERS' EQUITY

ACCOUNT *Nicole Wang, Capital*   No. *301*

DATE	PARTICULARS	P.R.	DEBIT	CREDIT	DR/CR	BALANCE

ACCOUNT *Lou Rivera, Capital*   No. *305*

DATE	PARTICULARS	P.R.	DEBIT	CREDIT	DR/CR	BALANCE

ANSWERS TO SECTION 12.5 CASE APPLICATION: MODIFYING ACCOUNTING SYSTEMS (cont.)

6. (cont.)

ACCOUNT *Government Grant*   No. *310*

DATE	PARTICULARS	P.R.	DEBIT	CREDIT	DR/CR	BALANCE

REVENUE

ACCOUNT *Rent Revenue*   No. *401*

DATE	PARTICULARS	P.R.	DEBIT	CREDIT	DR/CR	BALANCE

ACCOUNT *Gain on Trade*   No. *405*

DATE	PARTICULARS	P.R.	DEBIT	CREDIT	DR/CR	BALANCE

ACCOUNT *Special Revenue*   No. *410*

DATE	PARTICULARS	P.R.	DEBIT	CREDIT	DR/CR	BALANCE

ACCOUNT *Travel Revenue*   No. *415*

DATE	PARTICULARS	P.R.	DEBIT	CREDIT	DR/CR	BALANCE

ACCOUNT *Utilities Revenue*   No. *420*

DATE	PARTICULARS	P.R.	DEBIT	CREDIT	DR/CR	BALANCE

EXPENSES

ACCOUNT *Cash Short and Over*   No. *501*

DATE	PARTICULARS	P.R.	DEBIT	CREDIT	DR/CR	BALANCE

ANSWERS TO SECTION 12.5 CASE APPLICATION: MODIFYING ACCOUNTING SYSTEMS (cont.)

6. (cont.)

ACCOUNT *Income Tax Expense*   No. *505*

DATE	PARTICULARS	P.R.	DEBIT	CREDIT	DR/CR	BALANCE

ACCOUNT *Jail Expense*   No. *510*

DATE	PARTICULARS	P.R.	DEBIT	CREDIT	DR/CR	BALANCE

ACCOUNT *Loss on Sale*   No. *516*

DATE	PARTICULARS	P.R.	DEBIT	CREDIT	DR/CR	BALANCE

ACCOUNT *Loss on Trade*   No. *517*

DATE	PARTICULARS	P.R.	DEBIT	CREDIT	DR/CR	BALANCE

ACCOUNT *Mortgage Interest*   No. *525*

DATE	PARTICULARS	P.R.	DEBIT	CREDIT	DR/CR	BALANCE

ACCOUNT *Rent Expense*   No. *530*

DATE	PARTICULARS	P.R.	DEBIT	CREDIT	DR/CR	BALANCE

ACCOUNT *Special Assessments*   No. *535*

DATE	PARTICULARS	P.R.	DEBIT	CREDIT	DR/CR	BALANCE

ANSWERS TO SECTION 12.5 CASE APPLICATION: MODIFYING ACCOUNTING SYSTEMS (cont.)

6. (cont.)

ACCOUNT *Travel Expense*   No. *540*

DATE	PARTICULARS	P.R.	DEBIT	CREDIT	DR/CR	BALANCE

ACCOUNT *Utilities Expense*   No. *545*

DATE	PARTICULARS	P.R.	DEBIT	CREDIT	DR/CR	BALANCE

_____

_____

_____

ACCOUNTS	DEBIT	CREDIT

ANSWERS TO CHAPTER 12 REVIEW EXERCISES (text p. 564)

Exercise 1, p. 564   Using Your Knowledge

Analysis of errors:

	Changes to control account figure	Changes to subsidiary ledger figure
1.	_____	_____
2.	_____	_____
3.	_____	_____
4.	_____	_____
5.	_____	_____
6.	_____	_____
7.	_____	_____
Total Net Corrections	_____	_____

1. The correct total for the subsidiary ledger and the control is:

    Balance before corrections $32 456

    Net corrections to ledger   _____

    Corrected balance   _____

2. Correct control account figure   _____

    Total corrections required   _____

    Figure before corrections   _____

ANSWERS TO CHAPTER 12 REVIEW EXERCISES (cont.)

Exercise 2, p. 564

Source Document	In the Subsidiary Ledger						In the General Ledger									
	Which subsidiary ledger is affected?		Will the account be increased or decreased?		Will the account be debited or credited?		The accounting entry will be									
	A/R	A/P	Increase	Decrease	DR	CR	Bank		Accounts Receivable		Accounts Payable		Asset or Expense		Revenue	
							DR	CR	DR	CR	DR	CR	DR	CR	DR	CR
Purchase invoice																
Cash receipt on account																
Sales invoice																
Cheque copy on account																

ANSWERS TO CHAPTER 12 REVIEW EXERCISES (cont.)

Exercise 3, p. 565   **Comprehensive Exercise**

A., F.

GENERAL LEDGER

ACCOUNT *Bank*   No. *101*

DATE		PARTICULARS	P.R.	DEBIT	CREDIT	DR/CR	BALANCE
20— Mar.	31	Forwarded	–			DR	1 7 4 8 –

ACCOUNT *Accounts Receivable*   No. *105*

DATE		PARTICULARS	P.R.	DEBIT	CREDIT	DR/CR	BALANCE
20— Mar.	31	Forwarded	–			DR	7 2 2 0 –

ACCOUNT *Supplies*   No. *110*

DATE		PARTICULARS	P.R.	DEBIT	CREDIT	DR/CR	BALANCE
20— Mar.	31	Forwarded	–			DR	2 7 5 0 –

ANSWERS TO CHAPTER 12 REVIEW EXERCISES (cont.)

Exercise 3 (cont.)

A., F. (cont.)

ACCOUNT *Office Equipment*   No. *115*

DATE		PARTICULARS	P.R.	DEBIT	CREDIT	DR/CR	BALANCE
20— Mar.	31	Forwarded	–			DR	20 8 0 0 –

ACCOUNT *Accumulated Depreciation — Office Equipment*   No. *116*

DATE		PARTICULARS	P.R.	DEBIT	CREDIT	DR/CR	BALANCE
20— Mar.	31	Forwarded	–			CR	2 4 0 0 –

ACCOUNT *Automobile*   No. *120*

DATE		PARTICULARS	P.R.	DEBIT	CREDIT	DR/CR	BALANCE
20— Mar.	31	Forwarded	–			DR	29 5 0 0 –

ACCOUNT *Accumulated Depreciation — Automobile*   No. *121*

DATE		PARTICULARS	P.R.	DEBIT	CREDIT	DR/CR	BALANCE
20— Mar.	31	Forwarded	–			DR	4 8 0 0 –

ACCOUNT *Accounts Payable*   No. *205*

DATE		PARTICULARS	P.R.	DEBIT	CREDIT	DR/CR	BALANCE
20— Mar.	31	Forwarded	–			CR	6 2 6 4 70

ANSWERS TO CHAPTER 12 REVIEW EXERCISES (cont.)

Exercise 3 (cont.)

A., F. (cont.)

ACCOUNT *GST Payable*   No. *206*

DATE		PARTICULARS	P.R.	DEBIT	CREDIT	DR/CR	BALANCE
20— Mar.	31	Forwarded	–			CR	1 8 5 –

ACCOUNT *GST Recoverable*   No. *207*

DATE		PARTICULARS	P.R.	DEBIT	CREDIT	DR/CR	BALANCE
20— Mar.	31	Forwarded	–			DR	1 0 2 –

ACCOUNT *R. Bragg, Capital*   No. *301*

DATE		PARTICULARS	P.R.	DEBIT	CREDIT	DR/CR	BALANCE
20— Mar.	31	Forwarded	–			CR	47 3 7 4 15

ACCOUNT *R. Bragg, Drawings*   No. *302*

DATE		PARTICULARS	P.R.	DEBIT	CREDIT	DR/CR	BALANCE
20— Mar.	31	Forwarded	–			DR	12 0 0 0 –

ANSWERS TO CHAPTER 12 REVIEW EXERCISES (cont.)

Exercise 3 (cont.)

A., F. (cont.)

ACCOUNT *Fees Income*   No. *401*

DATE		PARTICULARS	P.R.	DEBIT	CREDIT	DR/CR	BALANCE
20— Mar.	31	Forwarded	–			CR	31 6 5 0 –

ACCOUNT *Car Expense*   No. *505*

DATE		PARTICULARS	P.R.	DEBIT	CREDIT	DR/CR	BALANCE
20— Mar.	31	Forwarded	–			DR	3 2 9 5 60

ACCOUNT *Miscellaneous Expense*   No. *515*

DATE		PARTICULARS	P.R.	DEBIT	CREDIT	DR/CR	BALANCE
20— Mar.	31	Forwarded	–			DR	3 7 5 40

ACCOUNT *Rent Expense*   No. *520*

DATE		PARTICULARS	P.R.	DEBIT	CREDIT	DR/CR	BALANCE
20— Mar.	31	Forwarded	–			DR	3 0 0 0 –

ACCOUNT *Telephone Expense*   No. *525*

DATE		PARTICULARS	P.R.	DEBIT	CREDIT	DR/CR	BALANCE
20— Mar.	31	Forwarded	–			DR	5 1 6 15

ANSWERS TO CHAPTER 12 REVIEW EXERCISES (cont.)

Exercise 3 (cont.)

A., F. (cont.)

ACCOUNT *Utilities Expense*   No. *510*

DATE		PARTICULARS	P.R.	DEBIT	CREDIT	DR/CR	BALANCE
20— Mar.	31	Forwarded	–			DR	9 5 0 20

ACCOUNT *Wages Expense*   No. *530*

DATE		PARTICULARS	P.R.	DEBIT	CREDIT	DR/CR	BALANCE
20— Mar.	31	Forwarded	–			DR	10 4 1 6 50

B., D.

ACCOUNTS RECEIVABLE LEDGER

ACCOUNT *Blue Cab Company*   *16 Fox Street*

DATE		PARTICULARS	P.R.	DEBIT	CREDIT	DR/CR	BALANCE
20— Mar.	31	Forwarded Invoice #74	–			DR	1 9 2 0 –

ACCOUNT *Champion Store*   *175 Main Street*

DATE		PARTICULARS	P.R.	DEBIT	CREDIT	DR/CR	BALANCE
20— Mar.	31	Forwarded Invoice #75	–			DR	7 5 0 –

ACCOUNT *Oasis Restaurant*   *325 Second Street*

DATE		PARTICULARS	P.R.	DEBIT	CREDIT	DR/CR	BALANCE
20— Mar.	31	Forwarded Invoice #76	–			DR	1 5 5 0 –

ANSWERS TO CHAPTER 12 REVIEW EXERCISES (cont.)

Exercise 3 (cont.)

B., D. (cont.)

ACCOUNT *Village Restaurant*   *400 Main Street*

DATE		PARTICULARS	P.R.	DEBIT	CREDIT	DR/CR	BALANCE
20— Mar.	31	Forwarded Invoice #77	–			DR	3 0 0 0 –

ACCOUNTS PAYABLE LEDGER

ACCOUNT *M. Ball, Consultant*   *430 Red Road, Bigtown*

DATE		PARTICULARS	P.R.	DEBIT	CREDIT	DR/CR	BALANCE
20— Mar.	31	Forwarded	–			CR	1 5 1 5 –

ACCOUNT *R. & R. Supply*   *151 King Street*

DATE		PARTICULARS	P.R.	DEBIT	CREDIT	DR/CR	BALANCE
20— Mar.	31	Forwarded	–			CR	2 7 4 0 –

ACCOUNT *Stirling Company*   *46 River Road*

DATE		PARTICULARS	P.R.	DEBIT	CREDIT	DR/CR	BALANCE
20— Mar.	31	Forwarded	–			CR	7 5 9 50

ACCOUNT *Tom's Garage*   *705 Victoria Street*

DATE		PARTICULARS	P.R.	DEBIT	CREDIT	DR/CR	BALANCE
20— Mar.	31	Forwarded	–			CR	1 2 5 0 20

ANSWERS TO CHAPTER 12 REVIEW EXERCISES (cont.)

Exercise 3 (cont.)

(**Note:** *The following transaction, missing from page 566 of the text, must be included.*

    15 *Cash Receipt*

       From Blue Cab Company, $1 920.00 on account.)

E.   **GENERAL JOURNAL**   PAGE 76

DATE	PARTICULARS	P.R.	DEBIT	CREDIT

Name _____   Date _____

Exercise 3 (cont.)

E. (cont.)   **GENERAL JOURNAL**   PAGE 77

DATE	PARTICULARS	P.R.	DEBIT	CREDIT

ANSWERS TO CHAPTER 12 REVIEW EXERCISES (cont.)

Exercise 3 (cont.)

F.

R. Bragg

General Ledger Trial Balance

April 30, 20—

ACCOUNTS	DEBIT	CREDIT

ANSWERS TO CHAPTER 12 REVIEW EXERCISES (cont.)

Exercise 3 (cont.)

G.

R. Bragg

Accounts Receivable Trial Balance

April 30, 20—

H.

R. Bragg

Accounts Payable Trial Balance

April 30, 20—

Exercise 4, p. 567

Indicate whether each of the following statements is true or false by placing a "T" or and "F" in the box provided. Explain the reason for each "F" response in the space provided.

a. The general journal is not normally used if the business has a synoptic journal.

b. There is a special column for every general ledger account in the synoptic journal.

c. The chief disadvantage of the synoptic journal is that you have to post column totals.

d. An accounting entry that takes more than one line cannot be recorded in the synoptic journal.

ANSWERS TO CHAPTER 12 REVIEW EXERCISES (cont.)

Exercise 4 (cont.)

e. There would be a special column for Rent Expense in the synoptic journal. ☐

f. The synoptic journal is balanced at the end of every page. ☐

g. The date used when formally posting the synoptic journal is the last day of the month. ☐

h. A credit to Sales in the synoptic journal would normally be entered in the Other Accounts credit column. ☐

i. All sales of merchandise are recorded in the sales journal. ☐

j. The cash payments journal is also known as the cash disbursements journal. ☐

k. Additional cash invested in the business by the owner would be recorded in the general journal. ☐

l. A bank debit advice requires an entry in the cash receipts journal. ☐

m. The five journal system inevitably leads to the clerks becoming specialists within the system. ☐

n. The general ledger would not balance if only four of the five journals were posted. ☐

o. A purchase partly for cash and partly on account would be recorded in the purchases journal. ☐

Explanations for "F" responses:

_____

_____

_____

_____

_____

_____

_____

_____

_____

_____

_____

_____

Exercise 5, p. 568

1. _____

_____

_____

_____

_____

_____

2. _____

_____

_____

ANSWERS TO CHAPTER 12 REVIEW EXERCISES (cont.)

Exercise 6, p. 568

A., B., C.

CASH RECEIPTS JOURNAL MONTH OF PAGE 61

DATE	PARTICULARS	OTHER ACCOUNTS CREDIT			GST PAYABLE CREDIT	PST PAYABLE CREDIT	SALES CREDIT	ACCOUNTS RECEIVABLE CREDIT	REF. NO.	BANK DEBIT
		ACCOUNT	P.R.	AMOUNT						

PURCHASES JOURNAL MONTH OF PAGE 74

DATE	PARTICULARS	OTHER ACCOUNTS CREDIT			GST RECOVERBLE DEBIT	PURCHASES DEBIT	REF. NO.	ACCOUNTS PAYABLE CREDIT
		ACCOUNT	P.R.	AMOUNT				

ANSWERS TO CHAPTER 12 REVIEW EXERCISES (cont.)

Exercise 6 (cont.)

A., B., C. (cont.)

CASH PAYMENTS JOURNAL　　　　　　MONTH OF　　　　　　PAGE 117

DATE	PARTICULARS	OTHER ACCOUNTS DEBIT			GST RECOVERABLE DEBIT	WAGES DEBIT	PURCHASES DEBIT	ACCOUNTS PAYABLE DEBIT	REF. NO.	BANK CREDIT
		ACCOUNT	P.R.	AMOUNT						

ANSWERS TO CHAPTER 12 REVIEW EXERCISES (cont.)

Exercise 6 (cont.)

A., B., C. (cont.)

SALES JOURNAL   **MONTH OF**   **PAGE** 82

DATE	PARTICULARS	GST PAYABLE CREDIT	PST PAYABLE CREDIT	SALES CREDIT	REF. NO.	ACCOUNTS RECEIVABLE DEBIT

GENERAL JOURNAL   **PAGE** 29

DATE	PARTICULARS	P.R.	DEBIT	CREDIT

C.

GENERAL LEDGER

ACCOUNT Bank   No. 105

DATE		PARTICULARS	P.R.	DEBIT	CREDIT	DR/CR	BALANCE
20— Dec.	31	Forwarded	–			DR	16 2 2 5 85

ANSWERS TO CHAPTER 12 REVIEW EXERCISES (cont.)

Exercise 6 (cont.)

C. (cont.)

ACCOUNT *Accounts Receivable* No. *110*

DATE		PARTICULARS	P.R.	DEBIT	CREDIT	DR/CR	BALANCE
20— Dec.	31	Forwarded	–			DR	8 2 3 1 70

ACCOUNT *Supplies* No. *115*

DATE		PARTICULARS	P.R.	DEBIT	CREDIT	DR/CR	BALANCE
20— Dec.	31	Forwarded	–			DR	3 1 2 50

ACCOUNT *Merchandise Inventory* No. *120*

DATE		PARTICULARS	P.R.	DEBIT	CREDIT	DR/CR	BALANCE
20— Dec.	31	Forwarded	–			DR	37 4 1 6 40

ACCOUNT *Equipment* No. *125*

DATE		PARTICULARS	P.R.	DEBIT	CREDIT	DR/CR	BALANCE
20— Dec.	31	Forwarded	–			DR	26 8 0 0 —

ACCOUNT *Accumulated Depreciation — Equipment* No. *126*

DATE		PARTICULARS	P.R.	DEBIT	CREDIT	DR/CR	BALANCE
20— Dec.	31	Forwarded	–			CR	12 4 0 0 —

ACCOUNT *Truck* No. *130*

DATE		PARTICULARS	P.R.	DEBIT	CREDIT	DR/CR	BALANCE
20— Dec.	31	Forwarded	–			DR	22 2 0 0 —

ANSWERS TO CHAPTER 12 REVIEW EXERCISES (cont.)

Exercise 6 (cont.)

C. (cont.)

ACCOUNT *Accumulated Depreciation — Truck*   No. *131*

DATE		PARTICULARS	P.R.	DEBIT	CREDIT	DR/CR	BALANCE
20— Dec.	31	Forwarded	–			CR	8 4 0 0 –

ACCOUNT *Accounts Payable*   No. *205*

DATE		PARTICULARS	P.R.	DEBIT	CREDIT	DR/CR	BALANCE
20— Dec.	31	Forwarded	–			CR	12 3 5 8 50

ACCOUNT *Bank Loan*   No. *210*

DATE		PARTICULARS	P.R.	DEBIT	CREDIT	DR/CR	BALANCE
20— Dec.	31	Forwarded	–			CR	18 0 0 0 –

ACCOUNT *PST Payable*   No. *215*

DATE		PARTICULARS	P.R.	DEBIT	CREDIT	DR/CR	BALANCE
20— Dec.	31	Forwarded	–			CR	3 6 0 –

ACCOUNT *GST Payable*   No. *220*

DATE		PARTICULARS	P.R.	DEBIT	CREDIT	DR/CR	BALANCE
20— Dec.	31	Forwarded	–			CR	3 1 5 –

ANSWERS TO CHAPTER 12 REVIEW EXERCISES (cont.)

Exercise 6 (cont.)

C. (cont.)

ACCOUNT *GST Recoverable*   No. *225*

DATE		PARTICULARS	P.R.	DEBIT	CREDIT	DR/CR	BALANCE
20— Dec.	31	Forwarded	–			DR	2 1 0 –

ACCOUNT *S. Scales, Capital*   No. *305*

DATE		PARTICULARS	P.R.	DEBIT	CREDIT	DR/CR	BALANCE
20— Dec.	31	Forwarded	–			CR	59 5 6 2 95

ACCOUNT *S. Scales, Drawings*   No. *310*

DATE		PARTICULARS	P.R.	DEBIT	CREDIT	DR/CR	BALANCE

ACCOUNT *Sales*   No. *405*

DATE		PARTICULARS	P.R.	DEBIT	CREDIT	DR/CR	BALANCE

ACCOUNT *Purchases*   No. *505*

DATE		PARTICULARS	P.R.	DEBIT	CREDIT	DR/CR	BALANCE

ANSWERS TO CHAPTER 12 REVIEW EXERCISES (cont.)

Exercise 6 (cont.)

C. (cont.)

ACCOUNT *Delivery Expense*   No. *510*

DATE	PARTICULARS	P.R.	DEBIT	CREDIT	DR/CR	BALANCE

ACCOUNT *General Expense*   No. *515*

DATE	PARTICULARS	P.R.	DEBIT	CREDIT	DR/CR	BALANCE

ACCOUNT *Rent Expense*   No. *520*

DATE	PARTICULARS	P.R.	DEBIT	CREDIT	DR/CR	BALANCE

ACCOUNT *Telephone Expense*   No. *525*

DATE	PARTICULARS	P.R.	DEBIT	CREDIT	DR/CR	BALANCE

ACCOUNT *Wages Expense*   No. *530*

DATE	PARTICULARS	P.R.	DEBIT	CREDIT	DR/CR	BALANCE

Name _____ Date _____

ANSWERS TO CHAPTER 12 REVIEW EXERCISES (cont.)

Exercise 6 (cont.)

C. (cont.)

ACCOUNTS RECEIVABLE LEDGER

ACCOUNT *C. Bruk*

DATE		PARTICULARS	P.R.	DEBIT	CREDIT	DR/CR	BALANCE
20— Dec.	31	Forwarded #325	–			DR	3 6 3 40

ACCOUNT *M. Howard*

DATE		PARTICULARS	P.R.	DEBIT	CREDIT	DR/CR	BALANCE
20— Dec.	31	Forwarded #296	–			DR	3 5 5 9 25

ACCOUNT *J. Joss*

DATE		PARTICULARS	P.R.	DEBIT	CREDIT	DR/CR	BALANCE
20— Dec.	31	Forwarded #306	–			DR	1 0 4 8 80

ACCOUNT *S. Persaud*

DATE		PARTICULARS	P.R.	DEBIT	CREDIT	DR/CR	BALANCE
20— Dec.	31	Forwarded #217	–			DR	1 5 5 25

ACCOUNT *D. Wilkins*

DATE		PARTICULARS	P.R.	DEBIT	CREDIT	DR/CR	BALANCE
20— Dec.	31	Forwarded #331	–			DR	3 1 0 5 –

ANSWERS TO CHAPTER 12 REVIEW EXERCISES (cont.)

Exercise 6 (cont.)

C. (cont.)

ACCOUNTS PAYABLE LEDGER

ACCOUNT *Smith's Service Station*

DATE		PARTICULARS	P.R.	DEBIT	CREDIT	DR/CR	BALANCE

ACCOUNT *Stirling Company*

DATE		PARTICULARS	P.R.	DEBIT	CREDIT	DR/CR	BALANCE
20— Dec.	31	Forwarded #245	–			CR	4 8 1 5 –

ACCOUNT *Triangle Electric*

DATE		PARTICULARS	P.R.	DEBIT	CREDIT	DR/CR	BALANCE
20— Dec.	31	Forwarded #4701	–			CR	4 2 8 0 –

ACCOUNT *Universal Vacuums*

DATE		PARTICULARS	P.R.	DEBIT	CREDIT	DR/CR	BALANCE
20— Dec.	31	Forwarded #6508	–			CR	1 0 7 0 –

ACCOUNT *Western Electric*

DATE		PARTICULARS	P.R.	DEBIT	CREDIT	DR/CR	BALANCE
20— Dec.	31	Forwarded #246	–			CR	2 1 9 3 50

ANSWERS TO CHAPTER 12 REVIEW EXERCISES (cont.)

Exercise 6 (cont.)

D.

Bristol Appliances Company

General Ledger Trial Balance

January 31, 20—

ACCOUNTS	DEBIT	CREDIT

ANSWERS TO CHAPTER 12 REVIEW EXERCISES (cont.)

Exercise 6 (cont.)

E.

Bristol Appliances Company
Accounts Receivable Trial Balance
January 31, 20—

Bristol Appliances Company
Accounts Payable Trial Balance
January 31, 20—

Questions for Further Thought, p. 571

1. _____
   _____
   _____
   _____

2. _____

3. _____
   _____

4. _____
   _____

5. _____
   _____

6. _____

7. _____
   _____

8. _____
   _____

9. _____
   _____
   _____

ANSWERS TO CHAPTER 12 REVIEW EXERCISES (cont.)

Questions for Further Thought (cont.)

10. _____

11. _____

12. _____

13. _____
_____

14. _____

15. _____
_____

Cases for Further Thought, p. 571

1. _____
_____
_____
_____
_____
_____
_____

2. _____
_____
_____
_____
_____
_____

3. _____
_____

4. _____
_____
_____
_____
_____
_____
_____
_____

5. _____

Name _____ Date _____

CASE STUDIES (text p. 572)

Case 1 *Gaining Control over Accounts Receivable*, p. 572

1. _____
   _____
   _____
   _____
   _____
   _____
   _____
   _____

2. _____
   _____
   _____
   _____
   _____
   _____
   _____
   _____
   _____
   _____
   _____
   _____
   _____
   _____

Case 2 *Looking After Number One: Good or Bad?*, p. 573

1. _____
   _____
   _____
   _____
   _____
   _____

2. _____

3. _____
   _____
   _____

CASE STUDIES (text p. 572)

Case 3 *A Personalized Synoptic Journal?*, p. 573

   1. _____
_____
_____
_____
_____
_____
_____

   2. _____
_____
_____
_____

Challenge Case 4 *No Journal!*, p. 574

   1. _____
_____
_____

   2. _____
_____
_____
_____

   3. _____
_____

   4. _____
_____
_____
_____
_____
_____
_____
_____

   5. _____
_____

   6. _____

Career   **ROBERTA LEI/STUDENT**

ANSWERS TO DISCUSSION QUESTIONS (text p. 577)

1. _____
   _____

2. _____
   _____

3. _____
   _____
   _____

4. _____
   _____

5. _____
   _____

6.

7. _____
   _____
   _____
   _____
   _____

Chapter 13 · Business Organizations and Decision-Making

ANSWERS TO SECTION 13.1 REVIEW QUESTIONS (text p. 589)

Partnerships

1. _____
   _____

2. _____
   _____

3. _____
   _____

4. _____

5. _____
   _____
   _____
   _____
   _____
   _____

6. _____
   _____
   _____

7. _____
   _____

8. _____
   _____
   _____

9. _____
   _____
   _____
   _____
   _____

10. _____
    _____

11. _____
    _____
    _____
    _____

12. _____

13. _____

14. _____

Name _____ Date _____

ANSWERS TO SECTION 13.1 REVIEW QUESTIONS (cont.)

15. _____
_____

16. _____
_____

17. _____
_____

18. _____

19. _____
_____

20. _____
_____

21. _____
_____
_____

22. _____
_____

ANSWERS TO SECTION 13.1 EXERCISES (text p. 590)

Exercise 1, p. 590

1. **Use the most appropriate words or phrases to complete the following statements. A list of words and phrases is given on page 591 of the text.**

    a. The partners of a business share in its _____ and _____.

    b. There is a separate _____ account and _____ account for each partner.

    c. You can usually tell if a business is a _____ from its name. You can also tell by examining its _____.

    d. The day-by-day accounting for a partnership is no different than for a _____.

    e. Accounting for the partners' _____ is the principal new aspect of partnership accounting.

    f. The capital accounts of a partnership must be maintained in agreement with the terms of the _____.

    g. Persons may pool their _____ when forming a partnership.

    h. Persons may bring together _____ when forming a partnership.

    i. A partnership is simple to _____.

    j. A partnership is not subject to _____.

    k. According to the law, a partnership is terminated by the _____, _____, or _____ of any partner.

ANSWERS TO SECTION 13.1 EXERCISES (cont.)

Exercise 1 (cont.)

l.   There is no _____ in regards to partnership debts.

m.   _____ means that the partners are legally bound by the actions of any one of them.

n.   The partnership agreement should be worked out with the help of a _____.

o.   The _____ of the various provinces come into play where there is no partnership agreement and a dispute arises.

Exercise 2, p. 591

A.   _____
     _____
     _____

B.   _____
     _____
     _____

Name _____ Date _____

ANSWERS TO SECTION 13.1 EXERCISES (cont.)

Exercise 3, p. 592

A. _____
_____
_____

B. _____
_____
_____

Name _____   Date _____

Exercise 3 (cont.)

C. _____

_____

_____

Exercise 4, p. 592

4. Three partnership situations are described below. **For each one, complete the chart to show how you would arrange for the partnership profits to be apportioned.**

   1. A and B operate a partnership in which:

     — the two partners maintain equal capital account balances,

     — both partners work full time in the business,

     — neither partner has any special background or experience.

   Complete the chart.

Give a salary to a partner or partners? Y or N?	
If yes, which one(s)?	
Give interest on capital balances? Y or N?	
Divide balance of net income equally? Y or N?	
If N, ratio to favour which partner?	

Name _____   Date _____

Exercise 4 (cont.)

2. A and B form a partnership in which:
   — A invests $200 000 in cash,

   B invests $20 000 in cash.

   — A does not participate at all in running the business,

   B works full time in the business.

   — A has many profitable business connections,

   B has a great deal of experience and talent in the industry.

   Complete the chart.

Give a salary to a partner or partners? Y or N?	
If yes, which one(s)?	
Give interest on capital balances? Y or N?	
Divide balance of net income equally? Y or N?	
If N, ratio to favour which partner?	

3. A, B, and C form a partnership in which:
   — A invests $500 000 cash in the business,

   B invests $100 000 cash in the business,

   C makes no financial investment.

   — A and B do not work in the business in any way,

   C works full time in the business.

   — A and B have no experience, talent, or connections,

   C is experienced, talented, and has connections.

   Complete the chart.

Give a salary to a partner or partners? Y or N?	
If yes, which one(s)?	
Give interest on capital balances? Y or N?	
Divide balance of net income equally? Y or N?	
If N, ratio to favour which partners?	

ANSWERS TO SECTION 13.1 EXERCISES (cont.)

Exercise 5, p. 594

a. _____
_____
_____
_____
_____
_____

b. _____
_____
_____
_____
_____
_____

c. _____
_____
_____
_____
_____
_____

d. _____
_____
_____
_____
_____
_____

e. _____
_____
_____
_____
_____
_____

ANSWERS TO SECTION 13.2 REVIEW QUESTIONS (text p. 602)

Corporations

1. _____
2. _____
_____

ANSWERS TO SECTION 13.2 REVIEW QUESTIONS (cont.)

3. _____

4. _____
_____
_____

5. _____

6. _____

7. _____
_____

8. _____

9. _____

10. _____

11. _____
_____

12. _____
_____
_____

13. _____

14. _____

15. _____
_____

16. _____
_____

17. _____

18. _____

19. _____

20. _____

21. _____

22. _____
_____

23. _____

24. _____
_____

25. _____

26. _____
_____

Name _____ Date _____

ANSWERS TO SECTION 13.2 REVIEW QUESTIONS (cont.)

27. _____
_____
28. _____
_____
29. _____
30. _____
_____
31. _____
_____
_____
_____
32. _____
_____
_____
_____
33. _____
34. _____
35. _____
_____
_____

ANSWERS TO SECTION 13.2 EXERCISES (text p. 603)

Exercise 1, p. 603

a. _____   g. _____

b. _____   h. _____

c. _____   i. _____

d. _____   j. _____

e. _____   k. _____

f. _____

Name _____ Date _____

Exercise 2, p. 604

2. A corporation began business on January 1, 20-1. Over the next seven years it made profits and paid out dividends as shown in the chart below.

   Complete the Retained Earnings column of the chart.

Year	Profits (Losses)	Dividends Paid	Retained Earnings at Year-end
1	($45 000)	nil	
2	($20 000)	nil	
3	$ 25 000	nil	
4	$ 48 000	nil	
5	$110 000	$ 50 000	
6	$156 000	$100 000	
7	$227 000	$120 000	

Answer the following questions.

A. Why were no dividends paid in the first three years?

   _____

B. Could a dividend have been paid in year 4?

   _____

C. In your opinion, why was a dividend not paid in year 4?

   _____

D. All of the retained earnings were not paid out in dividends. Give reasons why this would be the case.

   _____

   _____

   _____

   _____

Name _____   Date _____

Exercise 3, p 604

_____

_____

_____

Exercise 4, p. 605

4. **Complete each of the following statements by writing in the appropriate word or phrase from the list on page 605 of the text.**

   a. A dividend is distributed to the _____ in proportion to the number of shares held.

   b. Retained Earnings represents the company's net _____ of earnings.

   c. Only the _____ has the power to declare a dividend.

   d. When dividends are declared they are declared to _____ on a certain date.

ANSWERS TO SECTION 13.2 EXERCISES (cont.)

Exercise 4 (cont.)

e. A good system is necessary for keeping _____ up to date and accurate.

f. _____ are usually stated at so much a share.

g. Once declared, a dividend becomes a _____ of the company.

h. The Retained Earnings account normally has a _____ balance.

i. When a dividend is declared, it is set up in a _____ account.

j. When a dividend is declared, the _____ account is reduced.

Exercise 5, p. 605

Year	Number of Shares Sold	Cumulative Number of Shares Issued	Income for Year	Dividend Declared Dec. 15	Total Dividend for Year	Retained Earnings Dec. 31
1	10 000		$52 500	$1.00		
2	12 000		$50 250	$1.50		
3	12 500		$60 750	$1.60		
4	15 000		$75 200	$1.75		
5	20 000		$95 050	$1.85		

Exercise 6, p. 605

A. _____

B. _____

_____

_____

_____

C. _____

_____

_____

_____

ANSWERS TO SECTION 13.2 EXERCISES (cont.)

Exercise 7. p. 606

A.

Bank

Dividends Payable

Common Stock

Land

Preferred Stock

Building

Retained Earnings

Other Assets

ANSWERS TO SECTION 13.2 EXERCISES (cont.)

Exercise 7 (cont.)

B. _____

_____

_____

ANSWERS TO SECTION 13.3 REVIEW QUESTIONS (text p. 617)

Ratio and Percentage Analysis for Corporations

1. _____
2. _____
_____
3. _____
4. _____
5. _____
_____
6. _____
_____
7. _____
_____

ANSWERS TO SECTION 13.3 REVIEW QUESTIONS (cont.)

8. _____
   _____

9. _____
   _____

10. _____
    _____

11. _____
    _____
    _____
    _____

12. _____
    _____

ANSWERS TO SECTION 13.3 EXERCISES (text p. 618)

Exercise 1, p. 618   **Saturn Sales Company Ltd.**

Description	Ratio	Opinion
a. Current ratio		
b. Quick ratio		
c. Collection period		
d. Inventory turnover		
e. Rate of return on net sales		
f. Rate of return on owner's equity		
g. Debt ratio		
h. Equity ratio		
i. Times interest earned		

ANSWERS TO SECTION 13.3 EXERCISES (cont.)

Exercise 2, p. 619

CALVINO COMPANY
INCOME STATEMENT
YEAR ENDED DECEMBER 31, 20-8

Revenue

Sales	$170 000
Cost of Goods Sold	
Opening Inventory	$
Purchases	$128 500
Goods Available for Sale	
Closing Inventory	
Cost of Goods Sold	$129 000
Gross Profit	$
Operating Expenses	$
Net Income	$

CALVINO COMPANY
BALANCE SHEET
DECEMBER 31, 20-8

ASSETS

Current Assets

Bank	$ 3 700
Accounts Receivable	
Merchandise Inventory	10 500
Total Current Assets	$
Plant and Equipment	
Land	$ 35 000
Buildings and Equipment	
Total Plant and Equipment	$
Total Assets	$

LIABILITIES AND SHAREHOLDERS' EQUITY

Current Liabilities

Bank Loan	$ 15 000
Accounts Payable	
Total Current Liabilities	$
Shareholders' Equity	
Share Capital	$ 30 000
Retained Earnings	106 000
Total Shareholders' Equity	$
Total Liabilities and Shareholders' Equity	$

ANSWERS TO SECTION 13.3 EXERCISES (cont.)

Exercise 3, p. 621

A. 1. _____
    2. _____
    3. _____
    4. _____
    5. _____

B. 1. _____
    2. _____
    3. _____

C. _____
    _____
    _____
    _____
    _____
    _____

D. _____
    _____
    _____
    _____
    _____
    _____
    _____

Exercise 4, p. 621

Use a spreadsheet program to complete this exercise.

No answer is provided for this exercise.

ANSWERS TO SECTION 13.3 EXERCISES (cont.)

Exercise 5, p. 621

A.

Key Ratios and Statistics

Description	Pluto	Neptune
Current ratio		
Quick ratio		
Collection period		
Inventory turnover		
Rate of return on net sales		
Rate of return on equity*		
Debt ratio		
Equity ratio		
Times interest earned		

* Average equity figure not used.

B. _____
_____
_____
_____
_____
_____
_____

C. _____
_____
_____
_____
_____
_____

ANSWERS TO SECTION 13.4 COMPUTER EXERCISES (text p. 626)

Partnership Accounting Using Spreadsheets

Exercise 1, p. 626

1., 2.

Use your spreadsheet software for this exercise.

3. _____

4. _____

_____

_____

_____

_____

_____

_____

_____

5. _____

_____

_____

_____

_____

_____

_____

Name _____ Date _____

ANSWERS TO SECTION 13.5 REVIEW QUESTIONS (text p. 637)

Budgeting with Spreadsheets and Simply Accounting

1. _____
2. _____
   _____
3. _____
   _____
4. _____
   _____
5. _____
   _____
6. _____
   _____
7. _____
   _____
8. _____
   _____
   _____
9. _____
   _____
10. _____
    _____
    _____

ANSWERS TO SECTION 13.5 EXERCISES (text p. 637)

Exercise 1, p. 637

1. _____
   _____
   _____
   _____
   _____
   _____
   _____

ANSWERS TO SECTION 13.5 EXERCISES (cont.)

Exercise 2, p. 637   **Challenge**

A., B.

Use spreadsheet and word-processing software for these exercises.

ANSWERS TO SECTION 13.5 EXERCISES (cont.)

Exercise 2 (cont.)

A., B. (cont.)

ANSWERS TO SECTION 13.5 EXERCISES (cont.)

Exercise 3, p. 638   Extra Challenge

A. to C.

D. _____
_____
_____
_____

Communicate It (text p. 640)

_____
_____
_____
_____
_____
_____
_____
_____
_____
_____
_____
_____
_____
_____

ANSWERS TO CHAPTER 13 REVIEW EXERCISES (text p. 642)

Using Your Knowledge

Exercise 1, p. 642

Exercise 2, p. 642

A. _____

B. _____

C. _____

D. _____

_____

_____

_____

_____

_____

_____

_____

_____

_____

Exercise 3, p. 643

A. _____

_____

_____

_____

_____

B. _____

_____

_____

ANSWERS TO CHAPTER 13 REVIEW EXERCISES (cont.)

Exercise 3 (cont.)

C., D.

GENERAL JOURNAL   PAGE

DATE	PARTICULARS	P.R.	DEBIT	CREDIT

Exercise 4, p. 643

_____

_____

_____

_____

_____

_____

_____

_____

_____

_____

_____

_____

_____

_____

_____

_____

_____

_____

ANSWERS TO CHAPTER 13 REVIEW EXERCISES (cont.)

Exercise 5, p. 643

_____
_____
_____
_____
_____
_____
_____
_____
_____
_____

Exercise 6, p. 644

A. _____

B. _____
_____
_____
_____
_____
_____
_____

Exercise 7, p. 644

A. _____

B. _____

C. _____
_____
_____
_____
_____
_____
_____

ANSWERS TO CHAPTER 13 REVIEW EXERCISES (cont.)

Exercise 8, p. 644

Exercise 9, p. 645

ANSWERS TO CHAPTER 13 REVIEW EXERCISES (cont.)

Exercise 10, p. 645

A. _____

_____

_____

B. _____

_____

_____

Name _____ Date _____

ANSWERS TO CHAPTER 13 REVIEW EXERCISES (cont.)

Exercise 10 (cont.)

C.

_____

_____

_____

Name _____ Date _____

D.

GENERAL JOURNAL   PAGE ___

DATE		PARTICULARS	P.R.	DEBIT	CREDIT

Name _____ Date _____

ANSWERS TO CHAPTER 13 REVIEW EXERCISES (cont.)

Problems and Cases for Further Thought (text p. 647)

1. _____

2. _____

_____

_____

_____

3. _____

_____

_____

_____

_____

_____

4. _____

_____

_____

_____

5. _____

6. _____

_____

_____

_____

_____

_____

_____

7. _____

_____

8. _____

_____

9. _____

_____

ANSWERS TO CHAPTER 13 REVIEW EXERCISES (cont.)

10. _____

11. _____

12. _____

13. _____

CASE STUDIES (text p. 648)

Case 1 *Buy the Shares or the Assets?*, p. 648

1. _____

2. _____

CASE STUDIES (cont.)

Case 1 (cont.)

3. _____
_____
_____
_____

4. _____
_____
_____

Case 2 *Control of a Corporation,* p. 648

1. _____
2. _____
_____
_____
_____
_____

3. _____
4. _____
5. _____
_____
_____
_____
_____
_____

6. _____
_____
_____

7. _____
_____
_____
_____

Case 3 *A Problem of Sudden Termination,* p. 649

1. _____
2. _____
3. _____
4. _____
5. _____
6. _____

CASE STUDIES (cont.)

Case 3 (cont.)

7. _____
_____
_____
_____

8. _____
_____
_____
_____
_____
_____

9. _____

10. _____
_____

11. _____
_____
_____
_____

Challenge Case 4   *The Partner You Know or the Shareholder You Don't—Choosing between a Partnership or Corporation*, p. 651

Part A

1. _____
_____
_____
_____
_____
_____
_____

2. _____
_____
_____
_____
_____

CASE STUDIES (cont.)

3. Part A.

Year 1

_____

_____

_____

_____

_____

_____

Name _____ Date _____

CASE STUDIES (cont.)

Year 2

_____

_____

_____

_____

_____

_____

_____

CASE STUDIES (cont.)

Part B.

1.

2.

_____

_____

_____

3.

Name _____ Date _____

CASE STUDIES (cont.)

Part B. (cont.)

4. _____

_____

_____

5. _____

_____

_____

_____

Part C.

1. _____

_____

_____

_____

_____

_____

_____

_____

_____

_____

_____

_____

_____

_____

_____

_____

CASE STUDIES (cont.)

Part C. (cont.)

2. _____

_____

Challenge Case 5 *To Lend or Not To Lend*, p. 654

Part A.

1.

Key Ratios and Statistics	20-6	20-7	20-8
Working capital			
Current ratio			
Quick ratio			
Collection period			
Inventory trunover			
Debt ratio			
Equity ratio			
Times interest earned			
Rate of return on net sales			
Rate of return on owner's equity			

2. _____

_____

_____

_____

_____

_____

_____

_____

_____

_____

_____

_____

Name _____ Date _____

CASE STUDIES (cont.)

Part B.

  3.

_____

_____

_____

4. Extra Challenge

_____

_____

_____

CASE STUDIES (cont.)

Part B. (cont.)

5. **Extra Challenge**

The key ratios and statistics developed from the estimated statements are as follows:

RATIOS AND STATISTICS

Working capital   _____

Current ratio   _____

Quick ratio   _____

Collection period   _____

Inventory trunover   _____

Debit ratio   _____

Equity ratio   _____

Times interest earned   _____

Rate of return on net sales   _____

Rate of return on owner's equity   _____

The bank manager's thoughts might be as follows:

_____

_____

_____

_____

_____

_____

_____

_____

_____

_____

_____

_____

_____

_____

_____

_____

_____

_____

_____

_____

_____

CASE STUDIES (cont.)

Part B. (cont.)

_____

_____

_____

_____

_____

_____

_____

_____

_____

Name _____ Date _____

Chapter 14 **Payroll Accounting**

ANSWERS TO SECTION 14.1 REVIEW QUESTIONS (text p. 660)

Gross Pay

1. _____

2. _____

3. _____

4. _____

5. _____

6. _____

7. _____

8. _____

9. _____

10. _____

11. _____

12. _____

13. _____

14. _____

ANSWERS TO SECTION 14.1 EXERCISES (text p. 661)

Exercise 1, p. 661

Annual Salary	Payroll Period	Gross Pay per Period
$39 000	Weekly	
	Weekly	$ 800
$22 750	Biweekly	
	Biweekly	$1 250
$36 000	Semi-monthly	
	Semi-monthly	$1 800
$30 000	Monthly	
	Monthly	$3 200

Exercise 2, p. 661

Payroll Period	Gross Pay
a. Weekly	
b. Biweekly	
c. Semi-monthly	
d. Monthly	

Exercise 3, p. 662

Total Hours	Regular Rate	Regular Hours	Overtime Hours	Regular Pay	Overtime Pay	Gross Pay
46	$11.50					
43	$14.50					
44.5	$12.00					
54	$21.00					
47.25	$13.75					

ANSWERS TO SECTION 14.1 EXERCISES (cont.)

Exercise 4, p. 662

Day	Number of Units Completed	Salary	Piecework Earnings	Gross Pay
Monday	10			
Tuesday	9			
Wednesday (1/2)	5			
Thursday	11			
Friday	10			
Totals				

Exercise 5, p. 662

Time Card

Week Ended   July 23   20 --
Social Ins. No. 642 393 438
Name   Kashim Baksh

Day	Morning In	Morning Out	Afternoon In	Afternoon Out	Extra In	Extra Out	Total Hours
M	7:58	12:01	12:58	5:01			
T	8:07	12:00	12:57	5:02			
W	7:56	12:03	12:59	5:00			
T	7:59	12:02	1:01	5:03			
F	7:57	12:02	12:59	5:01			
S							
S							

	Hours	Rate	Earnings
Regular Time		14.00	
Overtime			
Gross Pay			

Time Card

Week Ended   July 23   20 --
Social Ins. No. 643 461 217
Name   Monica Peterson

Day	Morning In	Morning Out	Afternoon In	Afternoon Out	Extra In	Extra Out	Total Hours
M	7:58	12:01	1:00	5:02			
T	7:59	12:00	12:58	5:01	5:59	8:55	
W	7:57	12:01	12:59	5:02			
T	7:56	12:01	12:58	5:03			
F	7:59	12:01	12:59	5:01			
S	7:58	12:01					
S							

	Hours	Rate	Earnings
Regular Time		12.20	
Overtime			
Gross Pay			

ANSWERS TO SECTION 14.1 EXERCISES (cont.)

Exercise 6, p. 663

Salesperson	Sales for Month	Salary	Commission	Gross Earnings
Mary Hunt	$ 90 000			
Anna Nasser	$122 000			
Bob Rennie	$ 75 000			
Fay Savard	$316 000			
Paul Thors	$ 50 000			
Gloria Lem	$ 70 000			
Gladys Wilson	$ 26 000			

ANSWERS TO SECTION 14.2 REVIEW QUESTIONS (text p. 681)

Payroll Deductions and Net Pay

1. _____
2. _____
3. _____
4. _____
5. _____
6. _____
7. _____
8. _____
9. _____
   _____
10. _____
    _____
    _____
11. _____
12. _____
    _____
13. _____
    _____
    _____
14. _____
    _____
    _____

ANSWERS TO SECTION 14.2 REVIEW QUESTIONS (cont.)

15. _____

_____

_____

16. _____

17. _____

_____

18. _____

19. _____

_____

_____

_____

ANSWERS TO SECTION 14.2 EXERCISES (text p. 681)

Exercise 1, p. 681

A.

Employee	Biweekly Gross Pay	CPP Deduction	EI Deduction	RPP (5%) Deduction
F. Mazur	$2 180			
C. Koch	$2 200			
P. Parsons	$2 350			
G. Vittelli	$2 270			
Y. Van Del	$2 430			

B. _____ deductions: _____ @ _____ + final deduction of _____

Exercise 2, p. 682

PAYROLL JOURNAL   *For the two weeks ended*   20—

Employee	Net Claim Code	Earnings			Deductions											
		Regular	Extra	Gross	RPP	Union Dues	Income Tax Taxable Earnings	Income Tax Tax Deduction	CPP	EI	Ext. Health Ins.	Group Life	Total Ded'ns	Net Pay
J. Bell	8	2310 –		2310 –										

ANSWERS TO SECTION 14.2 EXERCISES (cont.)

Exercise 3, p. 682

To complete this exercise, use the payroll deduction tables found in your text, as well as the partial EI table below.

Employment Insurance Premiums							Cotisations à l'assurance-emploi	
Insurable Earnings Rémunération assurable			Insurable Earnings Rémunération assurable			Insurable Earnings Rémunération assurable		
From - De	To - À		From - De	To - À		From - De	To - À	
2048.23 - 2048.66	46.09	2080.23 - 2080.66	46.81	2112.23 - 2112.66	47.53	2144.23 - 2144.66	48.25
2048.67 - 2049.11	46.10	2080.67 - 2081.11	46.82	2112.67 - 2113.11	47.54	2144.67 - 2145.11	48.26
2049.12 - 2049.55	46.11	2081.12 - 2081.55	46.83	2113.12 - 2113.55	47.55	2145.12 - 2145.55	48.27
2049.56 - 2049.99	46.12	2081.56 - 2081.99	46.84	2113.56 - 2113.99	47.56	2145.56 - 2145.99	48.28
2050.00 - 2050.44	46.13	2082.00 - 2082.44	46.85	2114.00 - 2114.44	47.57	2146.00 - 2146.44	48.29
2050.45 - 2050.88	46.14	2082.45 - 2082.88	46.86	2114.45 - 2114.88	47.58	2146.45 - 2146.88	48.30
2050.89 - 2051.33	46.15	2082.89 - 2083.33	46.87	2114.89 - 2115.33	47.59	2146.89 - 2147.33	48.31
2051.34 - 2051.77	46.16	2083.34 - 2083.77	46.88	2115.34 - 2115.77	47.60	2147.34 - 2147.77	48.32
2051.78 - 2052.22	46.17	2083.78 - 2084.22	46.89	2115.78 - 2116.22	47.61	2147.78 - 2148.22	48.33
2052.23 - 2052.66	46.18	2084.23 - 2084.66	46.90	2116.23 - 2116.66	47.62	2148.23 - 2148.66	48.34
2052.67 - 2053.11	46.19	2084.67 - 2085.11	46.91	2116.67 - 2117.11	47.63	2148.67 - 2149.11	48.35
2053.12 - 2053.55	46.20	2085.12 - 2085.55	46.92	2117.12 - 2117.55	47.64	2149.12 - 2149.55	48.36
2053.56 - 2053.99	46.21	2085.56 - 2085.99	46.93	2117.56 - 2117.99	47.65	2149.56 - 2149.99	48.37
2054.00 - 2054.44	46.22	2086.00 - 2086.44	46.94	2118.00 - 2118.44	47.66	2150.00 - 2150.44	48.38
2054.45 - 2054.88	46.23	2086.45 - 2086.88	46.95	2118.45 - 2118.88	47.67	2150.45 - 2150.88	48.39
2054.89 - 2055.33	46.24	2086.89 - 2087.33	46.96	2118.89 - 2119.33	47.68	2150.89 - 2151.33	48.40
2055.34 - 2055.77	46.25	2087.34 - 2087.77	46.97	2119.34 - 2119.77	47.69	2151.34 - 2151.77	48.41
2055.78 - 2056.22	46.26	2087.78 - 2088.22	46.98	2119.78 - 2120.22	47.70	2151.78 - 2152.22	48.42

A.

PAYROLL JOURNAL *For the two weeks ended Februrary 15, 20—*

Employee	Net Claim Code Fed.	Net Claim Code Prov.	Earnings Gross	RPP 6.00%	Union Dues	Income Tax Taxable Earnings	Income Tax Fed. Tax	Income Tax Prov. Tax	Total Tax Dec'ns	CPP	EI	Ext. Health Ins.	Total Ded'ns	Net Pay
A. Vroom	10	10	2150 –		60 –							36 –		
C. Huang	1	1	2150 –		60 –							18 –		
R. Leidel	3	4	2300 –		60 –							36 –		
S. Tan	2	2	2375 –		60 –							36 –		
R. Morris	4	5	2425 –		60 –							36 –		

B.

_____

_____

_____

Exercise 4, p. 682

Refer to page 683 of your text for the list of words and phrases to be used.

a. An amount kept back from an employee's gross pay is known as a _____
_____ .

ANSWERS TO SECTION 14.2 EXERCISES (cont.)

Exercise 4 (cont.)

b. The amount of pay remaining after all deductions have been made is known as

_____.

c. Payroll calculations are summarized in a book known as the _____.

d. Keeping back an amount from an employee's pay is called _____ it.

e. Certain payroll deductions are made on behalf of the federal government. The
_____ system is used to keep track of all of these deductions
for all citizens of the country.

f. The deductions in question **e.** above are for _____,
_____, and _____.

g. To assist employers in making the deductions in question **f.** above, the government provides

_____.

h. The CPP deduction and the EI deduction are based on the _____
figure.

i. For the CPP, there is a _____ figure after which no further
deductions will be made for the year.

j. Employers, as well as employees, must _____ to the CPP and
EI funds.

k. A payroll made every two weeks is known as a _____ payroll.

l. A private pension plan that is approved by the government is known as a _____
pension plan.

m. An employee fills out a TD1 form in order to determine the _____.

n. The _____ number is based on the figure arrived at in question **m.**
above.

o. The deduction for income tax is not based on gross earnings. It is based on
_____ earnings.

ANSWERS TO SECTION 14.3 REVIEW QUESTIONS (text p. 687)

Recording the Payroll

1. _____

   1. _____

   2. _____

   3. _____

   4. _____

   5. _____

Name _____   Date _____

ANSWERS TO SECTION 14.3 REVIEW QUESTIONS (cont.)

2. _____
   _____
   _____
   _____
   _____
   _____

3. _____
4. _____
5. _____
6. _____
   _____
   _____

7. _____
   _____

8. _____
9. _____
   1. _____
   2. _____
   3. _____
10. _____
    _____

11. _____
    _____

Name _____ Date _____

ANSWERS TO SECTION 14.3 EXERCISES (text p. 688)

Exercise 1, p. 688

A., C., E.

GENERAL JOURNAL

PAGE

DATE	PARTICULARS	P.R.	DEBIT	CREDIT

ANSWERS TO SECTION 14.3 EXERCISES (cont.)

Exercise 1 (cont.)

B., C., D., E.

| Bank | Canada Pension Plan Payable | Employment Insurance Payable |

| Registered Pension Plan Payable | Employees' Income Tax Payable | Extended Health Insurance Payable |

| Union Dues Payable | Group Life Insurance Payable | Salaries Payable |

| Salaries Expense | Canada Pension Plan Expense | Employment Insurance Expense |

| Registered Pension Plan Expense |

ANSWERS TO SECTION 14.3 EXERCISES (cont.)

Exercise 1 (cont.)

F. **a.** _____

   b. _____

   c., d.

GENERAL JOURNAL   PAGE

DATE		PARTICULARS	P.R.	DEBIT	CREDIT

Exercise 2, p. 688

A. _____

B. _____

C. _____

D. _____

Exercise 3, p. 689

A. _____

B. _____

C. **a.** _____

   b. _____

   c. _____

   d. _____

D. _____

ANSWERS TO SECTION 14.4 REVIEW QUESTIONS (text p. 691)

Basic Payroll Records

1. _____
    _____

2. _____

3. _____
    _____

ANSWERS TO SECTION 14.4 REVIEW QUESTIONS (cont.)

4. _____
   _____
   _____

5. _____
   _____

6. _____
   _____

ANSWERS TO SECTION 14.4 EXERCISES (text p. 691)

Exercise 1, p. 691

A. a. Mary's gross pay

    b. Canada Pension Plan

    c. Employment Insurance

    d. Registered Pension Plan

    e. Income Tax

ANSWERS TO SECTION 14.4 EXERCISES (cont.)

Exercise 1 (cont.)

B. _____
_____

C. _____
_____

Exercise 2, p. 692

A. Box 14   _____

Box 16   _____

Box 18   _____

Box 20   _____

Box 22   _____

B. Explain the CPP deductions for November (not September, as indicated in the text).
_____
_____
_____

C. Explain why the EI deduction did not continue at the higher level reached in September.
_____
_____

ANSWERS TO SECTION SECTION 14.5 COMPUTER EXERCISES (text p. 700)

Using a Computer for Payroll

1., 2. Use Simply Accounting to complete these exercises.

Note: page 539 follows next.

ANSWERS TO SECTION 14.5 COMPUTER EXERCISES (cont.)

Exercise 2, p. 701

_____

_____

Exercise 3, p. 702

_____

_____

_____

_____

Communicate It (text p. 702)

_____

_____

_____

_____

_____

_____

_____

_____

_____

_____

_____

_____

_____

_____

_____

ANSWERS TO CHAPTER 14 REVIEW EXERCISES (text p. 704)

Exercise 1, p. 704   **Using Your Knowledge**

A., B.

PAYROLL JOURNAL

For the two weeks ended   20—

Employee	Net Claim Code	Earnings			Deductions													Net Pay
		Regular	Extra	Gross	RPP	Union Dues	Taxable Earnings	Income Tax		Total Tax Deduction	CPP	EI	Ext. Health Ins.	Group Life	Total Ded'ns	
								Federal Tax	Provincial Tax							

ANSWERS TO CHAPTER 14 REVIEW EXERCISES (cont.)

Exercise 1 (cont.)

C.

GENERAL JOURNAL

PAGE

DATE	PARTICULARS	P.R.	DEBIT	CREDIT

ANSWERS TO CHAPTER 14 REVIEW EXERCISES (cont.)

Exercise 2, p. 704

A., B.

PAYROLL JOURNAL

For the two weeks ended _____ 20—

Employee	Net Claim Code	Earnings			RPP	Union Dues	Deductions										Net Pay
		Regular	Extra	Gross			Taxable Earnings	Income Tax		Total Tax Deduction	CPP	EI	Ext. Health Ins.	Group Life	Total Ded'ns		
								Federal Tax	Provincial Tax								

ANSWERS TO CHAPTER 14 REVIEW EXERCISES (cont.)

Exercise 2 (cont.)

C.

GENERAL JOURNAL PAGE _____

DATE		PARTICULARS	P.R.	DEBIT	CREDIT

ANSWERS TO CHAPTER 14 REVIEW EXERCISES (cont.)

Exercise 3, p. 705 **Comprehensive Exercise**

a. _____
_____
_____
_____
_____
_____

b. _____
_____
_____
_____
_____

c. _____
d. _____
e. _____
f. _____
g. _____
_____
_____
_____

Exercise 4, p. 707 **Comprehensive Exercise**

Part A

Bank	CPP Payable	EI Payable	RPP Payable

ANSWERS TO CHAPTER 14 REVIEW EXERCISES (cont.)

Exercise 4 (cont.)

Employee's Income
Tax Payable

Extended Health
Insurance Payable

Union Dues Payable

Payroll Payable

Wages Expense

CPP Expense

EI Expense

RPP Expense

Part B

Expenses

Cash Paid Out + Amount Owed

Questions for Further Thought, p. 708

1. _____

2. a. _____

   b. _____

   c. _____

3. _____

4. _____

5. _____

ANSWERS TO CHAPTER 14 REVIEW EXERCISES (cont.)

Questions for Further Thought (cont.)

6. _____

7. _____
   _____
   _____
   _____

8. _____

Cases for Further Thought, p. 708

1. _____
   _____
   _____
   _____
   _____
   _____

2. _____
   _____
   _____
   _____
   _____
   _____

CASE STUDIES (text p. 709)

Case 1 *Wage Increases — What's Fair?*, p. 709

1. _____
   _____
   _____
   _____
   _____
   _____
   _____

2. _____
   _____
   _____
   _____
   _____
   _____
   _____
   _____

Name _____ Date _____

CASE STUDIES (cont.)

Case 2 *Wage Increases — How Much Can Be Offered?*, p. 709

1. _____
   _____

2. _____

3. _____

4. a. _____
   _____
   _____
   _____
   _____
   _____
   _____
   _____

   b. _____
   _____

Challenge Case 3 *A Profit-Sharing Proposal*, p. 710

1. _____
   _____
   _____
   _____
   _____

2. _____
   _____
   _____
   _____
   _____
   _____
   _____

3. a. _____
   b. _____
   _____

4. _____
   _____
   _____
   _____
   _____

CASE STUDIES (cont.)

Challenge Case 3 (cont.)

5. _____

_____

_____

_____

_____

_____

_____

6. _____

_____

_____

_____

_____

_____

_____

_____

_____

_____

_____

7. _____

_____

_____

_____

_____

8. _____

_____

_____

_____

_____

_____

_____

CASE STUDIES (cont.)

Challenge Case 3 (cont.)

9. _____

10. _____

11. _____

Summary Exercises

KALLEY'S DATABASE DEVELOPMENTS (Part 2), text p. 713

Near the end of its first year, Kalley's Database Developments is still processing all of its transactions in the General module. You will modify this accounting system so that Kalley's uses the Receivables and Payables modules, as well.

When completing this exercise, you will have few specific Simply Accounting instructions to guide you. Therefore, you should first complete the Summary Exercise for Travel Trailers on page 715 of the text so that you know how to work with the Receivables and Payables modules.

Required

1. Load the company files in the Kalley2 folder.

2. Create the vendor and customer accounts using the data listed below. Include information related to outstanding invoices (see the Historical Transactions tab). Also, record the payment terms when you create the vendor accounts (see the Options tab). Discounts are calculated before tax. Ignore any Simply Accounting fields for which you have no information.

Payables

Vendor	*Address*	*Terms*
Automated Office Supplies	796 Main St., Ottawa, ON K2M 7P2, 347-9807	n30
Fast Touch Software Ltd.	839 Front St., Ottawa, ON K1C 1Z8, 778-0743	2/10, n30
Mackie's Garage	4732 Cambie St., Ottawa, ON K2C 1Z8, 778-3967	n30
Risc Computers Ltd.	8659 Charles Ave., Ottawa, ON K1C 4M9, 778-4812	n30
T.B.A. Printing Ltd.	929 Inman Ave., Ottawa, ON K2A 5C5, 775-7219	n30
Virtual Computers	367 Coburn Dr., Ottawa, ON K2C 3L6, 765-6708	2/10, n30

Outstanding Invoices

Vendor	*Invoice No.*	*Amount*	*Date*	
Automated Office Supplies	2673A	$912.42	16-Mar-03	(Hint: Pre-tax amounts
Mackie's Garage	6941	$107.42	10-Mar-03	can be found by
Virtual Computers	8743	$312.87		dividing by 1.07.)

Receivables

Customers	*Address*	*Terms*
Culos & Weber	472 Daniels St., Ottawa, ON K8J 2B3 378-4464	2/10, n30 (entered by default)
Government of Ontario	Queen's Park, Toronto, ON M5G 1X5 416-362-1111	2/10, n30 (entered by default)
Guelph Public Library	121 Waterloo Ave., Guelph, ON N1H 3N9 519-821-6009	2/10, n30 (entered by default)
Sanz Electrical Engineers	897 7th., Guelph, ON N1H 6P3 519-821-2216	2/10, n30 (entered by default)
RMI Educational Services	607 Jamieson Ave., Ottawa, ON K5B 5C6 389-7311	2/10, n30 (entered by default)

Name _____ Date _____

KALLEY'S DATABASE DEVELOPMENTS (cont.)

Outstanding Invoices

Customer	Invoice No.	Amount	Date	
Culos & Weber	S036	$12 840.00	11-Jan-03	(Hint: Pre-tax amounts
Culos & Weber	S041	$7 490.00	3-Mar-03	can be found by
Sanz Electrical Engineers	S052	$3 210.00	25-Mar-03	dividing by 1.07.)
RMI Educational Services	S037	$535.00	12-Jan-03	
RMI Educational Services	S039	$642.00	18-Jan-03	
RMI Educational Services	S043	$428.00	5-Mar-03	
RMI Educational Services	S048	$428.00	15-Mar-03	

3. Link the appropriate accounts to the General module.

4. Pull down the History menu and choose Finish Entering History. (If you have made any mistakes in steps 2 and 3 above, they will be revealed at this stage.)

5. Use the General, Payables, and Receivables modules in Simply Accounting to record the transactions below.

	Date	Source Documents	No.	Name	Explanation	Amount	GST	Total
1.	Apr. 1	Cheque Copy	171	Myrtle Holdings Ltd.	Monthly rent	$1 900.00	133.00	$2 033.00
2.	Apr. 1	Purchase Invoice	8820	Virtual Computers	Toner for laser printer	245.98	17.20	263.20
3.	Apr. 1	Cheque Copy	172	Virtual Computers	Paid Invoice 8743			312.89
4.	Apr. 3	Remittance Advice	R044	RMI Educational Services	Received payment of Invoice S037			535.00
5.	Apr. 3	Sales Invoice	S053	Guelph Public Library	Sale on account	6 000.00	420.00	6 420.00
6.	Apr. 3	Remittance Advice	R045	Sanz Electrical Engineers	Received payment of Invoice S052, less a 2% discount			3 150.00
7.	Apr. 7	Cheque Copy	173	Automated Office Supplies	Purchased paper supplies	126.00	8.82	134.82
8.	Apr. 7	Cheque Copy	174	Mackie's Garage	Paid Invoice 6941			107.42
9.	Apr. 9	Cheque Copy	175	Virtual Computers	Paid Invoice 8820, less a 2% discount			258.28
10.	Apr. 9	Purchase Invoice	470	T.B.A. Printing Ltd.	For advertising pamphlets	1 250.00	87.50	1 337.50
11.	Apr. 12	Remittance Advice	R046	Guelph Public Library	Received payment of Invoice S053, less a 2% discount			6 300.00
12.	Apr. 14	Sales Invoice	S054	Government of Ontario	Sale on account	4 000.00	280.00	4 280.00
13.	Apr. 15	Cheque Copy	176	Shaun Kalley	Personal use of the owner			1 500.00
14.	Apr. 15	Cheque Copy	177	Automated Office Supplies	Paid Invoice 2673A			912.42
15.	Apr. 18	Credit Invoice	4910	T.B.A. Printing Ltd.	Allowance was granted on Invoice 470 because the wrong paper was used	250.00	17.50	267.50
16.	Apr. 18	Purchase Invoice	343	Fast Touch Software Ltd.	Purchased an assortment of software on account	439.72	30.78	470.50
17.	Apr. 18	Purchase Invoice	119B	Risc Computers Ltd.	Purchased recordable CDs	150.00	10.50	160.50
18.	Apr. 22	Owner's Memo	—	—	The owner took recordable CDs for his personal use	30.00	2.10	32.10
19.	Apr. 22	Cheque Copy	178	Solid Oak Ltd.	Purchased a desk	412.00	28.84	440.84
20.	Apr. 22	Credit Invoice	221C	Risc Computers Ltd.	Returned defective CDs for credit	60.00	4.20	64.20
21.	Apr. 27	Cheque Copy	179	Fast Touch Computers Ltd.	Paid Invoice 343, less a 2% discount			461.71
22.	Apr. 27	Cheque Copy	180	Mackie's Garage	Repaired automobile	346.00	24.22	370.22
23.	Apr. 30	Cheque Copy	181	Public Utilities Commission	Paid the utilities bill	175.00	12.25	187.25
24.	Apr. 30	Cheque Copy	182	AGB Telephone Company	Paid the telephone bill	63.00	4.41	67.41
25.	Apr. 30	Remittance Advice	R047	Government of Ontario	Received payment of Invoice S0544			4 280.00
26.	Apr. 30	Cheque Copy	183	Leanne Tan	Paid employee			2 100.00

KALLEY'S DATABASE DEVELOPMENTS (cont.)

6. Bank Reconciliation

The bank statement dated April 30th arrived and showed a final balance of $11 257.59. It also revealed the following outstanding cheques: Nos. 176, 180, 181, 182, and 183. The April 30th receipt of cash from the Government of Ontario did not appear on the bank statement.

To arrive at a final balance of $11 257.59, loan interest charges of $166.66 and service charges of $14.55 were deducted.

Required

Use the Account Reconciliation module of Simply Accounting to perform the bank reconciliation for April 30, 2002, and to make the journal entries that are needed.

7. Adjusting Entries

To prepare for the year-end financial statements, the following calculations were made:

1. A count of supplies revealed a total of $825.

   (First create a Supplies Expense account in the General ledger, account number 5375, "Group Account.")

2. Depreciation of equipment for the year was $650; depreciation of the Automobile was $700.

   (Create two expense accounts for depreciation. The account numbers you choose should place these accounts in alphabetical order. Then you will need two new contra accounts: Accumulated Depreciation—Equipment and Accumulated Depreciation—Automobile. You determine the account numbers. Classify these accounts as "Subgroup Accounts." Also, change the classification of the Equipment and Automobile accounts to "Subgroup Accounts." Finally, create two new "Subgroup Total" accounts named Total Equipment and Total Automobile with carefully chosen account numbers.)

3. The senior accountant advised that not all of the amount in the Service Revenue account had been earned as of April 30th. That is, some cash or accounts receivable had been received and some revenue had been recorded before Kalley's Database Developments had done any of the required work. (The business had been paid in advance.) The amount of revenue actually earned as of April 30th was calculated at $97 400.50.

   (The adjustment account that corresponds with Service Revenue is Unearned Revenue. Create this account in the Current Liabilities section. It is a liability because Kalley's has received cash or accounts receivable for work not yet done. The party that gave the cash or accounts receivable has a valid claim on Kalley's assets.)

8. Printing

Print the journal entries and financial statements required by your teacher.

The Receivables and Payables modules of Simply Accounting offer a number of reports that you can display and print. You can, for example, see the amount of money customers owe Kalley's Database Developments and how long they have owed it. Display each report produced in the Receivables and Payables ledgers. Take note of their similarities and differences. Print the reports that are requested by your teacher.

KALLEY'S DATABASE DEVELOPMENTS (cont.)

9. Communicate It

Shaun Kalley, the owner of Kalley's Database Developments, is concerned about how long two customers take to pay their accounts. He feels that collection letters need to be sent to Culos & Weber and RMI Educational Services. Before the correspondence is sent, he wants your thoughts on the following questions:

- Should the letters be essentially the same for each customer or should they be worded differently?
- Should Kalley's charge an interest penalty to either customer? What are the benefits and risks of doing so?
- Are there any GST implications when credit customers take a long time to pay their accounts?

Write a memo to Mr. Kalley to respond to the above questions. Then write a collection letter to each customer with overdue accounts. (Important: In your letters, use data from the Receivables ledger reports that you saw in question 8 above.)

10. Closing Routines

The first three closing entries that you learned in Chapter 9 are not necessary when you use Simply Accounting. All you need to do is advance the Session Date to the first day of the new fiscal year—May 1, 2003. Do this now. (Ignore the warnings that appear on your monitor.)

Display the trial balance for May 1st. Notice that all the revenue and expense accounts have been re-set to zero (closing entries 1 and 2). Also notice that net income has been transferred to the S. Kalley, Capital account (closing entry 3).

All you need to do is to transfer the balance of S. Kalley, Drawings to S. Kally, Capital. Do this now by making an entry in the General journal.

Note: page 560 follows next.

TRAVEL TRAILERS (text p. 715)

CASH PAYMENTS JOURNAL

DATE	PARTICULARS	OTHER ACCOUNTS DR			GST RECOV. DR	WAGES DR	DRAWINGS DR	ACCOUNTS PAYABLE DR	REF. NO.	BANK CR
		ACCOUNT	P.R.	AMOUNT						

TRAVEL TRAILERS (cont.)

CASH PAYMENTS JOURNAL

PAGE 85

DATE	PARTICULARS	OTHER ACCOUNTS DR			GST RECOV. DR	WAGES DR	DRAWINGS DR	ACCOUNTS PAYABLE DR	REF. NO.	BANK CR
		ACCOUNT	P.R.	AMOUNT						

CASH RECEIPTS JOURNAL

PAGE 37

DATE	PARTICULARS	OTHER ACCOUNTS CR			GST PAYABLE CR	PST PAYABLE CR	SALES CR	ACCOUNTS RECEIVABLE CR	REF. NO.	BANK DR
		ACCOUNT	P.R.	AMOUNT						

TRAVEL TRAILERS (cont.)

PURCHASES JOURNAL

DATE	PARTICULARS	OTHER ACCOUNTS DR			GST RECOV. DR	FREIGHT-IN DR	SUPPLIES DR	PURCHASES DR	REF. NO.	ACCOUNTS PAYABLE CR
		ACCOUNT	P.R.	AMOUNT						

Name _____   Date _____

TRAVEL TRAILERS (cont.)

SALES JOURNAL

DATE	PARTICULARS	GST PAYABLE CR	PST PAYABLE CR	SALES CR	REF. NO.	ACCOUNTS RECEIVABLE DR

TRAVEL TRAILERS (cont.)

GENERAL JOURNAL

PAGE 5

DATE		PARTICULARS	P.R.	DEBIT	CREDIT

TRAVEL TRAILERS (cont.)

GENERAL JOURNAL   PAGE 6

DATE		PARTICULARS	P.R.	DEBIT	CREDIT

TRAVEL TRAILERS (cont.)

ACCOUNT *Bank*   No. *101*

DATE		PARTICULARS	P.R.	DEBIT	CREDIT	DR/CR	BALANCE
20— May	31	Forwarded	–			DR	11 7 5 1 75

ACCOUNT *Accounts Receivable*   No. *110*

DATE		PARTICULARS	P.R.	DEBIT	CREDIT	DR/CR	BALANCE
20— May	31	Forwarded	–			DR	2 7 1 9 75

ACCOUNT *Merchandise Inventory*   No. *115*

DATE		PARTICULARS	P.R.	DEBIT	CREDIT	DR/CR	BALANCE
20— May	31	Forwarded	–			DR	125 4 2 3 –

ACCOUNT *Supplies*   No. *120*

DATE		PARTICULARS	P.R.	DEBIT	CREDIT	DR/CR	BALANCE
20— May	31	Forwarded	–			DR	1 1 5 1 –

ACCOUNT *Prepaid Insurance*   No. *125*

DATE		PARTICULARS	P.R.	DEBIT	CREDIT	DR/CR	BALANCE
20— May	31	Forwarded	–			DR	2 6 5 0 –

TRAVEL TRAILERS (cont.)

ACCOUNT *Equipment*   No. *130*

DATE		PARTICULARS	P.R.	DEBIT	CREDIT	DR/CR	BALANCE
20— May	31	Forwarded	–			DR	34 4 7 2 –

ACCOUNT *Accumulated Depreciation — Equipment*   No. *131*

DATE		PARTICULARS	P.R.	DEBIT	CREDIT	DR/CR	BALANCE
20— May	31	Forwarded	–			CR	6 0 0 0 –

ACCOUNT *Truck*   No. *140*

DATE		PARTICULARS	P.R.	DEBIT	CREDIT	DR/CR	BALANCE
20— May	31	Forwarded	–			DR	38 0 0 0 –

ACCOUNT *Accumulated Depreciation — Truck*   No. *141*

DATE		PARTICULARS	P.R.	DEBIT	CREDIT	DR/CR	BALANCE
20— May	31	Forwarded	–			CR	16 0 0 0 –

ACCOUNT *Accounts Payable*   No. *201*

DATE		PARTICULARS	P.R.	DEBIT	CREDIT	DR/CR	BALANCE
20— May	31	Forwarded	–			CR	21 3 8 6 09

TRAVEL TRAILERS (cont.)

ACCOUNT *Bank Loan*   No. 205

DATE		PARTICULARS	P.R.	DEBIT	CREDIT	DR/CR	BALANCE
20— May	31	Forwarded	–			CR	120 0 0 0 –

ACCOUNT *PST Payable*   No. 210

DATE		PARTICULARS	P.R.	DEBIT	CREDIT	DR/CR	BALANCE
20— May	31	Forwarded	–			CR	3 0 3 0 78

ACCOUNT *GST Payable*   No. 212

DATE		PARTICULARS	P.R.	DEBIT	CREDIT	DR/CR	BALANCE
20— May	31	Forwarded	–			CR	2 6 5 1 90

ACCOUNT *GST Recoverable*   No. 215

DATE		PARTICULARS	P.R.	DEBIT	CREDIT	DR/CR	BALANCE
20— May	31	Forwarded	–			DR	1 6 2 9 28

TRAVEL TRAILERS (cont.)

ACCOUNT *C. Fowler, Capital*   No. *305*

DATE		PARTICULARS	P.R.	DEBIT	CREDIT	DR/CR	BALANCE
20— May	31	Forwarded	—			CR	40 2 4 5 76

ACCOUNT *C. Fowler, Drawings*   No. *310*

DATE		PARTICULARS	P.R.	DEBIT	CREDIT	DR/CR	BALANCE
20— May	31	Forwarded	—			DR	15 0 0 0 —

ACCOUNT *Sales*   No. *405*

DATE		PARTICULARS	P.R.	DEBIT	CREDIT	DR/CR	BALANCE
20— May	31	Forwarded	—			CR	189 4 2 3 51

ACCOUNT *Discounts Earned*   No. *407*

DATE		PARTICULARS	P.R.	DEBIT	CREDIT	DR/CR	BALANCE
20— May	31	Forwarded	—			CR	1 0 3 4 20

TRAVEL TRAILERS (cont.)

ACCOUNT *Discounts Allowed*   No. *501*

DATE		PARTICULARS	P.R.	DEBIT	CREDIT	DR/CR	BALANCE
20— May	31	Forwarded	–			DR	3 5 7 –

ACCOUNT *Purchases*   No. *505*

DATE		PARTICULARS	P.R.	DEBIT	CREDIT	DR/CR	BALANCE
20— May	31	Forwarded	–			DR	96 5 8 1 75

ACCOUNT *Freight-in*   No. *510*

DATE		PARTICULARS	P.R.	DEBIT	CREDIT	DR/CR	BALANCE
20— May	31	Forwarded	–			DR	1 1 7 4 72

ACCOUNT *Bank Charges and Interest Expense*   No. *515*

DATE		PARTICULARS	P.R.	DEBIT	CREDIT	DR/CR	BALANCE
20— May	31	Forwarded	–			DR	4 5 1 6 50

TRAVEL TRAILERS (cont.)

ACCOUNT Delivery Expense   No. 520

DATE		PARTICULARS	P.R.	DEBIT	CREDIT	DR/CR	BALANCE
20— May	31	Forwarded	–			DR	5 6 5 0 20

ACCOUNT Depreciation of Equipment   No. 522

DATE		PARTICULARS	P.R.	DEBIT	CREDIT	DR/CR	BALANCE

ACCOUNT Depreciation of Truck   No. 523

DATE		PARTICULARS	P.R.	DEBIT	CREDIT	DR/CR	BALANCE

ACCOUNT Insurance Expense   No. 525

DATE		PARTICULARS	P.R.	DEBIT	CREDIT	DR/CR	BALANCE

ACCOUNT Utilities Expense   No. 530

DATE		PARTICULARS	P.R.	DEBIT	CREDIT	DR/CR	BALANCE
20— May	31	Forwarded	–			DR	4 3 5 0 40

TRAVEL TRAILERS (cont.)

ACCOUNT Miscellaneous Expense   No. 535

DATE		PARTICULARS	P.R.	DEBIT	CREDIT	DR/CR	BALANCE
20— May	31	Forwarded	–			DR	9 9 4 58

ACCOUNT Rent Expense   No. 540

DATE		PARTICULARS	P.R.	DEBIT	CREDIT	DR/CR	BALANCE
20— May	31	Forwarded	–			DR	6 2 5 0 –

ACCOUNT Supplies Expense   No. 545

DATE		PARTICULARS	P.R.	DEBIT	CREDIT	DR/CR	BALANCE

ACCOUNT Telephone Expense   No. 550

DATE		PARTICULARS	P.R.	DEBIT	CREDIT	DR/CR	BALANCE
20— May	31	Forwarded	–			DR	1 3 7 6 20

Name _____ Date _____

TRAVEL TRAILERS (cont.)

ACCOUNT *Wages Expense*   No. *555*

DATE		PARTICULARS	P.R.	DEBIT	CREDIT	DR/CR	BALANCE
20— May	31	Forwarded	–			DR	45 7 2 4 11

ACCOUNT *Income Summary*   No. *598*

DATE		PARTICULARS	P.R.	DEBIT	CREDIT	DR/CR	BALANCE

ACCOUNTS RECEIVABLE LEDGER

ACCOUNT *B. Fraser*   *15 Gray St., London, ON N6A 4T9*

DATE		PARTICULARS	P.R.	DEBIT	CREDIT	DR/CR	BALANCE
20— May	31	Forwarded (May 10) #634	–			DR	4 0 2 50

ACCOUNT *W. Hoyle*   *49 First St., Winnipeg, MB R3B 2H9*

DATE		PARTICULARS	P.R.	DEBIT	CREDIT	DR/CR	BALANCE
20— May	31	Forwarded (May 12) #635	–			DR	8 6 25

TRAVEL TRAILERS (cont.)

ACCOUNT *A. Newman*   *250 Fort Road, Fort Erie, ON L2A 4H1*

DATE		PARTICULARS	P.R.	DEBIT	CREDIT	DR/CR	BALANCE
20— May	31	Forwarded (Apr 30) #629	–			DR	2 8 7 50

ACCOUNT *Schell Brothers*   *96 Garrison Ave., Halifax, NS B3H 2B5*

DATE		PARTICULARS	P.R.	DEBIT	CREDIT	DR/CR	BALANCE
20— May	31	Forwarded (May 4) #633	–			DR	1 1 6 1 50

ACCOUNT *N. Thompson*   *20 Wilson Ave., Red Deer, AB T4N 3Y3*

DATE		PARTICULARS	P.R.	DEBIT	CREDIT	DR/CR	BALANCE
20— May	31	Forwarded (May 1) #630	–			DR	6 8 4 25

ACCOUNT *L. Walker*   *4 Dennis Ave., Acton, ON L7J 2M6*

DATE		PARTICULARS	P.R.	DEBIT	CREDIT	DR/CR	BALANCE
20— May	31	Forwarded (May 2) #631	–			DR	9 7 75

TRAVEL TRAILERS (cont.)

ACCOUNT *Double-G Industries*   *17 LaSalle St., Hull, QUE J8X 4H6*

DATE		PARTICULARS	P.R.	DEBIT	CREDIT	DR/CR	BALANCE
20— May	31	Forwarded #420	–			CR	11 3 1 5 25

ACCOUNT *Maynard's Delivery*   *49 Mill St., Barrie, ON L4M 4Y2*

DATE		PARTICULARS	P.R.	DEBIT	CREDIT	DR/CR	BALANCE

ACCOUNT *Modern Mobile Homes*   *680 Gray Rd., Wesleyville, NF A0G 4R0*

DATE		PARTICULARS	P.R.	DEBIT	CREDIT	DR/CR	BALANCE
20— May	31	Forwarded #2213	–			CR	2 2 4 7 –

ACCOUNT *National Hardware*   *64 Venture St., Aylmer, ON N5H 1H5*

DATE		PARTICULARS	P.R.	DEBIT	CREDIT	DR/CR	BALANCE
20— May	31	Forwarded #2309	–			CR	2 9 8 2 09

TRAVEL TRAILERS (cont.)

ACCOUNT *Parker Manufacturing*   *10 Bergen St., Kamloops, BC V2C 2A9*

DATE		PARTICULARS	P.R.	DEBIT	CREDIT	DR/CR	BALANCE

ACCOUNT *Windsor Manufacturing*   *47 Armstrong Ave., Nanaimo, BC V9R 5T5*

DATE		PARTICULARS	P.R.	DEBIT	CREDIT	DR/CR	BALANCE
20— May	31	Forwarded #404	–			CR	4 8 4 1 75

TRAVEL TRAILERS (cont.)

_____

_____

_____

ACCOUNTS	DEBIT	CREDIT

TRAVEL TRAILERS (cont.)

Travel Trailers

Accounts Receivable Trial Balance

Travel Trailers

Accounts Payable Trial Balance

TRAVEL TRAILERS (cont.)

WORK SHEET

Travel Trailers

Six Months Ended June 30, 20—

ACCOUNTS	TRIAL BALANCE		ADJUSTMENTS		INCOME STATEMENT		BALANCE SHEET	
	DEBIT	CREDIT	DEBIT	CREDIT	DEBIT	CREDIT	DEBIT	CREDIT

TRAVEL TRAILERS (cont.)

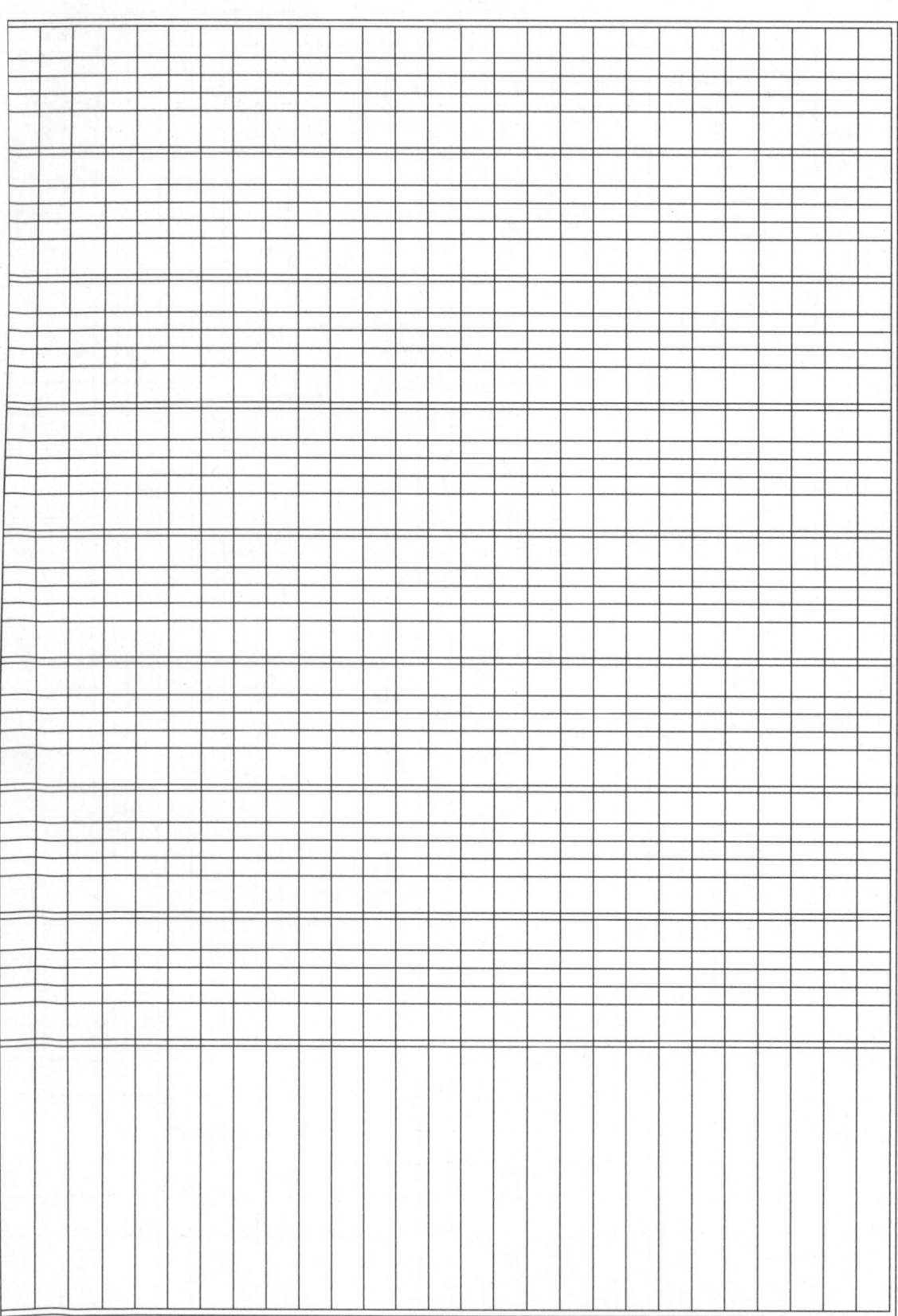

TRAVEL TRAILERS (cont.)

Travel Trailers

Income Statement

TRAVEL TRAILERS (cont.)

Travel Trailers
Balance Sheet

SUNSHELL DESIGNS (cont.)

Extending Your Computer Knowledge (cont.)

1. _____
2. _____
3. _____
4. _____

_____

_____

_____

_____

_____

Communicate It (text p. 743)

_____

_____

_____

_____

_____

_____